ADVANCES IN
PERSONALITY ASSESSMENT
Volume 2

ADVANCES IN PERSONALITY ASSESSMENT
Volume 2

Edited by
James N. Butcher
University of Minnesota

Charles D. Spielberger
University of South Florida

IEA LAWRENCE ERLBAUM ASSOCIATES, PUBLISHERS
1983   Hillsdale, New Jersey   London

Lawrence Erlbaum Associates, Inc., Publishers
365 Broadway
Hillsdale, New Jersey 07642

ISSN   **0278 2367**

ISBN   **0-89859-216-X**

Printed in the United States of America
10   9   8   7   6   5   4   3   2   1

Contents　　　　·

Preface

Personality assessment continues to be an enormously rich and diverse field with many new and exciting empirical and theoretical contributions. This series was stimulated by a growing need for an authoritative, up-to-date resource for clinicians and researchers to publish timely articles in personality assessment. Volume 2 of the *Advances in Personality Assessment* series is devoted to invited papers from a number of distinguished researchers in its field.

The range of papers included in the present volume highlights the diversity of the developments in the field, the high quality of conceptualization, and the progress in empirical research. Piotrowski's chapter describes his current thoughts on the objective evaluation of dream content. Gynther summarizes recent work on subtle and obvious content in personality items, and Eysenck and Eysenck explore new developments in cross-cultural personality assessment. The chapter by Viglione and Exner provides an update of research on Exner's Comprehensive Rorschach System, and Claridge summarizes the extensive work on Eysenck's Psychoticism Scale. Schraa, Jones, and Dirks review recent developments in normative research and its relevance to personality assessment. Finally, Spielberger, Jacobs, Russell, and Crane outline an interesting new approach to measuring angry feelings and unveil a new personality measure—the *State-Trait Anger Scale.*

Future plans for the *Advances in Personality Assessment* include volumes that explore cross-cultural research on personality assessment, and new concepts and techniques. The goal of the series will continue to be the rapid dissemination of important new developments in theory and research on all aspects of personality assessment. Special emphasis will be given to the following types of papers: (a) reports of significant theoretical and methodological advances of broad interest; (b) authoritative reviews of current research on widely used measures of personality; (c) comprehensive investigations of the predictive and construct validity of standard personality assessment methods; (d) descriptions of the construct and validation of promising new assessment procedures; and (e) invited papers by distinguished contributors to the field.

James N. Butcher
Charles D. Spielberger

1 The Perceptanalytic Dream System (PDS) as a Tool in Personality Assessment[1]

Zygmunt A. Piotrowski
in collaboration with Albert M. Biele[2]

PDS had its origin in the fortuitous discovery that the perceptanalytic interpretive TAT rules (Piotrowski Psychoanal. Rev., 1950, 1952), appropriately modified, yield even more valid results when applied to manifest dreams (Piotrowski 1971, 1973). PDS gives a personality assessment, shows the intrapsychic incompatibilities, the affective and behavioral reactions to disturbing conflicts and frustrations, and reveals how the dreamer consciously or unconsciously envisages the resolution of his subjective difficulties. The basic postulate requires that dream events be evaluated as if they were events observed consciously in active life. However, the dream report (the dreamer's description of his unconsciously produced and privately perceived visual-motor events) must first be translated, with the aid of PDS rules, into the standard conscious and universal verbal language. The most useful as well as reliable and valid PDS rules are Assent–Dissent and Primacy of Verbs and Abstract Nouns. Second in reliability and validity are the rules of Symbolism and Implied Evidence. Any suitable generalizations about human personality and its development, Freudian, Jungian, sociological, and so forth can be used to complement the PDS assessment (Rule of Complementarity). PDS employs two axioms, *A* and *B,* which differ in purpose, importance and validity of conclusions. The second part of this article contains a dream, a demonstration of its blind PDS interpretation (Z.A.P.) and psychotherapeutic notes relevant to the validation of the blind interpretation (A.M.B.).

[1]Financial aid from the Benjamin A. and Evelyn P. Strouse Foundation to carry on the dream project is gratefully acknowledged.

[2]The late Albert M. Biele, M.D., was Clinical Professor of Psychiatry at the Thomas Jefferson University Medical College.

1

It is astonishing that what is now the Perceptanalytic Dream System (PDS) was written for a very different purpose and without any thought of night dreams (Piotrowski, 1950, 1952, 1952a). These interpretive rules were originally published for use with the Thematic Apperception Test stories. The discovery that these rules produced even more highly valid and significant results with night dreams was a case of serendipity. Albert M. Biele provided the dreams which I interpreted "blind", that is, without any knowledge of the dreamer or his problems. Dr. Biele also evaluated the accuracy of the personality assessment that emerged (Piotrowski & Biele, 1973). One day I used the TAT rules and the relevance and high validity of the TAT rules applied blindly, was surprising and repeatedly demonstrated.

How was this possible when the roles of conscious and unconscious thinking were so different in producing dreams and TAT stories? The TAT pictures are interpreted consciously and deliberately, giving the subject an opportunity to improve, suppress or greatly change his spontaneous associations to the stimulus pictures, and thus dissemble his genuine ideas and inclinations. The sleeping dreamer, on the other hand, produces his imagery unconsciously. He is asleep and involved in no active interhuman contact with anyone else. Although he perceives his dream events consciously, he misinterprets their reality value and significance. While dreaming, he typically mistakes his dream events for empirical reality, but does not get confused and disoriented. It seems that when he withdraws his interest from empirical reality, he cannot be confused and misguided by it; besides, he wants to rest and sleep without being disturbed.

However, the similarities between dream and TAT products may be more important than the differences. Whether he dreams or makes up stories about the TAT characters, the subject imagines people intertwined in diverse relationships with one another but without any possibility of real interaction with them. The subject feels like an observer, not a participant in the social activities that take place before his mental eyes. As an observer, he does not feel responsible for what is happening and therefore cannot be proven wrong or guilty.

In both situations the stimuli are vague, day residuals in dreams and ambiguous pictures in the TAT. When a subject interprets these stimuli in a definite and specific way (using only some of the numerous possible responses of equal plausibility) he unwittingly reveals his preferences and anticipations. When asleep and physically inert, the dreamer receives no significant sensory impressions from the surrounding physical environment. Experiencing nothing inconsistent with his imagery, it is easy for him to mistake dream imagery for actual sensory impressions. This illusion allows the person to react in dreams very much the way he behaves in daily psychosocial relations (Piotrowski, 1980). While sleeping and dreaming, the individual does not have as many modes of mental functioning at his disposal as he does when he is awake, conscious and able to control his mind deliberately.

The differences in the production of night dreams and TAT stories seem to account for the better results when the PDS is applied to dreams. The stimuli of dreams are the subject's unknown day residuals, different in every dreamer and perhaps even in every dream. The TAT stimuli consist of a set of pictures with reliably recognizable human figures; these elicit, time and again, conscious trite phrases concerning human interrelationships. The higher the share of conscious and critical thinking during a projective test performance, the less valuable is the information obtained. Moreover, the subject may make a guess as to the use which will be made of his test responses. He may then carefully modify his responses to influence the analysis of his TAT performance in a desired direction. Finally, dreaming is a personal, spontaneous and unconsciously created series of visual-motor images without concurrent interference by anyone else. The TAT examination is usually someone else's idea that is carried out under his direction.

DESCRIPTION OF PDS

The PDS interpretive rules are logically the same as those we use in our waking life when we assess the personality of socially interacting individuals (Piotrowski, 1971). However, two prerequisites must be met. The primary one demands "translating" the dream's pictorial language into the standardized public verbal language (Piotrowski, 1982). The second prerequisite calls for a careful discernment between dream elements which have a graphic, pictorial referent and those which are expressed solely in words and have no pictorial correlates. The latter are more conscious than those expressed in visual-motor imagery, and therefore less reliable as indicators of the dreamer's intrapsychic dynamics. Thus, the PDS rules offer a method of "translating" the private visual-motor imagery into the public verbal language, but training and education are necessary to achieve skill combined with validity (Piotrowski, 1972, 1972a).

Contrary to a widespread impression, there is little real bizarreness in dreams. This misperception seems to result from failure to unravel the meaning of a concrete object, or giving it a fanciful interpretation. Overlooking the great difference in manner of expression between the pictorial and the verbal language can also lead to this erroneous conclusion. Verbal speech is better in describing interpersonal relations (the closeness, distance, strife or attraction) since it can employ spatial and temporal terms. Pictorial language is better in describing intraindividual feeling states (varieties and degrees of inner tension, self-confidence, fears and kinds of depression).

Two general premises have dominated the interpretation of dreams since antiquity; for the sake of brevity let them be called *Axiom A* and *Axion B*. *Axiom A* is the more valid and important one psychologically. It states that the personality traits of all dream figures are projected traits of the dreamer himself. The novelty of PDS is the idea that each dream figure represents a different trait set, with each set differing in the degree of assent or dissent by the dreamer (See Rule of Assent and Dissent). Each trait set reveals a distinguishable, quasi-autonomous sub-personality that can occasionally be observed even in the dreamer's overt behavior. *Axiom B* postulates that each dream figure manifests the dreamer's opinion, emotions, attitudes and intentions regarding the type of person represented by the particular dream figure. Thus, the dreamer expects old, young, male, female, and all types of persons, to behave in real life situations as they do in his dreams (whether or not he is aware of this assumption). Obviously, no dream illustrates all the personality traits of a dreamer. This makes it possible for both *Axioms,* applied to the same dream, to result in valid conclusions (Piotrowski, 1952a).

Dreams are remarkably truthful because they have an efficient way of obviating repression without complicating and confusing the dream message. Whenever a mental content disturbs the dreamer and he wishes to avoid becoming aware of its implications, it can be attributed to a dream figure other than the dreamer himself. According to PDS, all the traits that dreamers assign to themselves in their own dreams are assented and acknowledged by the dreamer to be their own genuine characteristics. When attributed to figures quite different from the dreamer, they can easily be disowned, saving the dreamer from tension. Thus, repressed traits can be manifested in dreams of which the individual is aware without arousing any repression or causing distortions. The diversity of dream figures provides a means of indicating multiple degrees of repression, yet reveals the traits in distinct ways. The diversity of dream figures provides, then, a multi-point scale of the unconscious (Piotrowski, 1977). For PDS needs and purposes, the unconscious can be defined as a persistent, organized and planned pursuit of certain goals of which the individual is unaware because anxiety interferes with the full realization of the goals pursued (Piotrowski, 1957). The degree and scope in which mental contents are kept in states of the unconscious can vary. We may be in possession of some relevant and valid information without realizing its consequences, which we would grasp clearly and immediately in higher states of consciousness. Additionally, the meaning of dreams is sometimes incomprehensible to the dreamer but self-evident to others. It appears preferable to use the terms assent and dissent instead of the complex and debatable conscious and unconscious (Piotrowski, 1973).

The personality which is assessed by the PDS reveals the psychological traits (that is, affects, thoughts, intentions and actions) that influence the individual's direct and indirect psychosocial interaction with his environment (Piotrowski, 1957). Dreams serve an important psychobiological function. They help to formulate and dramatize intrapsychic conflicts; usually they also indicate a way of solving the conflict (Piotrowski, 1971). The conflicts, with their concurrent anxiety and decrease in self-confidence, intensify concern for the future. Imagination is useful when one is striving for a way out of the difficulties, and the lack of sensory-motor contact with the physical environment facilitates this creative process. The central nervous system can pay full attention to the dreamer's intrapsychic processes with hardly any interference by empirical, environmental stimuli.

Some dreams may have their origin in the physiology of the organism (e.g., seriously incapacitating illnesses, pregnancy). All physical changes in the person affect their security and standing among others. They contribute to internal conflicts, associated with the inevitable readjustment to social relations and mode of existence in general. Nothing takes place in a vacuum. Our mental processes reflect the whole living organism, its body as well as its mind.

SEVEN INTERPRETIVE RULES

Rule of Assent and Dissent.   To assent a trait manifested in a dream is to affirm it as a genuine personal characteristic regardless of whether the trait is an asset or a liability in life, whether it signifies health or illness and whether it is good or evil. Even when an individual has not thought about it, but assents it once he has been made aware of the nature of the trait, the trait is considered "assented." To dissent a trait is to doubt or genuinely deny that one possesses it. There are degrees of assent and dissent. Rating a trait on this scale is done in terms of differences in physical traits between the dreamer (as he or she looks in that period of the dream) and the dream figure to which the rated trait was attributed. The most significant difference is in sex, then age, health, power, education, and so forth. The most dissented traits are assigned to animated inanimate objects which move on their own (e.g., airplanes not controlled by anyone, tall building cranes without a driver); they too are classified as dream figures. The nature of the intrapsychic conflict is then inferred from a comparison of the assented with the dissented traits. It seems that people are more willing to talk about their assented traits than their dissented ones. Caution is advised in broaching traits ascribed to animated inanimate dream figures.

Rule of Primacy of Verbs and Abstract Nouns.   Both verbs and abstract nouns occurring in night dreams should be taken literally because they validly reveal the dreamer's intentions, attitudes and action-tendencies. Abstract nouns are verbs in disguise; for example, "concentration" means paying active attention to one thing and excluding all others. Concrete nouns, on the other hand, indicate the means for realizing our desires. There are many more means of achieving gratification than basic needs; there are also many varieties of means to satisfy the same wish or desire. It follows, then, that there are more concrete nouns than verbs in any developed verbal language.

Rule of Multiple Meanings of Concrete Nouns.   The meaning of a concrete noun in a dream cannot be logically incompatible with that of the verb with which the concrete noun forms a meaningful verb phrase. Therefore, the verbs should be interpreted first before their logical complements, the concrete nouns, can be unraveled with satisfactory validity. For example, a man dreams that he would like to escape from another man of similar age who is threatening him with a spear. In this particular situation, the spear, pointed dangerously at him, symbolizes his mildly dissented hostility towards men and his fully assented fear of the consequences of his own aggressiveness (*Axiom A*). It may also symbolize the dreamer's view that men in general tend to be challenging, competitive and aggressive toward each other (*Axiom B*). In another dream, the dreamer does not feel seriously endangered, but is amused and intrigued by a long and narrow slit in the spear's arrowhead; another interpretation is more appropriate. In this case, the spear could be a symbol of the male organ, which does not necessarily invalidate the first interpretation of the spear. Both are probable. However, the slit in the arrowhead is an unrealistic and unexpected visual detail. Since such a spear had not actually been seen in waking life, we must assume that it had its origin in the dreamer's autistic, wishful fantasy, and probably reveals something imagined but not actually experienced in reality. In some dreams butterflies with claws appear. As a dream figure, such a butterfly represents a cluster of one of the dreamer's part-personalities: there are people who are gentle and superficially attractive but who nevertheless painfully hurt others on occasion.

Rule of Implicit Evidence.   Endings of dreams are of great interest because they show what the dreamer contemplates doing about the conflict visualized in the dream. Nightmares are aborted dreams; they end in panic before any possible solution has been envisaged. In nightmares the anxiety is so great that it disrupts the dream and restores full consciousness. When facing a great danger toward the end of the dream, it makes a difference whether or not the dreamer fights back, and how he does it. Thus, dream endings have prognostic significance.

Rule of Complementarity.   The dream interpretation can be enriched by the application of any sound psychological and psychopathological principle. For example, sadness or depression is not often directly mentioned in dream reports. However, one frequently finds visualized instances of frustration. Frustrations are followed by depressions or indicate a depressive state. Dream indication of a strong attachment to father or mother can indirectly reveal emotional difficulties in marriage or in other close relationships with adults.

Rule of Generalization.   This question does not arise with *Axiom A*, but comes up when *Axiom B* is employed. How wide or narrow should the area of applicability of *Axiom B* conclusions be? In a dream, if a man behaves in a certain manner, is it the dreamer's belief that all men of that age range behave in the manner of the male dream figure, or only a selected group of men, or possibly only one man? This question is of a theoretical rather than practical significance because it is not difficult nor onerous to obtain a reliable answer from the dreamer in an interview.

Rule of Difference Between Covert and Overt Behavior.   This rule is also of theoretical rather than practical significance, particularly to the psychotherapist who learns a great deal about the difference between covert and overt behaviors from the patient himself and from his own observations. Nevertheless, it may become an important practical question whether or not the dreamer will actuate some of his tendencies in the future. Prediction of overt behavior is the most difficult personological problem. We have only a modest beginning. More numerous and more diverse factors, including environmental, must be considered and appraised making predictions of overt behavior when assessing intrapsychic processes. The greater the incompatibilities, the more difficult it is to plan and act effectively. Dreams do not augur well when at the end of them there is an increase in anxiety, depression, abandonment or surrender. Prognosis is favorable when at the end of dreams matters are handled more successfully and with less inner tension than they had been at the beginning of the dream.

A SAMPLE DREAM

Dan was a young, married but childless man who asked Albert M. Biele, M.D. for psychotherapy. He complained of depression, anxiety, agoraphobia, and feelings of personal inadequacy. He was in a graduate school at the time, and needed to function more efficiently in order to receive his doctorate at the end of the academic year. Science and personal research were his greatest interests. During the initial session, he was encouraged to dream and to write down his night dreams immediately upon awakening. He came to the next session with the following dream:

> I was in some kind of building with a wooden floor. My wife and I and another man were there. The man pointed down to the floor, to a lizard or catfish. We talked about it. I reached down, picked it up, and it grabbed hold of me with a hind claw. I shook my hand and it (the animal) fell off. (What kind of lizard?) This lizard was a mudpuppy, an amphibian like creature. And I felt better when I shook it off. (What kind of mudpuppy?) It had funny looking gills on the side of its head, not nice arches, almost like a tree or finger-type gills. (Where was it?) On the floor that was made with wide wooden boards with cracks between them. The animal was in a crack between the boards.

The spontaneously recorded part of the dream was communicated in seven terse sentences. Dr. Biele asked three questions in the hope that Dan would recall some additional information about the fundamental visual-motor aspects of the dream, which he did.

The dream analysis was done mainly within the logical framework of *Axiom A*. It must be kept in mind that the fundamental interpretive PDS rule applies the same principles of assessment that are used in evaluating personality from observations of an individual's conscious behavior in interpersonal relationships. The important prerequisite is that the visual-motor language of the dream must be translated into the public verbal language with the aid of the following four rules:

Assent and Dissent, Logical Primacy of Verbs and Abstract Nouns, Desymbolization of Concrete Nouns and Implicit Evidence. Thus, the mudpuppy does not denote (in terms of *Axiom A*) a primitive amphibian animal, but one part of the dreamer which functions quasi-autonomously in certain circumstances; real mudpuppies have no claws, but the one in Dan's dream does. This implies that Dan reacts in an unexpected and hostile manner when deprived of the freedom of movement, which belies the usual impression of calm and restraint. The anomalous and wicked "hind claw" also marks him as a defensively aggressive person, who is weak and feels exposed to the control of others. He dissents these traits very strongly; aquatic cold-blooded animals are very near the full-dissent end of the assent-dissent dimension. The mudpuppy caused the strongest affect-laden experience in the dream. Hence, we are justified in concluding that the dissented traits manifested by the mudpuppy are of great dynamic significance. The dream discloses that Dan behaves in a shocked and agitated way when he comes into a close and positive association with another man, taking a dependent role. Dan carried out the other man's suggestion, bending in the process.

Dan's wife was also in the dream but only as a passive observer. However, including her in his dream, Dan revealed some positive affect for her. He did not mind her seeing his involvement with the other man and the outcome if it. Thus, indirectly, the wife had been implicated by him in his disordered relationships with men. In the dream, the attributes of the mudpuppy are more dissented than those of his wife. Dan's withdrawing tendencies then are of two kinds. Dan finds it unacceptable to be a mere observer without initiative, reduced to a subordinate role in interpersonal relationships that matter to him. This withdrawal is characterized by avoiding the complications of psychosocial relationships and is colored depressively. In the second kind of withdrawal, which is much more dissented, Dan is alert, ready to strike out immediately should he feel endangered. Resentment is usually associated with such a striking defensive attitude, and engenders acute anxiety states.

All traits which Dan attributed to himself are fully assented. This means that he is aware of possessing those traits or can be made aware of them without inner opposition. Outstanding among them is the great difference in attitude toward men and women (represented by his wife). Dan paid no attention to his wife during the entire dream. By contrast, he was very sensitive to the man and unhesitatingly responded to him carrying out his suggestion. The intimate meeting with the man ended for Dan painfully.

Dan's intrapsychic conflict, conspicuously revealed in his dream, was to be attracted to men but to incur pain when yielding to the temptation. The preference for men is striking against the background of Dan's disregard of his wife and her passivity. Married men who are ambivalent about their attraction to men and who neglect their wives are, as a rule, inadequate sexually. A homosexual inclination is one form of inadequate heterosexuality (Piotrowski, 1967). An analysis of the "mudpuppy" seems useful. PDS states that the symbolic meaning of words complements the content of the verb phrase of which it is a logical part and should be compatible with the main message of the dream. Let us consider the following observations, all of which pertain to the apparently casual meeting of the two men. Their common object of interest was a defenseless and frail little creature which loses its tail easily when touched but which Dan's unconscious endowed with a vicious hind claw. This fictitious "claw" makes it an exceptional mudpuppy, weak but well capable of taking care of itself when threatened, suggesting that being affected by men is not as dangerous and unmanageable as it seems to Dan, for otherwise why would he dissent the mudpuppy's defense reaction so strongly? The matter that drew the men together must be of concern to men only because otherwise there would be no need or desire to keep the wife away from the conversation and the mudpuppy. These itemized observations, viewed as aspects of the same functional whole, make it very probable that the brisk little salamander symbolizes the phallus of a man with sexual difficulties. Continuing this line of reasoning we may assume that the "crack between the boards" indicates a body orifice which gets involved in sexual activities. It could be a bisexual symbol (of the vagina, anus, or both). As an amphibian, the mudpuppy is not warmblooded but coldblooded; it symbolizes a very limited capacity for warm positive emotions toward others. Moreover, amphibious means literally "leading a double life."

Dan was the only dream figure which changed its place on the dream stage. He was stimulated by two of the other dream figures. In terms of *Axiom A* this means that lack of control over two of his dissented action tendencies caused Dan to move, act and suffer a painful frustration. Assented frustration indicates a depression (Rule of Complementarity). Dan knows that he causes his own misery by insufficiently controlling his homosexual inclination. When this inclination is only moderately gratified, Dan can tolerate it easily (the man who pointed to the mudpuppy), but when a body contact is made, anxiety becomes acute (touching the mudpuppy), and contact is broken immediately and aggressively. Dan is not only tempted (on a fully assented level), he also tempts on a slightly dissented level (in the person of the man who actively attracted Dan). By contrast, Dan's attitude toward his wife is quite subdued but he seems to appreciate and to trust her. He had placed her in the dream to watch his weakness for men, but also his intense struggle to limit its manifestation to socially acceptable forms, such as private talks with men (*Axiom B*). Dan, in the role of his wife, displayed dependency on his marital mate, his expectation that she would be tolerant and would not leave him alone to fight his psychosexual deviance. He dissents unpleasant and offensive scenes, watching them impassively (*Axiom A*). Had the dream scene been acted out in reality, it would have been offensive to the wife (Rule of Complementarity).

The parents did not appear in the dream, but parents have such a strong influence upon the development of their children's personality that psychosocial roles acquired while living with parents affect future relationships with women and men. Therefore, in Dan's dream, the wife is likely to disclose some traits shared also by Dan's mother (Rule of Complementarity). The most apparent of these traits would be standing by her son's side as if ready to help if necessary, but maintaining some emotional distance from him. Similarly the father's traits could be conjectured from the "other man's" characteristics (Rule of Generalization). The conspicuous trait would be to get other people (including his son) into trouble by motivating them to do things they will later regret. This implies a certain disregard for Dan's welfare (*Axiom B*). If this is a valid deduction, Dan should be wary of men (*Axiom A*). He might resent men's suggestions and orders.

The dream ended as it had begun. The situation remained unchanged. Dan posed a problem but did not solve it. Each dream figure resumed its position of isolation it had at the beginning of the dream. Dan was in great need for help to break out of the circle of indecision caused by well matched incompatible strong drives which were mutually inhibiting one another. The desire for therapy seems genuine to allay an intense anxiety and enervating vacillation. The advantage of the strongly dissented mudpuppy traits is preventing actual homosexually colored body contacts and thus save Dan great social embarrassment and near panic; however, they make Dan feel and act in a coldblooded hostile manner. Dan's standards of social behavior are strongly determined by prevailing norms of personal conduct. The socially inoffensive and positive attitudes, revealed in the dream, are assented or but slightly dissented, while the socially most disruptive hostility that can be manifested in violent acts is very strongly dissented (on the U8 level). In other words, Dan fights hard against his socially and personally most agitating and frightening behavior dramatized by the mudpuppy. Prognosis for a successful psychotherapy seems good.

DR. BIELE'S CLINICAL VALIDATION

The following text concerning Dan consists of excerpts from the 105-page typoscript left by Dr. Biele. All sentences in quotes are Dan's. Occasional sentences in parentheses are Dr. Biele's but have been condensed by ZAP. The rest of the text are direct quotations from Dr. Biele:

The purpose was to ascertain to what extent the 'blind PDS' could disclose the major pathology in the first two or three sessions following the initial consultation. The case is not presented as a study of therapeutic technique. The dreamer contacted the author and urgently requested a consultation because of an acute anxiety attack. He reported that he could not leave the apartment, dreading the occurrence of a panic state. The wife had to accompany him so that he would be able to leave his apartment. She also had to escort him to classes. He was hesitant, guarded and had extreme difficulty in presenting his problem. He was distressed that his symptoms were occurring just when he was about to start his last year in a graduate school. He felt that it was crucial to his well-being that *these attacks* be brought under control. He was most concerned about his academic work, even though he was a grade A student throughout his school years, yet often felt defeated. "When people tell me to do things, I resent it. Sometimes I do what I'm told, but I have mental reservations. I like to find the other person wrong." Dan was openly guarded about the relationship that might develop between him and his therapist, a matter that occupied his attention from the very onset of therapy until his departure.

"The roughest period of my life until now was adolescence." He began to think at that time that he was lacking in masculinity. He took showers in a gym only when he was assured that he would be alone. Since his marriage he tended to be socially withdrawn. He felt more *safe* being withdrawn. After several months in therapy, Dan reported that he had been holding back in his sessions. (He then started to discuss his psychosexual difficulties continually). "I just don't feel like a man." He repeatedly expressed a desire to overcome his problem. After a number of weeks, during which he experienced the most intense anxiety up to this point, he disclosed with great difficulty that he was afraid he might have some homosexual tendencies. "I'm afraid of what you will think of me. Even though you haven't forced me, I feel you are making me talk about something that is very frightening." His exploration of both his homosexual fears and hemosexual impulses gave rise to extreme anxiety. He was in such distress that it seemed wise to have two sessions in one day. (He mentioned repeatedly that bodily contact in a spirited ball game evoked the specific fear about his *latent homosexuality*. He also talked a lot and freely about his hostile aggressiveness whenever he felt set upon physically or mentally. He had the greatest difficulties to curb this form of irrational defense. Later in treatment Dan had a frank homosexual dream which was of crucial importance.) Dan interpreted this dream himself: "It's the old story. When I try to turn my wife off or don't feel up to having sex with her, then the old homosexual fear comes back." With this one spontaneous associative response to the dream, there was a dramatic and lasting reduction in his anxiety and depression. Toward the end of the ten-month treatment Dan commented spontaneously: "I can think about it (homosexual impulses), but I don't get panicky. It occurs to me when I am in the gym, just like before, but now I can look at the guys and the problem is sort of academic." (There was a conspicuous gain in relevant insight). He had available to him, through his insight, experiences, cognizance of mild constrained anger or anxiety that was generated in a series of current interpersonal situations. Prior to therapy these impulses were unrecognized.

(The helpful role of the wife is abundantly documented). Dan described her as "a very good person", unusually efficient, held in high regard by her employers and able to handle all the domestic matters with the same degree of efficiency. She accomplishes all this with such ease that he feels all the more humiliated and becomes intensely angry. His wife is his most reliable shield against stresses.

"She is a very good, very loving, very loyal person." Dan "kept her in place" by being uncooperative, resisting her pleas to be of some help and making her daily life a little more difficult. "I wanted to make her realize that I was the man!" He is "dependent on mother" as well. The persistence of this "paradoxical tie to mother" perplexes him. He became painfully aware that his way of life was similar to his mother's style of which he had been critical. Dan's father was prone to impulsive rages during which he would "stomp around the room, red faced." He was chronically depressed, and irritable with little or no provocation, whereas mother rarely displayed any overt anger. Dan became extremely disquieted when he stated that he was "very much like my father" (Rule of Generalization).

The blind analysis of Dan's dream revealed his pathology and his resistances far more readily and precisely than that which was obtained from the clinical data available at the beginning of treatment. The material (in this clinical assessment) is limited exclusively to the hard clinical data that was observable. Such data could have been validated by any clinician who could have viewed and heard the sessions.

REFERENCES

Piotrowski, Z. A. A new evaluation of the Thematic Apperception Test. *Psychoanalytic Review,* 1950, *37,* 101–127.

Piotrowski, Z. A. The Thematic Apperception Test of a Schizophrenic interpreted according to new rules. *Psychoanalytic Review,* 1952, *39,* 230–251.

Piotrowski, Z. A. (The TAT Newsletter). J. Project. Techn., 1952a, *16,* 512–514.

Piotrowski, Z. A. *Perceptanalysis: A fundamentally reworked, expanded and systematized Rorschach method.* Ex Libris, Philadelphia, 4th print., 1979. (Orig. publ. 1957).

Piotrowski, Z. A. Inadequate heterosexuality. *Psychiatric Quarterly,* 1967, *41,* 360–365.

Piotrowski, Z. A. A rational explanation of the irrational: Freud's and Jung's own dreams reinterpreted. *Journal of Personality Assessment,* 1971, *35,* 505–518.

Piotrowski, Z. A. Testing of intelligence and personality. In A. M. Freedman & H. I. Kaplan (Eds.) *Diagnosing mental illness.* New York: Atheneum, 1972, pp. 41–85.

Piotrowski, Z. A. From inkblots to dreams: Perceptanalysis generalized. Rorschachiana Japonica, 1972a, *14,* 1–10.

Piotrowski, Z. A. The Piotrowski dream interpretation system illustrated by an analysis of a specific dream. *Psychiatric Quarterly,* 1973, *47,* 609–622.

Piotrowski, Z. A. The movement responses (rorschach). In: *Rorschach psychology.* Maria Rickers-Ovsiankina, ed. 2nd, enl. edit. Huntington NY: R. E. Krieger, 1977, pp. 189–227.

Piotrowski, Z. A. Computerized perceptanalytic rorschach: The psychological x-ray in mental disorders. In: *Technology in mental health care delivery systems.* J. B. Sidowski, J. H. Johnson, T. A. Williams, eds. Norwood NJ: Ablex Publishing Corporation, 1980, pp. 85–108.

Piotrowski, Z. A. Unsuspected and pertinent microfacts in personology. *American Psychologist,* 1982, *37,* 190–196.

Piotrowski, Z. A. & Biele, A. M. Blind analyses of manifest dreams preceding death. American Psychiatric Association Scientific Proceedings, 176th annual meeting, 1973, 308–309.

2 Current Research in the Comprehensive Rorschach System

Donald J. Viglione, Jr.
U.S. Navy

John E. Exner, Jr.
Rorschach Workshops

Current Rorschach research cast in the Comprehensive System is reviewed in this chapter. The first group of such studies is a series of test-retest reliability investigations over various time periods with children. These data are integrated with the developmental norm data presented elsewhere to derive hypotheses about the emergence of various Rorschach variables during childhood. Two other test-retest studies indicate that under certain conditions the Rorschach is relatively impervious to efforts to improve one's performance. In another study, persistence in a meaningless task was related to "a cognitive overload" predicament as represented in an excess of a particular Rorschach response category. Evidence is also presented indicating that empirically relevant state anxiety has essentially no effect on the Rorschach among normals. In light of these and former findings, an intercorrelational matrix of major Rorschach variables is examined and its implications specified. Finally, preliminary findings on the differential diagnosis of borderline, schizotypal, and schizophrenic conditions are presented.

This chapter presents current Rorschach research cast in the Comprehensive System (Exner, 1974, 1978; Exner, Weiner, Schuyler, 1979). The Comprehensive System is an integration of the five major Rorschach systems in common usage in the United States (Exner, 1969). It incorporates the most useful and reliably scorable indices from these other approaches. Supplementing these are selected variables whose interscorer reliability has been demonstrated and that have meaningful psychological correlates. Much of the understanding of the inherited variables comes from other systems, but a great portion of the validation work remains to be accomplished. In addition, although most of the previous research has been adequately designed and interpreted, much has not met acceptable standards. Consequently, Exner and his coworkers have undertaken the task of further delineation of the constructs associated with these variables and configurations among them. The studies presented in this chapter represent the continuation of this work.

The studies in this chapter address separate avenues of research which are united by the principles of the Comprehensive System. They differ in focus, some emphasizing major interpretive issues, others psychometric, clinical, or environmental influences. All are united by the understanding of the Rorschach as primarily a problem-solving task which activates one's consistent style of coping behavior. The problem posed by the test is to temporarily ignore the fact that a given inkblot is precisely that and to violate reality by answering the question, "What might this be?". It is only an inkblot as younger clients are quick to remind us, but we demand that they solve the problem of the Rorschach. When the subject is forced to convert the ambiguity and complexity of the inkblot into something else, an intriguing pattern of psychological activity is stimulated. The data gleaned from the subject's responses, or solutions, provide a glimpse of how the individual works with the world, how he responds to ambiguity and challenge. These data are quantified in the various scores and more indirectly expressed in the words and other behaviors that are observed. The impressive temporal consistency of the various Rorschach scores, as derived from test-retest studies (Exner, 1978; Exner, Armbruster, & Viglione, 1978), suggests that these solutions to the Rorschach problem are representative of one's relatively stable, idiographic style of coping with the world.

This problem-solving point of view differs from the view that projection constitutes the fundamental process underlying the formation of Rorschach responses (Frank, 1939). Certainly, the "projective process" plays an important role in the Rorschach, but the main feature is associated with the manner in which the person has been accustomed to dealing with stimuli—one's psychological habits. It is also important to note that the projective hypothesis is often associated with the mistaken belief that the inkblots present unstructured and consequently, simple "blank-screen" stimuli. On the contrary, the challenge of the Rorschach is that its ten inkblots are complex, ambiguous forms that require the subject to perform involved translation and decision operations (Arnheim, 1969; Exner, 1978; Exner, Armbruster, & Mittman, 1978).

The interpretive foundation for the Comprehensive System is found in what Exner (1978) has called the "4-Square", which incorporates the basic information describing one's characteristic response or problem-solving style. The four indices of the 4-Square are:

1. *Erlebnistypus* (*EB*, the ratio of human movement to weighted color responses.)
2. Experience Actual (*EA*, the sum of human movement and weighted color responses.)

3. Experience Base (*eb,* the ratio of non-human movement to shading and gray-black responses.)
4. Experience Potential (*ep,* the sum of non-human movement, shading, and gray-black responses.)

These four items are symmetrical: two ratios (*EB, eb*) each with a corresponding sum (*EA, ep*). The *EB* yields information on whether a given individual tends towards ideational or affective coping responses to stress (Rorschach, 1921). The psychological action as represented by both human movement and color responses is deliberately initiated for coping purposes. Beck (1960) was the first to recognize the significance of this fact by combining both sides of the *EB* to form the sum *EA,* as a general index of the "amount" of organized resources available for coping. Earlier, Klopfer (Klopfer, Ainsworth, Klopfer, & Holt, 1954) had postulated that other Rorschach determinants, namely non-human movement and some of the shading and gray-black responses, correspond to psychological activity outside of deliberate control. Exner extended Klopfer's ratio to encompass all shading and gray-black responses and formed the *eb.* Following Beck's lead, Exner (1974) added the two sides of the *eb* to produce *ep,* which reflects the proportion of psychological activity not readily accessible to deliberate control and often experienced as stimulation acting on or impinging on the individual. These four variables taken as a whole encompass the basic information about the psychological habits and capabilities of an individual and represent the critical interpretive departure from earlier systems.

THE STIMULUS-INPUT AND THE EMERGENCE OF THE RESPONSE-STYLE

The emergence of the response style or coping style of an individual is generally assumed to occur during what has been referred to as the reaction time or first response time. These intervals average about 7″ across all 10 cards. It may seem surprising that within such a short interval that the predominant psychological habits of an individual come to bear in solving the problem of the Rorschach. This reaction time is often thought to be related to impulsivity or ability to delay. This conclusion is based on a "linear" understanding of the response process as consisting of stimuli presentation, gradual response development, and response report with the impulsive response being a premature report of an ill-formed response. Recent data (Exner, Armbruster, & Mittman, 1978) suggest that numerous responses are formulated during these reaction time intervals and that the associated processes are more complex than this "linear" model would assume. Indeed a more complex "network" or "branching" model may better describe the development of the response as an expression of the psychological habits of the individual. A number of responses may be simultaneously developed in a parallel processing fashion characteristic of visual imagery (Singer, 1974), under the influence of the psychological habits.

Exner (1980) has presented other data from Card I that suggest that much of the response development may occur well within the first half second after stimulus presentation. Within this very short interval the subject may scan the blot many times, pausing intermittantly along the way. It is possible that much of the problem of the Rorschach is resolved during the first half second, and that the remainder of the 6″ response time to Card I is spent in elaboration, refinement, selection, and rehearsal of the response to be delivered. The scan itself may be molded by the problem-solving habits of the individual, as is suggested by Exner's (1978) discussion of "underincorporation" and "overincorporation." If the majority of the stimulus input and much of the response "work" is completed during the first half second, there are a couple of implications that deserve attention. First of all, the remainder of the reaction time is quite long in comparison, but may be necessary to reduce the complexity that a "branching" or "network" process produces. Secondly, this would necessitate a modification in the understanding of "impulsivity" on the Rorschach. More central to the theme of this chapter is the implication that these response styles are automatic, psychological habits that manifest practically instaneously upon exposure to the inkblot stimuli. Such a possibility attests to the power and pervasiveness of the psychological style of the individual as it presents itself in the solution of the Rorschach problem, and is truly remarkable. On the other hand, in everyday perception such instaneous processing is the rule rather than the exception, and the Rorschach is fundamentally a perceptual task.

This emphasis on the problem-solving aspects of the test is not meant to cast aside the notion that the test is also a "projective" instrument. The richness of each protocol is intimately tied to the personal world of the subject. The lengthy interval after the stimulus input may be associated with the expression of the unique concerns of the subject. Typically, this material is invaluable to interpretation but research of this area has generally led to disappointing results. In addition to the obvious methodological faults associated with some of this work, this lack of satisfactory results may be attributable to the research practice of equating the idiographic aspects of the Rorschach to content scores. With the demise of this "symbolic" approach and the "easy" research it generates, more sophisticated approaches of exploring the unique, personal aspects of the test and understanding how these features merge with the psychological habits of the individual to form a response will ensue. Does the personal psychology of the individual affect the stimulus input, response formation, elaboration, selection, or rehearsal processes? These are important research questions and deserve further attention.

RELIABILITY OF THE TEST AMONG CHILDREN

As noted above, numerous temporal consistency studies on the Rorschach have been reported for adults and illustrate that the majority of variables included in the Comprehensive System, among them the *EB, EA,* and *ep,* are very sturdy over various time intervals ranging from seven days to three years (Exner, Armbruster, & Viglione, 1978; Exner, 1978). The most extensive of these involved the retesting of 100 nonpatients after a three-year period. The resultant test-retest correlations ranged from $r = .90$ for the Affective Ratio (*Afr,* the number of responses for the last three cards, which are chromatic, divided by the number of responses on the first seven cards, which are predominantly black and gray) to $r = .66$ for the sum of the gray-black and shading responses (*Sh*). As a result of this study, it was hypothesized, that the majority of the Rorschach variables represent enduring traits and *Sh,* animal movement (*FM*) and inanimate movement (*m*) reflect more temporary state effects. The group of studies in this section highlight the consistency of the Rorschach variables as they develop in the maturing child. The gradual crystallization of response hierarchies, ego functions, personality traits, or whatever hypothetical constructs a given viewpoint endorses should be reflected in the increasing stability of these data with advancing age.

In the first study (Thomas & Exner, 1980) two groups of children were retested after relatively long periods. One group consisted of 30 nonpatient, 6-year-olds who were tested shortly after they entered the first grade and retested approximately 2 years later. The second group consisted of 25, 9-year-olds, tested for the first time in fourth grade and retested approximately 2½ years later. The test-retest correlations for these two groups, plus those for the 100 adults retested after three years (Exner, Armbruster, & Viglione, 1978) are presented in Table 2.1.

The greatest differences exist between the child groups and the adults: sixes and nines resemble each other more than they do the adults, in terms of the stability of their response styles over long periods. Nines are only marginally, if at all, more consistent than sixes. No conclusive patterns of development can be discerned from these data, although the aspects of perceptual accuracy ($X+\%$, the percentage of all responses that are good form, and *P,* popular responses) apparently stabilize quite early. The increase in correlations of *EA* and *ep* from the sixes to the nines suggests that the *EA:ep* relationship begins to crystallize by the ninth year. The Egocentricity Index ($3r+(2)/R$, a function of pairs and reflections) and the active movement total (*a*) are quite sturdy among these children. Generally, the modest correlations for both children's groups suggest that early solutions to the Rorschach problem may not accurately predict later configurations at a subsequent stage in development. On the other hand, these

TABLE 2.1
Test-Retest Correlation Coefficients of Two Groups of Children
and One Adult Group Over Long Periods

Groups		First test age 6, retest after 24 mos. N = 30	First test age 9, retest after 30 mos. N = 25	100 adults retested after 36-39 mos.
		r	r	r
Variable	Description			
R	Responses	.67	.61	.79
P	Popular responses	.77	.74	.73
Zf	Z frequency	.55	.68	.83
F	Pure form	.52	.69	.70
M	Human movement	.48	.62	.87
FM	Animal movement	.49	.60	.72
m	Inanimate movement	.13	.09	.31
a	Active movement	.86	.81	.86
p	Passive movement	.42	.29	.75
FC	Form color responses	.14	.34	.86
CF+C	Color domonant responses	.27	.35	.79
SumC	Sum of weighted color responses	.42	.58	.86
Sh	Total of all gray-black & shading responses	.08	.29	.66
Percentages & Ratios				
L	Lambda	.18	.39	.82
X+%	Extended good form	.84	.86	.80
Afr	Affective Ratio	.51	.79	.90
3r+(2)/R	Egocentricity index	.78	.74	.87
EA	Experience Actual	.19	.45	.85
ep	Experience Potential	.20	.57	.72

data do not help determine whether children would display the high degree of response consistency that adults manifest over short intervals (Exner, 1978).

A second study was designed and executed to investigate this question. In this study, 25, 8-year-olds were tested and then retested after seven days for comparison to a group of 25 adults whose seven-day test-retest correlations were presented earlier (Exner, 1978). The results are presented in Table 2.2. The correlations of the two groups resemble each other closely and are consistently very high. Thus, the solutions offered by both adults and children remain quite stable over short periods. Combining these results with the above study, the relative lack of consistency among children's Rorschach behavior over long periods reflects developmental changes rather than either fluctuations in the response style or unreliability of the test. Given the increasing sturdiness of the test with age, and the crystallization of personality characteristics, one may safely assume that the short-term consistency demonstrated in this study maintains over brief periods after age eight. These data, however, do leave the questions open about consistency over brief period for children under eight and for all children for intervals longer than 7 days and shorter than 2 years.

A study by Alinsky and Exner in 1980 yields information about the second question. Two groups of 20 subjects were collected, all non-patients, one group containing 7-year-olds and the other 9-year-olds. They were retested 260 to 290 days after the first Rorschach administration. The resultant data are presented in Table 2.3. These data reveal a striking similarity between the 15-year-olds' test-retest correlations and the adults' data presented in Table 2.1. Apparently the response features and corresponding psychological habits are crystallizing or have crystallized by mid-adolescence. The exceptions are those features (*m, Sh*)

TABLE 2.2
Test-Retest Correlation Coefficients of a Group of Children and a
Group of Adults Over Seven Day Periods

Groups		Age 8 $N = 25$	Adults $N = 25$
		r	r
Variable	Description		
R	Responses	.88	.86
P	Popular responses	.86	.84
Zf	Z frequency	.91	.88
F	Pure form	.79	.68
M	Human movement	.90	.81
FM	Animal movement	.75	.63
m	Inanimate movement	.49	.28
a	Active movement	.91	.91
p	Passive movement	.86	.84
FC	Form color responses	.90	.93
CF+C	Color dominant responses	.89	.82
SumC	Sum of weighted color responses	.88	.85
Sh	Total of all gray-black & shading responses	.70	.51
Percentages & Ratios			
L	Lambda	.82	.73
X+%	Extended good form	.95	.88
Afr	Affective Ratio	.91	.93
3r+(2)/R	Egocentricity Index	.94	.91
EA	Experience Actual	.85	.83
ep	Experience Potential	.75	.62

TABLE 2.3
Test-Retest Correlation Coefficients of Two Groups of
Children Over Nine Month Periods

Groups		First test age 7 N = 20	First test age 15 N = 20
		r	r
R	Responses	.71	.80
P	Popular responses	.88	.83
Zf	Z frequency	.62	.79
F	Pure form	.82	.74
M	Human movement	.46	.82
FM	Animal movement	.53	.70
m	Inanimate movement	.06	.17
a	Active movement	.77	.85
p	Passive movement	.39	.64
FC	Form color responses	.28	.81
CF+C	Color dominant responses	.46	.71
SumC	Sum of weighted color responses	.37	.70
Sh	Total of all gray-black & shading responses	.11	.48
Percentages & Ratios			
L	Lambda	.24	.76
X+%	Extended good form	.86	.83
Afr	Affective Ratio	.61	.89
3r+(2)/R	Egocentricity Index	.70	.86
EA	Experience Actual	.23	.73
ep	Experience Potential	.18	.64

which have been associated with state phenomenon. In contrast to the adolescent and adult groups, the younger children's data lack evidence of response-style consistency. Most striking is the contrast between the various color variables (*FC, CF+C, Sum C*), *EA,* and *ep* between the younger and older children. Apparently, these features are reaching the "permanence" of psychological habits during the time interval between 7 and 15 years of age. All three groups share the same high correlations for *X+%* and *P* noted earlier, thus further supporting the early stabilization of perceptual accuracy and acceptance of conventionality.

As a group these studies yield valuable information for the issue of reliability of various indices and childhood development. First of all, the findings concerning *X+%* and *P* clearly negate the mistaken attribution of low scores on these variables as reflecting the typical problems of children in perceiving reality. On the contrary, children accurately process environmental stimuli as is clearly reflected in normative data presented earlier by Ames (1966) and Exner (1978).

It is true that these data also indicate that children tend to mediate less complicated stimuli, but do so accurately nevertheless. On a more general level children's response tendencies, as reflected in their solutions to the Rorschach problem, do change over long periods of time. The younger the child, the more
change can be expected. However, the greater sturdiness over shorter periods
indicates that these changes are gradual rather than precipitous and apparently
related to development and crystallization of response styles. Rorschach data
from a given testing early in childhood probably accurately describes coping
tendencies concurrent with the testing but might not accurately predict later
behaviors or ultimite, adult psychological habits. On the other hand, the evidence does suggest these habits are easily recognizable in Rorschach data configurations produced in late adolescence.

These correlational data also permit an elaboration of Exner's (1978) discussion on the developmental trends of the various 4-Square components. Deriving
his conclusions from cross-sectional, normative data, he concluded that increases
in *M* and *C* result in a gradual increase in *EA* relative to *ep* through the ages 5 to
16. The *ep* components, *FM, m,* and *Sh,* stay relatively stable during this time.
Although these normative data reveal group mean, developmental trends they are
of little value in predicting an individual's future scores based on previous
testing. By adding the correlational data, a clearer picture of the developmental
trends is possible. Such test-retest data yield information about the consistency
over time of a given score relative to its group mean. Table 2.4 presents these
developmental data: the normative data collapsed over three-year periods as well
as the representative correlational data. Certainly, the complex of findings is
incomplete, but they do permit tentative conclusions.

TABLE 2.4
Comparisons of Developmental Norms and Correlational
Data of Various Age Groups

	Developmental Means					Test-retest correlations				
Ages	*5-7*	*8-10*	*11-13*	*14-16*	*Adults*	*6-8*	*7-8*	*9-12*	*15-16*	*Adults*
Variable										
M	1.2	1.9	2.6	2.7	3.5	.48	.64	.62	.82	.87
SumC	3.5	2.9	3.5	3.3	3.7	.41	.37	.58	.70	.86
FC	0.8	1.2	2.0	2.0	3.6	.42	.28	.29	.81	.86
CF+C	2.3	2.2	2.1	2.2	1.7	.27	.46	.35	.71	.79
EA	4.7	4.8	6.1	6.0	7.2	.19	.23	.45	.73	.85
FM	a	a	a	a	2.4	.49	.53	.60	.70	.72
m	2.9^b	3.0^b	3.3^b	3.1^b	0.7	.13	.06	.09	.17	.31
Sh	1.7	1.7	1.7	1.7	3.3	.08	.11	.29	.48	.66
ep	4.6	4.7	5.0	4.8	6.4	.20	.18	.57	.64	.72

[a] Not available, included in *m* totals
[b] Includes FM

Beginning with the normative data for M, one notices a rather rapid mean increase until early adolescence, followed by a more gradual increase until adulthood. In contrast the correlational data suggest that M might crystallize by the sixteenth year. Apparently, an individual is likely to give more M after this time but his or her standing relative to the peer group is likely to persist. To summarize these findings, the evidence suggests decreasing fluctuation of individual M scores around its initially, rapidly increasing and thereafter more slowly increasing group mean. The normative data reveal that $SumC$ manifests what appears to be a less gradual increase than M. The correlational findings suggest that $SumC$ appears to stabilize about its group more slowly than does M. Consequently, although the absolute level of $SumC$ for a given peer group may not increase very much, the ranking of the individuals within the group is subject to fluctuation. $SumC$, on the whole does not appear to become a firm, trait-like feature until adulthood. This inconsistency might be related to the change from color dominant $(CF+C)$ responses to form color responses (FC) with maturation. Throughout most of childhood, the temporal inconsistencies of both M and $SumC$ are reflected in EA. The mean increase is probably mostly a function of increases in M. Taken somewhat concretely, EA apparently does not "crystallize" until M ceases to increase and $SumC$ ceases to fluctuate. These data also suggest that the predictability of EB from earlier Rorschach data is limited. However the developmental trend of increasing introversiveness $(M > SumC)$ suggests that an introversive style in mid-adolescence is more likely to persist than in an extratensive $(M < SumC)$ style. In cases where $FC > CF+C$, this prediction is even more likely to be borne out.

In general, the ep elements are more state-like than EA elements, but their mean levels do not change during childhood. m is grossly inconsistent throughout the lifespan. FM, on the other hand, gradually reaches a level of moderate stability relative to its apparently consistent group mean (if we can assume that FM and m account for the same proportion of $FM+m$ across ages). Sh, highly inconsistent relative to a stable group mean, apparently arrives at a moderate consistency in adulthood. It is interesting to note that increases in Sh, unlike other variables, do not occur until at least age 16. It is also important to realize that although the $FM+m$ mean is constant through development, it exceeds most other variables in early childhood. Thus, its predominance later in life might signal immaturity. As a modification of an earlier statement, it appears that m, is exclusively a state variable, and FM and Sh become mixtures of state and trait features. Throughout development, ep reflects the fluctuations of its components and is probably best described as a mixed state-trait variable in adulthood. The EA to ep relationship probably does not stabilize until early adulthood, after the increases in Sh and M are achieved and $SumC$ and FM "mature."

Two other studies with children are closely associated with the issue of temporal consistency of the Rorschach. They explore the sturdiness of the response style despite instructions to alter one's responses upon retest. The basic response style of an individual should be recognizable in the underlying structure of a set of responses although the precise description of the percepts may vary with conditions. If this hypothesis is borne out, the temporal consistency of this style as expressed in Rorschach behavior across various contexts is further supported. The first of these studies (Hulsart, 1979) was designed to test this hypothesis among severely disturbed children who were encouraged to improve their performance upon retesting. The subjects were 55 impatient children between the ages of 11 and 15, who were screened for intellectual deficiency and neurological impairment. They were retested 2 days after their original Rorschach administration. At both testings they were required to give two responses per card and upon retesting were informed that a staff member personally important to the child had reviewed the original findings and had concluded that the subject could improve his or her performance. Subjects were instructed to do the "very best that you can. . . ''. As controls, 27 inpatient children were given the standard introduction except for the instruction to produce two responses per card without encouragement to improve their retest performance.

Although many of the retest responses offered by the experimental group differed from the initial responses, there were no significant differences among any of the major structural variables either between or within groups. This demonstration of the reliability of the Rorschach is tempered by the possibility of methodological problems. The key word "best" may have been interpreted differently by various children. The instruction to the experimental group may have been too ambiguous or too threatening so as to inhibit modifications of responses. Another possible confounding factor is that the subjects' severe pathology could have overwhelmed any effects of "attempts" to alter one's approach to the test. These considerations led to a new study (Thomas & Exner, 1980), designed to eliminate these methodological criticisms.

The resultant study incorporated the same procedure of initial testing, intervention to alter performance of experimental subjects, and retesting. The subjects were 60, 8-year-olds, randomnized into two groups, each consisting of both 15 males and 15 females. Every subject was led to anticipate being tested at least twice. Experimental subjects were specifically instructed to give different answers on their second administration. This instruction was justified by the claim that examiners tend to hear the same answers over and over and that their training would be improved by hearing different kinds of responses. All examiners used the standard procedure for administration, except that the standard encouragement given for Card I in cases where only one response is forthcoming was lengthened to include ". . . and I hope you'll find at least two things in each one."

In addition to mean differences, test-retest correlations were presented for these reliability data. These correlations for both the experimental and control groups were uniformly high ($r = .75$ or more) and nearly identical for ten of the 19 important variables (those listed in Tables 1–3). The exceptions are pure form responses, F (experimental $r = .59$, control $r = .81$), Lambda, L, the proportion of all responses that are pure form ($r = .67$, $r = .82$), m ($r = .27$, $r = .48$), Sh ($r = .44$, $r = .71$), and ep ($r = .38$, $r = .70$). The differences in F, m, Sh account for the differences in L and ep. It was also found that the experimental group gave significantly more F and m but fewer Sh in the second test. It is important to note that the retest correlations for the control group are remarkably similar to those produced by the 8-year-olds retested after seven days, which are presented in Table 2.3. Of the five major ratios (EB, eb, $EA:ep$, $FC:CF+C$, $a:p$, active to passive movement) only eb shifted in "directionality." This change in eb is a result of the changes in m and Sh, which have already been described as the most state-like of all the Rorschach variables at this age. The four stable ratios yield critical information regarding the response style and are relatively impervious to modification as demonstrated by this study and previous work with adults (Exner, Armbruster, & Viglione, 1978). Incidentally, the results for these variables are very similar to the Exner *et al* study. It is true that these four ratios do change during childhood, as we hypothesized above, but they seem resistant to situationally induced change over short intervals at any time during the life span.

The changes in m and Sh may be due to situational variables. It may be that the experimental intervention influenced the amount of unorganized psychological activity by increasing it in the ideational sphere (m) but reducing it in the affective sphere (Sh). This is consistent with the cognitive focus of the instructions which may have "translated" some affective "pressure" to cognitive "pressure." The difference in F and L are a bit more perplexing, but Exner (1978) has presented findings that suggest that certain individuals tend to "flip" from low F or L to high or vice versa under certain circumstances. Certainly, the possibility remains that these variables may be subject to modification through conscious effort and are simply less reliable than others.

A critical issue in this study is whether the independent variable was effective, that is whether the subjects in the experimental group did give different answers when taking the test over. This was evaluated by comparing frequencies of identical and different answers. Identical answers were defined as responses with the same content using the same or nearly the same location area. In other words, the percept of two men fighting to the Popular area on Card III would be considered identical to two men working at night, given to the same area, even though the second answer might include the additional determinants C', achromatic color, or Y, diffuse shading. Conversely, if the answer on retest were two dancing women, the two responses would be considered to be different. The resultant data clearly indicate that the experimental subjects do appear to have followed directions. Only 14% of their answers were identical while 86% of the control subjects' were repeated. These findings clearly support the conclusions that a consistency will exist in perceptual-cognitive operations of a person even though manifest behaviors are altered, thus lending further support to the stability of the problem-solving style as manifest in Rorschach data.

Based on the accumulation of temporal consistency findings, one can offer some broad conclusions concerning the nature of the test. First of all these data reaffirm what is one of the central themes of this chapter: that the Rorschach is one way of gaining information about the consistent psychological habits or operations that underlie one's behavior (Exner, 1980). Furthermore, these tendencies are discernible even though the verbalizations that contain them may change. This is akin to the psychological consistency that underlies seemingly inconsistent behaviors in everyday life. The complexity and ambiguity of the test apparently also offer the flexibility to reflect the dominant features of one's psychological habits. They are manifest in the underlying structure which organizes the solutions to the Rorschach problem and quantifies the major scores.

THE 4-SQUARE

Much of the validation work for the Comprehensive System has focused on the 4-Square interrelationships. Recently the *EA:ep* relationship has undergone increased scrutiny and the studies presented in this section represent a continuation of this work. The temporal consistency data reviewed above indicated that the *EA:ep* gradually stabilizes through development and reaches permanence by adulthood (Exner, Armbruster, & Viglione, 1978). Normative data shows that *EA* increases relative to *ep* as children mature and that more normals than patients have *EA* greater than *ep*. These results have been understood to show that the *EA:ep* relationship represents a stable, personality characteristic reflecting the relative ''amount'' of psychological activity organized in a way that is available for coping purposes versus that which is related to more immature experiences that impinge on the individual. Treatment studies have shown increases in *EA*, alone (Beck, 1960) and relative to *ep* (Exner, 1978), among patients who improved in therapy. For patients who begin treatment with *ep* greater than *EA*, a reversal occurs in the majority of cases, that is *EA* becomes greater than *ep*, in retest records when intervention continues for more than a brief period (Exner, 1978). Exner has suggested that such changes occur because treatment either facilitates the organization of resources in ways to make them more available or relieves stress as reflected in *ep* or both. This is not to say that *ep* activity is always disruptive and pathological. In fact, about 30% of the adult reference sample presented by Exner in 1978 had *ep* greater than *EA*. In addition, *ep* activity in moderate amounts probably represents the excitation and stimulation underlying motivational processes.

Persistence and frustration-tolerance are often thought to be associated with coping resources and purportedly increase with maturation and therapeutic improvement. Based on the empirically-demonstrated relationship between *EA:ep* and such gains, it has been hypothesized that these Rorschach variables encompass important information about persistance and frustration-tolerance. Exner and Bryant (1975, 1976) investigated this hypothesis in two small-sample studies. The findings suggest that when *EA* is greater than *ep,* individuals are likely to persist for longer periods on difficult tasks. Subjects in the first study with more *EA* than *ep* took more trials and more frequently successfully completed a mirror-tracing task than did subjects with more *ep.* Conversely, this second group terminated their effort much more often. Subjects in the second study with more *EA* tended to persist longer at a pursuit rotor task. There remains some doubt whether the task in the first study was truly frustrating, but it is more clear that the pursuit rotor task did interfere with goal-achievement and thus was truly frustrating (Kimble & Gamezy, 1968; Lindzey, Hall, & Thompson, 1975). These results suggest that *EA:ep* is related to frustration tolerance and persistence as hypothesized by Exner in 1978.

When confronted with a frustrating task, one's alternatives are to exert a continued effort toward mastery or to discontinue the work. As Wiener-Levy and Exner (1981) point out, the theoretical expectation is that individuals with fewer coping resources available and more psychological activity outside of direct control, *EA* less than *ep,* would be more likely to remove themselves prematurely from a frustrating situation. On the other hand, those with *EA* greater than *ep* might persist in their coping attempt. Wiener-Levy and Exner designed a study to evaluate the Exner and Bryant results and implications more precisely. They expanded their study to investigate whether the magnitude of the difference between *EA* and *ep* was important in addition to the direction of the *EA:ep* ratio. To investigate these questions, 80 undergraduates were selected and were screened to exclude those with obvious perceptual-motor deficiencies. Pursuit rotor data were collected immediately after the Rorschach administration by a second experimenter who had no information about the Rorschach results. Subjects were randomly assigned to either a high or low frustration condition and were classified into four groups according to the magnitude of the difference between *EA* and *ep.* The less frustrating condition required the subject to track a pursuit rotor as it revolved 60 times per minute. The more frustrating condition differed in that the direction of the rotation reversed each minute and the angular velocity increased by five revolutions upon each reversal. Post-experimental data, however, indicated that the two conditions did not differ in the amount of self-report frustration they induced. In addition to persistence as measured by time until quitting, time off-target was measured as a dependent variable. During such off-target periods, a timing device emitted a distinct sound that served as extrinsic, negative feedback to the subjects. After a 2 minute practice period, the experimenter informed the subjects that the study involved the identification of unusual individuals who can ultimately stay on target 70% of the time, a goal which unbeknown to the subjects was practically unapproachable.

Contrary to expectation, it was found that as *ep* became increasingly large relative to *EA* subjects persisted for longer periods even though all groups performed at approximately the same level of accuracy. There were no significant findings for the frustration level interaction or for the interaction between the two independent variables. This negative finding is not surprising because, as stated above, the two conditions were not experienced differently by the subjects. Through examination of the components of *EA* and *ep,* it was found that *ep* ($r = .39, p < .01$) rather than *EA* ($r = .02$, n.s.) was strongly associated with persistence. Further investigation revealed that *m* ($r = .36, p < .01$), *Sh* ($r = .36, p < .01$), but not *FM* ($r = .11$; n.s.) accounted for practically all of the variance between *EA-ep* and persistence ($r = -.40, p < .01$). The only other Comprehensive System variable that correlated significantly with persistence was white space responses (*S, r = .38, p < .01*).

Wiener-Levy and Exner explain the difference between their findings and the Exner and Bryant results in terms of feedback processes. The subjects in the Exner and Bryant studies relied only on intrinsic feedback processes while the subjects in the present study were afforded unequivocal, extrinsic feedback in the form of a relatively loud tone whenever off-target. The authors contend that the most appropriate response by the subjects in this study would be to terminate the effort since the task was actually meaningless and the goal of 70% accuracy was obviously not being approached. In comparison the Exner and Bryant study utilized a less complex stimulus field and task, with the subjects experiencing performance improvement into the sixth minute. Persistence on such a task would be appropriate to the situation.

As noted earlier, *EA* appears to reflect resources that are available to the individual for use when a situation requires some form of coping. It may also be true that low *m* and *Sh,* as components of *ep,* are related to and increased capacity to process external simulus inputs, that is, more elements of the stimulus field are mediated. Conversely, in instances where *m* and *Sh* are excessive, the opposite may be true as the disturbing, internal *activity* tends to interfere with available, coping resources. With such excessive internal stimulation, it seems likely that external inputs cannot be processed as efficiently, a condition that decreases complex, problem solving capabilities. *m* is associated with ideation provoked by the experience of situational stress and *Sh* with experiences of negative affect (Exner, 1978). Wiener-Levy and Exner concluded that these elements tend to create an "overload" situation that may interfere with processing in one of three ways: (1) by distracting subjects from attending to external feedback, (2) through misinterpretation of such feedback, or (3) by establishing a state of hyperalertness. Such conditions would reduce the probability of accurate assessment of complex information provided by the task at hand and also reduce the likelihood of appropriate response—in this study, quitting the task. The authors conclude that *m* and *Sh* are probably less related to frustration-tolerance than of limitation to cognitive capabilities in the problem-solving style of the individual.

As described in the previous section, *m* and to a lesser extent *Sh* are state variables. In addition they have been shown under certain conditions to be related to, but not necessarily directly related, to stress and anxiety (Exner, 1978;

Auerbach and Spielberger, 1972; Frank, 1978). State-anxiety (Spielberger, 1975) can interfere with cognitive processing and represents one way of understanding the impact that Sh and m had on the subjects in the Wiener-Levy and Exner study. The negative and confusing findings in the Rorschach—anxiety research indicates that a more specific delineation of the types of stress, anxiety, and conditions under which the relationships manifest. Viglione and Exner (in press) designed a study to more specifically assess whether increases in Sh would be associated with laboratory, social-evaluative stress and concommitant state-anxiety. If such were the case, one could establish a relationship between external stress and temporary performance "deficits" through increases in Sh. m was not addressed directly in the Viglione and Exner study but the results are presented here.

Viglione and Exner contrasted the Rorschach protocols of subjects under low (control) and high (experimental) social-evaluative stress. Subjects with verbal intelligence deficiencies and current life stress were excluded from the study. There were 30 subjects in each treatment group, with approximately the same proportion of undergraduate and non-psychology graduate students. Upon arriving at the experimental room, all subjects were administered a portion of the STAI X-1, a measure of state-anxiety (Spielberger, Gorusch, & Lushene, 1970). After this baseline measurement was collected the control and experimental procedures diverged: social-evaluative aspects were emphasized in the experimental procedure and minimized in the control. After being told that most of the subjects got about half of a series of anagrams correct, control subjects received 16 easily solvable anagrams and experimental subjects 12 unsolvable and 4 solvable ones. The groups were provided with positive and negative feedback respectively. After these experiences, a second partial STAI X-1 was administered to determine whether the intervention did result in more state-anxiety among experimental subjects than control subjects. With the expectation that more anagrams would be administered afterwards, both groups were administered a Rorschach by a second experimenter who was unaware of the nature and purpose of the study.

The results of the study revealed that the state-anxiety score increase among experimental subjects ($\bar{x} = 6.13$) significantly exceeded, $F (1,55) = 19.55$, the control increase ($\bar{x} = .07$). These findings clearly indicate that the social-evaluative stress intervention was effective. However, both groups did not differ in the frequency of m and Sh. In addition, post-experimental inventory results supplied by both the subjects and examiners indicated that the state-anxiety, induced by the experimental intervention, apparently quickly dissipated once the Rorschach was begun.

Thus, these results conflict with earlier results suggesting a relationship between Sh, m and social-evaluative stress. Although the social-evaluative stress did result in significant increases in state-anxiety, it did not substantially alter Sh and m. Closer examination of individual variables, including the components of Sh, yielded no significant findings. Sequence analysis did reveal that the two groups differed in terms of their first response to Card I but not the next response or the first response to Card II. Experimental subjects gave a more conservative first response with fewer M, human contents (H), and synthesized responses ($DQ+$). In addition, the nonsignificant difference between groups on this response reflected a more conservative quality among experimental subjects. Viglione interpreted this more conservative response as an attempt by experimental subjects to overcome experimentally-induced helplessness. By offering a less ambitious initial response, being successful, these subjects overcame their helplessness, and the associated state-anxiety. As a result, the experimental subjects more closely resembled the control subjects and offered basically identical solutions to the Rorschach problem. This hypothesized relationship between both m and Sh and helplessness derives some support from Exner's 1978 discussion of the relationship. One might expect the performance deficits, associated with m and Sh, produced in the Wiener-Levy and Exner study to manifest when the subject feels helpless.

These results have important implications for the issue of reliability. In general, the results indicated that the test is quite resistant to the type of state-anxiety changes produced in this experiment. The test, itself, may offer opportunities to adjust or alter temporary states that might have otherwise affected Rorschach performance. This feature of the test, which is probably related to the flexibility of the test cited earlier, may contribute to the temporal stability of the test. As Frank (1978) has contended, the relationship between stress and various Rorschach determinants may only hold when the stress is sufficiently powerful to induce state changes throughout the administration of the test. An alternative explanation is that this relationship maintains when the subject goes sufficiently far along the Selye's (1956) alarm-resistance-exhaustion sequence. Only under such conditions will situational variables alter Rorschach performance. In adults these effects are probably first noticeable in m and secondarily Sh. The lack of temporal consistency among children suggests that their Rorschach behaviors and response habits are more susceptible to disruption by situational variables. This is understanable by the fact that their resources are less developed and sophisticated, and that helplessness as a result is more easily stimulated.

SOME RELEVANT INTERCORRELATIONS

Exner (1974, 1978) has emphasized that the response style of an individual is revealed through the configuration of the various indices rather than by isolated variables. Accordingly, it is crucial to understand the relationships among these indices. One source of such information is intercorrelations among these variables. Such data (Viglione, Gillespie, & Exner, 1980) were derived from the 100 non-patients from the temporal consistency study noted earlier in this chapter (Exner, Armbruster, and Viglione, 1978). Because these data are derived from non-patients, the intercorrelational matrix encompasses what might be called

TABLE 2.5

Mean Intercorrelations of 16 Rorschach Variables with R Partialed for Test and Retest of 100 Non-Patient Adults

	M	SumC	EA	FM	FM+m	Sh	ep	FC	CF+C	X+%	P	F	L	Afr	3r+(2)/R	Zf
M	–															
SumC	-.46*	–														
EA	a	a	–													
FM	.19	-.33*	-.13	–												
FM+m	.20	-.34*	-.17	a	–											
Sh	-.12	.23	.10	.10	.13	–										
ep	.03	-.08	-.05	a	a	a	–									
FC	-.15	a	a	-.32*	-.40*	-.14	-.35*	–								
CF+C	-.47*	a	a	-.23	-.18	.37*	.12	.09	–							
X+%	-.08	.06	-.06	-.06	-.17	.00	-.06	.18	-.05	–						
P	.04	-.01	.03	-.08	-.02	-.04	-.04	.03	-.03	-.02	–					
F	.02	-.22	-.36*	-.17	-.15	-.23	-.25	-.20	-.14	.10	-.07	–				
L	-.17	-.25	-.41*	-.14	-.14	-.22	-.24	-.23	-.16	.03	-.08	a	–			
Afr	-.27	.46*	.16	-.24	-.27	.27	-.01	.21	.42*	.11	.03	-.06	.09	–		
3r+(2)/R	-.12	.38*	.26	-.14	-.17	.27	.06	.21	.28	.09	.09	-.15	-.19	.64*	–	
Zf	.43*	.14	.42*	.14	.13	.07	.13	.10	-.01	.08	.01	-.20	-.24	.11	.04	–

^{a}artificially inflated and consequently excluded

*$p \leq .01$, $r \geq .26$, at both testings

"successful" response styles of these relatively well-adjusted individuals. Various patient populations might produce different configurations.

Before examining the matrix, some technical considerations need be addressed. Because the frequency of any given Rorschach score is directly related to the number of responses (R), all intercorrelations involving these scores are artificially inflated. To compensate for this confounding, the effects of R have been statistically removed through partialling techniques. In addition, correlations that are artificially inflated through spurious relationships are omitted. For example, the correlation of EA and M is excluded because M is included in EA. The partial correlations presented in Table 2.5 are actually coefficients that correspond to the mean amount of variance accounted for by the test and retest correlations of the original study. For example, a correlation of .80 accounts for .64 of the variance between two variables and a correlation of .60 accounts for .36, for a mean of .50. The corresponding correlation to .50 is about .70, so that .70 would appear in Table 2.5. Because of the large number of significance tests, 128, conservative significance levels were utilized. To be considered significant, both the test and retest correlations were required to reach the $p < .01$ level. Thus, both at test and retest significant correlations were greater than $r = \pm .26$.

Perusing Table 2.5, one might first notice that F and L are negatively correlated with all other determinants. (One seeming exception is the correlations with $X+\%$, but this variable is a computed percentage rather than an individually scored determinant.) This finding lends statistical support to the use of L, as the quotient of F divided by the number of all "non-F" responses. Interpretively, it supports the understanding of F and L as suggestive of an unwillingness to process the more complex features of the inkblots and also a reluctance to experience the emotional and ideational complements inherent in other determinants, especially those included in EA (F, $r = -.36$; L, $r = -.41$).

These data also reveal some interesting, and perhaps confusing, information about the 4-Square components. Most striking is the substantial negative correlation between the two sides of the EB, M and $SumC$, $r = -.46$. This inverse relationship lends support to the notion that among normals either M, ideational, or $SumC$, emotional, resources dominate, that is, when one side of EB is large the other side tends to be small. This statement is equivalent to saying that ambitents, M and $SumC$ approximately equal, are atypical among non-patients. Further inspection of the $SumC$ components reveals that the relationship between M and $CF+C$, $r = -.47$, rather than that between M and FC, $r = -.15$ largely accounts for the inverse relationship between M and $SumC$. It must be noted that among normals pure color responses, C, are rare, so that in this sample $CF+C$ largely consists of CF. This finding suggests that the ability to respond in an emotionally dominant but sufficiently modulated manner is central to the extratensive style. FC, on the other hand, might not be specifically related to any style. This lack of specificity might be related to the fact that the majority of *FC*, as presented in Table 2.4, does not develop until after age 12 when the basic foundation of the Experience Type, or psychological coping style is already partially fixed. However, these results cannot be taken to mean that extratensives maintain less emotional control than others. On the contrary, Exner (1978) has presented data that shows that they are no more likely than other experience types to have *CF+C* exceed *FC* and that *FC* generally exceeds *CF* among normals.

As expected *EA* and *ep* are not correlated. However, various components of these sums are substantially intercorrelated. These correlations can be essentially reduced to (1) an inverse relationship between *FC* and *FM+m*, $r = -.40$, (2) a positive relationship between *Sh* and *CF+C*. It may be that *FC* and *FM+m* "compete" in some way. For example, excessive *FM+m* may make it difficult to discharge emotion in a modulated fashion. Alternatively, considering the developmental data, excessive *FM+m* in childhood may inhibit the develop of *FC* in adolescence. *CF* responses may signal an ability to sustain the irritating or disrupting, emotional activity associated with *Sh*. Along a developmental perspective *CF* may promote the development of *Sh* in late adolescence or early adulthood.

A few other findings are noteworthy. *Zf*, organizational activity, is highly correlated with *EA* and *M*, $r = .42$ and $r = .43$, but not with *SumC*, $r = .14$. This is understandable in light of their both involving ideational activity. A "comforting" negative finding is that both *X+%* and *P* are not substantially correlated with any other Rorschach variables. This supports the oft-stated belief that perceptual accuracy and the willingness to perceive convention are independent of other Rorschach response parameters. Surprisingly, *X+%* and *P* are not intercorrelated, $r = -.02$. This suggests that the ability to perceive reality accurately does not mean that non-patients will respond to conventionality. Earlier, in the chapter the developmental data linked *X+%* and *P* in that they both stabilize early. Certainly, there is some interdependency because all *P* are good form in and of themselves. However among normal adults, of whom one can expect high *X+%*, *P* might be related to other factors. This understanding of these variables allows for the expression of nonconformity by examinees (Exner, 1978).

The correlations of *Afr* and *3r+2/R* are also interesting. Those between *Afr* and the various color response categories (*SumC*, $r = .46$; *FC*, $r = .21$, and *CF+C*, $r = .42$) might be considered to be artificially inflated. On the other hand, because a given color response can occur on Cards II and III and because not all responses to Cards VIII, IX, and X are color responses these intercorrelations are included. In any event, the results show that *Afr* is associated with the extratensive style in general: high correlation with *SumC* and *CF*, low correlations with *FC*, negative correlation with *M*, $r = -.27$. Thus the data reveal a consistency between response style and the "amount" of exposure one has to emotionally provocative stimuli among non-patients. The greatest single correlation is between *Afr* and *3r+(2)/R*, $r = .64$. Apparently, the tendency to mediate emotionally provocative stimuli is strongly associated with a tendency to focus on one's self. If we can assume that such individuals feel better about themselves, this relationship might explain why they can withstand more *Sh*, even though the correlation between *3r+(2)/R* and *Sh* is not quite significant at both test and retest ($r = .27$).

These data have various implications for interpretation of individual protocols. First of all, these results in the context of other results presented in this chapter suggest that excessive *F* and *L* may be related to some type of attempt to conceal psychopathology. Secondly unusual combinations such as simulataneous elevations of *FC* and *FM+m*, contrasting levels of *CF* and *Sh*, extratensive styles with low *Afr*, among others, deserve special attention in the interpretive process. These issues are worthy of further empirical attention.

As emphasized a number of times, these data are derived from an adult, nonpatient sample. One would expect different response configurations among other age groups and patient groups. For example, among patient groups with reality distortion, such as schizophrenics, one might expect a positive association between *X+%* and *P* since perceptual accuracy will have a greater effect on conventionality. Contrasts among intercorrelational matrices from various ages and diagnostic categories would provide a better understanding of the indices.

USEFULNESS OF THE TEST IN DIFFERENTIAL DIAGNOSIS

During the past decade, researchers and theorists have vociferously debated the issue of the nature and limits of "borderline" personality pathology (Liebowitz, 1979; Grinker, 1979; Gunderson & Kolb, 1978; Kernberg, 1979; Spitzer & Endicott, 1979). Much effort has been expended in determining whether the "borderline personality" is distinct from what was formerly referred to as borderline schizophrenia" (Knight, 1953). The American Psychiatric Association, as presented in the Diagnostic and Statistical Manual of Mental Disorders (DSM-III, 1980) does distinguish between Schizotypal Personality Disorder, which encompasses those features commonly associated with the concept of borderline schizophrenia, and the Borderline Personality Disorder. According to DSM-III, the Schizotypal Personality Disorder is marked by magical thinking, ideas of reference, social isolation, recurring illusions, oddities of speech, inappropriate rapport, suspiciousness, and excessive social anxiety. In contrast, the borderline personality excludes evidence of peculiarities of thought and perception but does include impulsivity and unpredictable behavior, difficulty with anger, unstable and intense interpersonal relationships, lack of emotional control, identity disturbance, intolerance of being alone, chronic feelings of emptiness or boredom and a tendency towards physically destructive acts.

The taxonomy presented in DSM-III implies a clear differentiation between the two disorders is practically possible and clinically useful. However, these implications are yet to be evaluated. Gunderson and Kolb (1978), for example, suggested that the differential diagnosis between the two is not always easily accomplished. Similarly, Spitzer and Endicott (1979) have allowed for the possibility of a mixed or secondary diagnosis such as "Borderline Personality with Schizotypal features." If these clinical entities are truly distinct, fundamentally different patterns of psychological activity should underlie them. These patterns should manifest on the Rorschach as distinct configurations of response parameters, which would correspond with dissimilar problem-solving tendencies. This possibility of distinct coping styles as a reflection of contrasting symptomotology deserves further study.

As an initial investigation of this research question, Exner (1978) compared the Rorschach protocols of 21 borderline patients with 25 schizophrenics. This small study revealed that the borderline patients gave fewer distorted human movement responses $(M-)$ and Special Scores (indicative of cognitive impairment), a greater Egocentricity Index, more S, P, and texture responses (T), and demonstrated a tendency towards "underincorporation" (lower Zd), and a more frequent occurrence of ep being significantly greater than EA. Both groups had lower than average $X+\%$, but the borderline individuals tended to use weak, or more aptly described as unusual (FQw), rather than distorted $(FQ-)$ forms as the schizophrenics did. Generally, these findings are consistent with the differences between borderline pathology and schizophrenia as highlighted by DSM-III. They suggest a greater tendency for reality distortion $(X+\%, FQw)$ and thought disturbance $(M-$, Special Scores) among schizophrenics. The Zd, T, Egocentricity, S, and EA:ep, findings might be interpreted as representative of the hypothesized borderline features outlined in DSM-III.

The findings of the 1978 study are compelling and suggest that the borderline syndrome may be distinct from schizophrenic-like disturbances such as the schizotypal disorder. However the small sample size and the considerable similarity of the two groups as compared to normals among some Rorschach data necessitates a more complete investigation of the topic.

Such a study is in progress and is designed for 120 subjects drawn from recently admitted patients, equally divided among independently diagnosed borderline, schizotypal, and schizophrenic subjects. Data for 56 subjects have been collected, including 19 borderlines, 15 schizotypals, and 22 schizophrenics. The small sample size prohibits complete and conclusive analysis but does allow ANOVA comparisons among means for 16 major variables from the Rorschach Structural Summary. These means are presented in Table 2.6. For comparison purposes, representative means for non-patients are also included. They have been derived from the normative data presented by Exner in 1978 unless otherwise noted.

This table reveals that the only variable which discriminates between the borderline and both other groups is T, with borderlines giving significantly more.

TABLE 2.6

Means and Standard Deviations for 16 Rorschach Variables
for Three Patient Groups and Also for Non-Patients

Groups		Borderline $N = 19$		Schizotypal $N = 15$		Schizophrenic $N = 22$		Non-patient $N = 325$	
		M	SD	M	SD	M	SD	M	SD
Variable	Description								
R	Responses	21.8	4.9	19.6	6.3	23.4	5.8	21.8	5.1
Zf	Z frequency	7.1	3.9	7.3	4.5	9.6	4.2	9.4	2.3
X+%	Extended good form percentage	.67	.16	.63	.11	$.59^a$	.13	.81	.12
F+%	Good form percentage	.76	.11	.70	.07	$.64^a$	.15	.89	.08
FQw	Unusual forms, "weak"	5.2	2.6	4.3	2.1	3.5	1.6	2.5^d	e
FQ-	Distorted forms, "minus"	1.9	1.1	2.9	1.9	6.4^c	2.1	0.9^d	e
S	Space responses	3.8^b	1.3	1.4	0.7	1.9	0.8	1.1	0.7
DQv	Vague responses	4.1	1.3	3.6	1.4	2.2^a	0.9	e	e
L	Lambda	.56	.13	.71	.15	$.46^b$	.21	.82	.30
	Egocentricity Index	.64	.14	$.38^a$	.11	.41	.10	.37	.06
Afr	Affective Ratio	$.80^b$	.11	.63	.08	$.84^b$	.13	.69	.06
P	Popular responses	4.9	1.3	4.6	1.1	3.6	1.3	6.4	2.7
SS	Special Scores	3.6	1.1	3.9	1.9	6.5^a	2.1	0.7	0.3
Sh	Shading and black-gray	5.3	2.3	3.3	1.9	4.1	2.9	3.3	1.8
T	Texture	2.4^c	1.1	0.7	0.6	0.8	0.6	1.2	0.9
H	Human Content	5.2	2.3	3.2	1.6	3.9	1.8	4.7	1.4

Note: No Tests of significance between patient groups and non-patients.

[a] Significantly different from Borderline group
[b] Significantly different from Schizotypal group
[c] Significantly different from both other patient groups
[d] Estimated from data in Exner, 1974
[e] Unavailable

Borderlines also offered more *S* responses and had a greater Egocentricity Ratio than schizotypals. In comparison to schizophrenics, borderlines had higher $F+\%$ (percentage of good form among pure form responses) and $X+\%$, more *DQv* (vague responses, percepts lacking form requirements) and fewer Special Scores. Schizotypal subjects had lower *Afr* than both borderlines and schizophrenics and a higher *L* than schizophrenics. Schizophrenics gave significantly more distorted responses (FQ−) than both other groups.

A *Chi* square analysis for differences among frequencies which 12 important structural variables appear among the records of the three patient groups was also completed. These frequencies and the corresponding percentages for each group are presented in Table 2.7.

TABLE 2.7
Frequencies of Which 12 Rorschach Variables Appear in
the Protocols of Three Diagnostic Groups

Groups	Borderline $N = 19$		Schizotypal $N = 15$		Schizophrenic $N = 22$	
	Freq.	%	Freq.	%	Freq.	%
Variable						
EB Introversive $M \geq SumC + 2$	2^b	.10	9	.60	11	.50
EB Extratensive $M \leq SumC - 2$	10	.52	2^a	.13	7	.31
EB Ambient $\| M - SumC \| \leq 2$	7	.36	4	.26	4	.18
$ep > EA$	17	.89	13	.86	8^b	.36
$CF+C > FC$	12	.63	6	.40	13	.59
$M^p > M^a$	7	.36	5	.33	8	.36
M- (minus form)	3	.15	6	.40	16^b	.72
$Zd < -3.0$	10	.52	6	.40	5^a	.22
FQ-	4	.21	7	.46	21^b	.95
$FABCOM+ALOG > DV+INCOM$	3	.15	4	.26	17^b	.77
CONTAM	0	.00	1	.06	4	.18
$(H) + (Hd) > H + Hd$	9	.47	9	.60	12	.54

[a] Significantly different from borderline group.
[b] Significantly different from both other groups.

These data reveal that the borderline and schizotypal samples are very similar, except for basic response style, where the borderline subjects are largely extra-tensive and ambient while the schizotypal group is predominantly introversive and ambient. This is contrast to the schizophrenic group in which 18 of the 22 illustrate a marked style, 18 either introversive or extratensive with only four ambient. Most of the statistically significant differences occur between the schizophrenics and both other patient groups. There are significantly fewer cases in which ep exceeds EA; but more records in which the minus form quality is more frequent than weaks, more records with $M-$ present and more records with severe Special Score outnumbering less severe ones. The schizophrenics also show significantly less "underincorporation" in their organizing efforts than do borderlines.

These preliminary results suggest three major trends evident in the data. The first dimension concerns the relative dominance of severe disturbance among the three clinical entities. It seems clear that the schizophrenic group does differ markedly from the borderline group in a number of ways. They manifest a greater perceptual distortion ($F+\%$, $X+\%$, $FQ-$), and a more serious disturbance in thinking ($M-$, Special Scores). Generally, these features correspond to the reality distortions and cognitive impairment endemic to schizophrenics. Borderlines, on the other hand, manifest an idiosyncratic but not distorted approach to reality and mild or possibly circumscribed cognitive difficulties. Although the schizotypal subjects do not differ significantly from the borderlines on any of these variables, they fall consistently between the borderlines and schizophrenics.

A second trend is most evident among the borderline group and might be referred to as emotional immaturity and coping style reliability. Among the 19 borderline subjects 17 are either extratensive or ambient and 17 have more *ep* than *EA*. These findings in combination with the high *Afr* and excessive *CF+C*, indicate that the majority of this group apparently has problems in effective utilization of emotional resources and modulation of emotional responses. The predominance of *DQv* and less severe Special Scores delineates a type of thinking that is less sophisticated and differentiated than is common among adults. The complex of their excessive self-centeredness (Egocentricity Index), needs for closeness (*T*), and anger or oppositionalism (*S*) results in a chaotic interpersonal world. The tendency to miss critical cues or "underincorporate" (*Zd*) in the context of the other findings adds an impulsive feature. Collectively, these features describe a coping style marked by limited psychological development and substantial conflict, which is consistent with the social and emotional turbulence inherent in the DSM-III description. If only the schizophrenics and borderlines are considered these findings support those published earlier (Exner, 1978) suggesting that these groups are distinct clinical entities, with the former characterized by serious difficulties in perception and thinking and the latter by gross immaturity. However, the third trend as represented by the third group, the schizotypals, complicates the differential diagnosis issue.

The schizotypal group differs significantly from the borderline group for only five of the 28 variables analyzed: fewer *S* and *T*, lower Egocentricity Index and *Afr*, and a greater frequency of introversiveness. A literal interpretation of these differences suggests that, as contrasted with the borderline, they are less oppositional, experience far intense needs for closeness, are less self-centered, are less prone to be overly responsive to emotionally toned stimuli, and are more prone to use forms of deliberate ideation in their coping behaviors. When compared to the schizophrenic group, the schizotypals differ significantly for only seven variables. There are more cases in which *ep* exceeds *EA*, suggesting less stabilization of the personality features; they give fewer of the more serious Special Scores and fewer $M-$ responses, reflecting a less disturbed kind of thinking; they have the lower *Afr* suggesting less responsiveness to emotional stimuli, and they have a substantially lower *L*, indicating a greater ability to "back away" from stimulus complexity. In contrast to both groups, the schizotypal style is characterized by greater control and psychological distancing, features increasing the reliability and effectiveness of the coping style.

Returning to the original issue of differential diagnosis, whether these groups are truly distinct entities identifiable by differing configurations of psychological habits as represented by the Rorschach data, one must realize that these small samples do not justify a definitive answer. However, the data do force some speculations. Although the schizotypal and schizophrenic groups are similar in many ways, the sharp difference between the two in the amount of perceptual distortion, psychological control, and serious cognitive disturbance indicates that they may actually be distinct entities with divergent psychological habits. Similarly, despite many points of agreement between the schizotypal and borderline groups, their contrasts in style, self-involvement, emotional responsiveness, and needs for closeness, suggests the schizotypal is considerably unlike the borderline. Thus, in general, these early results support the practicality and utility of the DSM-III classifications but do cast doubt on the advantage of mixed borderline and schizophrenic diagnoses. They also open the possibilities for further exploration of other diagnostic issues from DSM-III. For example, it would be interesting to contrast the Rorschach response style of Avoidant and Schizoid Personality Disorder groups with each other and the three groups used in this study. In addition, the new distinctions within Somatoform and Affective Disorders deserve further study. One important research question is whether the group differences manifest among individuals. In other words, at what level of accuracy do the various features of the groups in question discriminate between individuals from the three groups?

FINAL THOUGHTS

The studies summarized in this chapter in various ways yield information about the Rorschach as a problem-solving task. The data concerning the reaction time and stimulus input attracts more attention to the processes involved in the development and delivery of a response. The complex of developmental studies allows a glimpse of the problem-solving style as it matures and stabilizes. Weiner-Levy and Exner's study provides an initial description of the limits of that coping ability in instances of excessive *ep*. They conclude that excessive *Sh* and *m* result in overstimulation that overloads or confuses cognitive processing, and the Viglione and Exner data suggests that helplessness may be critical to such difficulties. The incomplete data contrasting borderline with schizotypal subjects allow us to better understand these confusing clinical entities by specifying the psychological styles underlying their behavior. The intercorrelational matrix among the non-patients reflects the expected configurations among various Rorschach indices.

The conclusions from these studies need further replication and investigation and lead one to wonder about other aspects of the Rorschach, Of general concern is the mechanism by which the problem-solving style of an individual merges with one's personal interests and concerns to form a verbalized response. Further specification of the correspondencies between various configurations of 4-Square variables and their relationship to coping capacities would also be helpful. Comparison of various other DSM-III diagnostic categories would yield a more thorough understanding of various types of pathology. It might also give a psychological context to the lists of behavioral features used as criteria by DSM-III. To follow up on the hypotheses generated by the intercorrelational study, well-designed studies contrasting emotional and behavioral tendencies of individuals with unusual configurations of Rorschach variables might be undertaken. Specifically, the relationship between P and form accuracy as related to nonconformity and also the relationship of L to defensiveness and simulation deserve further study.

In general, it would seem that considerable data are being accumulated from which the Rorschach can be understood better than may have been the case in the past. While the Rorschach is more than 60 years old, much of our understanding regarding its nature and usefulness has occurred only recently, during the period when advances in technology, data processing, and data analysis have permitted the sorts of research methods necessary to broach these issues. Obviously, much more is to be learned about the test and an extended research endeavor continues to be required.

REFERENCES

Alinsky, D. & Exner, J. *Temporal consistency among seven and fifteen year olds retested after nine months.* Workshops Study 352 (unpublished), Rorschach Workshops, 1980.

Ames, L. B. Changes in Rorschach responses throughout the human life span. *Genetic Psychology Monographs,* 1966, *74,* 89–125.

Arnheim, R. *Visual thinking.* Berkeley: Univ. of California Press, 1969.

Auerbach, S. M. & Spielberger, C. D. The assessment of state and trait anxiety with the Rorschach test. *Journal of Personality Assessment,* 1972, *36,* 314–335.

Beck, S. J. *The Rorschach experiment: ventures in blind diagnosis.* New York: Grune and Stratton, 1960.

Exner, J. E. But its only an inkblot. *Journal of Personality Assessment,* 1980, *44,* 562–577.

Exner, J. E. *The Rorschach: A Comprehensive System,* (Vol. 1). New York: John Wiley and Sons, 1974.

Exner, J. E. *The Rorschach: A Comprehensive System, current research and advanced interpretation.* (Vol. 2). New York: John Wiley and Sons, 1978.

Exner, J. E. *The Rorschach Systems.* New York: Grune & Stratton, 1969.

Exner, J. E., Armbruster, G. L., & Mittman, B. The Rorschach response process. *Journal of Personality Assessment,* 1978, *42,* 27–38.

Exner, J. E., Armbruster, G. L., & Viglione, D. The temporal stability of some Rorschach features. *Journal of Personality Assessment,* 1978, *42,* 474–482.

Exner, J. E., & Bryant, E. *Pursuit rotor performance and the EA:ep relation.* Workshops Study 212 (unpublished), Rorschach Workshops, 1975.

Exner, J. E. & Bryant, E. *Mirror star tracing as related to different Rorschach variables.* Workshops Study 222 (unpublished), Rorschach Workshops, 1976.

Exner, J. E., Weiner, I. & Schuyler, W. *A Rorschach workbook for the Comprehensive System.* Bayville, N.Y.: Rorschach Workshops, 1976.

Frank, G. On the validity of hypotheses derived from the Rorschach: II, The relationship between shading and anxiety. *Perceptual and Motor Skills.* 1978, *46*, 531–538.

Frank, L. K. Projective methods for the study of personality. *Journal of Psychology,* 1939, *8*, 389–413.

Grinker, R.R. Diagnosis of borderlines: A discussion. *Schizophrenia Bulletin,* 1979, *5*, 47–52.

Gunderson, J. G. & Kolb, J. E. Discriminating features of borderline patients. *American Journal of Psychiatry,* 1978, *135*, 792–796.

Hulsart, B. *The effects of a "second chance" instructional set on the Rorschach records of emotionally disturbed and culturally deprived children.* Unpublished doctoral dissertation, Long Island University, 1979.

Kernberg, O. F. Two reviews of the literature on borderlines: An assessment. *Schizophrenia Bulletin,* 1979, *5*, 53–58.

Kimble, G. & Gamezy, N. *Principles of general psychology.* (3rd Ed.). New York: The Ronald Press, 1968.

Klopfer, B., Ainsworth, M., Klopfer, W., & Holt, R. *Development in the Rorschach technique, I: Theory and practice.* Yonkers-on-the-Hudson, N.Y.: World Book Co., 1954.

Knight, R. Borderline state. *Bulletin of the Menninger Clinic,* 1953, *17*, 1–12.

Liebowitz, M. R. Is borderline a distinct entity? *Schizophrenia Bulletin,* 1979, *5*, 23–28.

Lindzey, G., Hall, C., & Thompson, R. *Psychology,* New York: Worth, 1975.

Rorschach, H. *Psychodiagnostics.* Bern:, 1921 (Translation, Hans Huber, Verlag, 1942).

Selye, H. *The stress of life.* New York: McGraw Hill, 1956.

Singer, J. *Imagery and daydream methods in psychotherapy and behavior modification.* New York: Academic Press, 1974.

Spielberger, C. D. Anxiety: State-trait process. In Spielberger, C. D. (Ed.), *Stress and anxiety* (Vol. 1). Wiley, 1975.

Spielberger, C. D., Gorusch, R. L., & Lushene, R. E. *Manual for the Stait-Trait Anxiety Inventory.* Palo Alto: Consulting Psychologists Press, 1970.

Spitzer, R. L. & Endicott, J. Justification for separating schizotypal and borderline personality disorders. *Schizophrenia Bulletin,* 1979, *5*, 95–100.

Task Force on Nomenclature and Statistics, American Psychiatric Association. *Diagnostic and Statistical Manual of Mental Disorders,* (3rd Ed.). Washington, D.C.: American Psychiatric Association, 1980.

Thomas, E. & Exner, J. *The effects of instructions to give different responses during retest on the consistency of scores for eight year olds.* Workshops Study 372 (unpublished), Rorschach Workshops, 1980.

Viglione, D. J. & Exner, J. E. The effect of state-anxiety and social-evaluative stress on the Rorschach. *Journal of Personality Assessment,* in press.

Viglione, D. J., Gillespie, R. A., & Exner, J. E. *Some intercorrelations of Rorschach structural features.* Rorschach Workshops Study, 311 (unpublished), 1980.

Weiner-Levy, D. & Exner, J. E. The Rorschach EA-ep variable as related to persistence in a task frustration situation under feedback conditions. *Journal of Personality Assessment,* 1981, *45*, 118–124.

3 Recent Advances in the Cross-Cultural Study of Personality

H. J. Eysenck and S. B. G. Eysenck
Institute of Psychiatry, University of London

Cross-cultural comparisons of personality raise three problems which have to be distinguished. The first is whether identical dimensions of personality can be postulated in the cultures being compared. The second relates to the possibility of measurement in the second culture, given that the answer to the first question is in the affirmative. The third question relates to the possibility of effecting a direct comparison between the two cultures; this cannot necessarily be done properly even if the answer to the first problem is in the affirmative. Solutions are suggested to the methodological problems raised, and substantive research in the field is reviewed. It is shown that different methods, such as, questionnaire studies and analyses of demographic indices, give similar results in demonstrating marked differences in personality between different cultures, particularly with respect to extraversion-introversion and neuroticism-stability. Evidence suggests that differences in neuroticism are related to differences in stress, and differences in extraversion and psychoticism (inversely) to differences in *per capita* income. It is concluded that very similar or identical dimensions can be found in all the different cultures and nations surveyed, and that meaningful differences between them on the major dimensions of personality can be discovered.

INTRODUCTION

Since the publication of Wundt's *Völkerpsychologie* in nine volumes (Wundt, 1904–1919) there have been periods of increasing interest in cross-cultural studies, alternating with periods of decreasing interest. The middle years of this century saw very little work published on this topic, but there has been a revival

41

of interest in the last twenty years, as indexed by the number of textbooks and lists of readings published in recent years (e.g. Berry & Dasen, 1974; Brislin, Lonner & Thorndike 1973; Dawson & Lonner, 1974; Lewinson, 1977; Malpass, 1977; Marsella, Tharp & Ciborowski, 1979; Triandis et al, 1980; Warren, 1977) and books dealing explicitly and empirically with the topic of this chapter (Butcher & Pancheri, 1976; Hofstede, 1980; Lynn, 1971; Spielberger & Diaz-Guerrero, 1976). In this chapter we shall be concerned with only one of the many problems that are raised by the comparison of different cultures and nations, namely differences in personality between one national/cultural group and another. In doing so we shall be equally concerned with methodological problems as with substantive results.

We may begin by stating that there are three problems rather than one in comparing personalities from one culture to another, and the failure to realise this has led to many difficulties and complications. The first problem is the simple descriptive or structural one: do the same dimensions suffice adequately to describe certain areas of personality in the two cultures being compared? This question is absolutely fundamental, and a positive answer is required before any further steps can be taken; yet it is usually aborted, and the assumption made that the same dimensions, traits, or factors which account for the major part of the variance in one population will suffice to do so in a second population also. As we shall see, this hypothesis can be shown to be erroneous in many instances, although it can be shown to be correct in others; clearly empirical investigations are needed before we can proceed with the investigation of our second problem.

The second problem, given that identical (or very similar) dimensions, traits or factors are found to account for a major part of the variance in the two cultures, relates to the problem of *measurement* in the two cultures. Even though the *factors* in the two cultures may be identical, it can and does occur that individual *items* in the scales show different factor loadings. When this happens, clearly a different *weight matrix* (or scoring key) has to be constructed for measurement in the second, as compared with the first culture, choosing appropriate factor loadings to determine the nature of the weight matrix. Thus in this case we are concerned with constructing a suitable measurement instrument for *culture 2;* we cannot simply take the original weight matrix in order to do so, and although changes may be minimal, they should nevertheless be made in line with the above discussion.

This leads us to the third problem, namely the actual cross-cultural comparison between the two cultures or nations involved. Clearly if different weight matrices are needed in order to score the test in the two cultures, the test scores are not strictly comparable. This is true whether we use the same weight matrix or different weight matrices; if we use the same weight matrix, then scores will be based on items having different loadings, and being therefore not strictly comparable. If the weight matrices differ, then clearly again no direct comparison can be made. What is required is a single *reduced weight matrix,* including only those items having identical (or near identical) loadings for the two sets of factors. Proper comparison should only be based on such reduced weight matrices, as will be explained more in detail in later sections.

CROSS-CULTURAL VALIDITY OF PERSONALITY DIMENSIONS

Our first problem, as previously mentioned, is the question of *comparative dimensionality* in the two different populations. Psychometrically, dimensions of personality, factors or traits are defined in terms of factor analytic investigations which identify groups of items sharing common variance, and setting them off against other groups of items not sharing this common variance. It cannot be assumed that the same items will be found to share common variance when different cultures are being studied, and the assumption that they do so must be empirically verified. A few examples may suffice to indicate the importance of this prescription.

Matesanz and Hampel (1978) conducted factor analyses of inter-item correlations for the FPI (Freiburger Persönlichkeitsinventar, a German personality questionnaire which contains measures for a number of traits as well as the major type factors extraversion–introversion and neuroticism-stability.) Questionnaires were applied to German and Spanish probands, and separate factor analyses carried out. These demonstrated that while there was considerable invariance for extraversion (E) and neuroticism (N), the other traits of the FPI gave quite different results in the two countries. It is clear that it would be unacceptable to simply administer the Spanish version of the FPI to groups of Spanish probands, and score them according to the original manual. This procedure might be admissible for E and N, but it would be completely meaningless as far as the other traits in the questionnaire are concerned. Even for E and N, as we shall see, there may be difficulties in spite of the apparent identity of factors in the two matrices.

As another example, consider the work of Furnham and Henry (1980). These authors use the Rotter Locus of Control Scale to test three groups of South African nurses (African, European, Indian), who were carefully matched in terms of age, sex, education, occupation, homogeneity, living conditions and language competence, and considered to be functionally equivalent. Although no significant differences were found between the scores of these three groups, a factor analysis of each group's results indicated a different factor structure emerging for each group. As the authors point out, ''methodologically it is important to ensure that the items on the measuring instrument are interpreted similarly by all groups and that a similar factor structure emerges from each group before embarking on research.'' [P.27.] This clearly is a minimum requirement; it is unfortunate that it has so often been neglected in past work.

A third example comes from the extensive work that has been done, nationally and internationally, on the 16PF scale of Cattell. He himself has of course always been fully aware of the necessity of comparing factor structures across cultures before using the test, and has indeed suggested a rigorous and original method of carrying out such comparisons (Cattell, 1970.) Even in his own hands (Cattell, Schmidt, & Pawlik, 1973) cross cultural comparisons were more often found to be incongruent than congruent, and the large number of people who have tried to match factors in other countries (even closely similar ones to the original American culture, such as England, Germany, New Zealand, etc.) showed on the whole a far-reaching failure to obtain congruence (e.g. Adcock, 1974; Adcock & Adcock, 1977, 1978; Amelang & Borkenau, 1981; Comrey & Duffy, 1968; Eysenck, 1972; Eysenck & Eysenck, 1969; Greif, 1970; Howarth & Browne, 1971; Levonian, 1961; Schneewind, 1977; Sells, Demaree, & Will, 1968, 1970; Timm, 1968; etc.) These many results indicate that Cattell's factors are not replicable in other countries (and often not in the United States of America either), that items scored for one factor in his manual may have much higher loadings on other factors in other countries, that unitary factors in his analysis emerge truncated or separated into two or three, or associated with other factors, in other analyses, and so on. Clearly the many studies which have simply translated his scale and used the original weight matrices may give meaningless results in other countries.

Few people have given thought to the problems involved (e.g. Carlier, 1980; Irvine, 1978; and Cattell, 1970.) Cattell has attempted to provide a universal method when the need arises to compare factor score estimates across groups differing in some respect, and where *items* factored in all the groups are identical. He describes an *equipotent* method of analysis, which throws scores from different groups into a combined standard score distribution, and operates on the scores of each group with its own factor estimation weights, but with the matrices for all the groups brought to equipotency. He has also suggested a more satisfactory *isopodic* procedure which uses covariance factoring, after first reducing artificial metric differences among variables by what he calls "universe standardising" conversions. An even more radical method would involve application of the mean standardised covariance matrix to the raw score deviations of members of all groups, brought into a combined distribution on each variable. Cattell's suggestions have not been followed up in actual practice, and might prove somewhat difficult to execute; nevertheless he has clearly recognised the problem and suggested a possible solution.

An alternative method, used in our own work, has been suggested by Kaiser, Hanka, and Bianchini (1969). This method, which is too heavily statistical to be described here, enables us to interpret similarity between sets of factors derived for identical items from different populations in terms of indices of factor comparisons which range from 0 (no similarity at all) to 1.00 (perfect agreement). We have used these indices in many studies, using the somewhat arbitrary criterion of .95 for *similarity,* and .98 for essential *identity* of factors between populations. Obviously indices of factor comparisons below .95 are still indicative of similarity provided they exceed .80, but for the purpose of making sure that factors in different cultures are strictly comparable, we will use the term "similar" only for indices of .95 or above, and the term "identical" only for indices of .98 and above. Here too of course actual identity would demand indices of 1.00, but we have followed the above definition of these two terms.

In our work we have used carefully translated versions of the Eysenck Personality Questionnaire (EPQ; Eysenck & Eysenck, 1975), which measures the major dimensions of personality (psychoticism, extraversion, and neuroticism, as well as a lie or dissimulation dimension.) These three (or four) major dimensions have usually emerged from large-scale factor analytic investigations of personality, although sometimes under different names (Royce, 1973), and they form the major dimensions in our own system of personality description (Eysenck & Eysenck, 1969, 1976). We will not here discuss the background to this system, or our reasons for adopting it; a detailed statement is found in Eysenck (1981).

Translated questionnaires were then applied to samples of 500 males and 500 females, sometimes more, occasionally somewhat less, making up a reasonable sample of the population of that country. We have found (Eysenck & Eysenck, 1975) that social status variables are not very relevant to personality; this is fortunate, as it makes the selection of a reasonable sample very much easier. Age and sex are relevant, and hence require to be controlled. The concept of a "reasonable sample"; as opposed to a random or quota sample, is discussed elsewhere (Eysenck, 1975). Here we may ask to what extent a "reasonable sample" would give similar or identical results to those obtained from a proper quota sample, when both are taken in the same country. Such a comparison is reported by Eysenck (1979), and the results are given in Table 3.1. It will be seen that identity is obtained on all comparisons.

Apart from the indices of factor comparison, our published data usually give the alpha coefficient reliability of the scales in the two countries, intercorrelations between factors in the two countries, and where available information on scores of specially selected additional groups such as criminals, psychotics, neurotics, and so forth. As the EPQ comes in two forms (adult and junior), we have worked both with adults and with children. Detailed comparisons for many

TABLE 3.1
Indices of Factor Comparisons for Standardization and
Quota Samples (From Eysenck, 1979)

| Groups | Factor Comparisons | | | |
	Psychoticism	Extraversion	Neuroticism	Lie
English Male vs Quota Male	.991	1.000	.997	.997
English Female vs Quota Female	.993	1.000	.999	.998
Quota Male vs Quota Female	.987	.999	.999	.995

different countries are given below in Table 3.2 (for adults) and Table 3.3 (for children), giving in each case the reference to the authors of the study and the particular country in which the work was carried out.

These tables speak for themselves. It will be seen that the vast majority of indices indicate the essential *similarity* of factors in the different countries, and an astonishingly high number speak for *identity*. This is true both for males and females, in the adult samples, and for boys and girls, in the children's sample. Not wishing to gild the lily we will refrain from commenting at too great length on the results, except to say that they are strongly in support of the view that *essentially the same dimensions of personality emerge from factor analytic studies of identical questionnaires in a large number of different countries,* embracing not only the European cultural groups, but also many quite different types of nations. This of course was to be expected in view of the strong genetic components underlying these major dimensions of personality (Fulker, 1981). We have given a more detailed discussion of the results of our work elsewhere (Eysenck & Eysenck, 1981), and will not repeat the major points made there. Altogether, we feel that we have succeeded in demonstrating that sufficient identity obtains as far as the structure of personality is concerned in these different populations to allow us to proceed to a consideration of the other two points.

The occasional low values pose a problem. In some cases, such as the low values of the females in Nigeria, the cause may be the small number of cases (101) involved; it has been our experience that numbers substantially below 500 in a given group lead to unstable factor loadings, and hence to poor indices of factor comparison. The same may apply to the adult Japanese groups but really cannot be the reason as far as the low indices of factor comparisons for the Hungarian females on *P* are concerned. Such occasional deviations are difficult to explain, but they do not detract from the generally high level of the indices found in these tables.

Various publications listed in Tables 3.2 and 3.3 give details about the weight matrices to be applied in different countries, and these data are of no general interest and will not be discussed here. We may just note that in most cases a few items change loadings drastically, either losing the loading they had in the original British population analysis, or else shifting the loading from one factor to another. Some of these losses and shifts could be explained by inadequate translations; in our early work we found it reassuring that whenever an error in translation was discovered there was a drastic change of loading for that item, indicating that factor analysis is capable of uncovering such errors. Studies involving such errors have to be repeated of course, before publication is possible.

More interesting are changes in loading due to cultural differences, and we have usually found that it is possible to account for these observed changes in terms of fairly obvious suggestions as to causation made by representatives of the country in question, who were involved in the translation and/or administration

TABLE 3.2

Indices of Factor Comparisons for Adult Samples of Males and Females,
Compared with British Samples

EPQ	AUTHORS	COUNTRY	YEAR	M n	F n	Males P	E	N	L	Females P	E	N	L
Adult 1	E.C. Dimitriou & S.B.G. Eysenck	Greece	1978	639	662	.941	.992	.983	.977	.892	.999	.961	.999
Adult 2	H.J. Eysenck et al	France	1980	428	383	.987	.998	.992	.993	.983	.996	.996	.996
Adult 3	S.B.G. Eysenck, O. Adelaja & H.J. Eysenck	Nigeria	1977	329	101	.980	.990	.990	.980	.660	.910	.920	.930
Adult 4	S.B.G. Eysenck, N. Humphery & H.J. Eysenck	Australia	1980	336	318	.933	.997	.994	.993	.995	.996	.994	.988
Adult 5	S. Iwawaki, S.B.G. Eysenck & H.J. Eysenck	Japan	1980	719	599	.946	.990	.978	.981	.994	.994	.997	.992
Adult 6	L. Lojk, S.B.G. Eysenck & H.J. Eysenck	Yugoslavia	1979	491	480	.994	.990	.987	.997	.967	.970	.999	.982
Adult 7	M.A. Rahman & S.B.G. Eysenck	Bangladesh	1980	544	531	.998	.984	.998	.980	.989	.991	.996	.991
Adult 8	N. Tarrier, S.B.G. Eysenck & H.J. Eysenck	Brazil	1980	636	760	.998	.992	.997	.999	.992	.981	.996	.990
Adult 9	H.J. Eysenck, B.S. Gupta & S.B.G. Eysenck	India	to appear	509	472	.981	.986	.985	.997	.968	.992	.991	.964
Adult 10	S.B.G. Eysenck	Sicily	1981	376	409	.982	.995	.998	.994	.934	.978	.994	.992
Adult 11	S.B.G. Eysenck, V. Escolar & A. Lobo	Spain	to appear	435	595	.972	.998	.990	.980	.966	.999	.994	.994
Adult 12	S.B.G. Eysenck & A. Matolcsi	Hungary	”	548	414	.997	.995	.998	.981	.936	.999	.961	.991
Adult 13	S.B.G. Eysenck & J. Chan	Hong Kong	1982	270	462	.962	.995	.997	.950	.993	.995	.998	.996

TABLE 3.3

Indices of Factor Comparisons for Junior Samples of Boys and Girls,
Compared with British Samples

EPQ	AUTHORS	COUNTRY	YEAR	M n	F n	Factor Comparisons Males				Factor Comparisons Females			
						P	E	N	L	P	E	N	L
Junior 1	S.B.G. Eysenck, B. Kozeki & M. Kalmanchey-Gelenne	Hungary	1980	1150	1035	.913	.996	.930	.997	.735	.949	.923	.994
Junior 2	S.B.G. Eysenck & N. Seisdedos	Spain	1978	976	1002	.967	.995	.996	.993	.974	.984	.986	.990
Junior 3	S. Iwawaki, S.B.G. Eysenck & H.J. Eysenck	Japan	1980	261	228	.855	.990	.982	.875	.955	.987	.989	.893
Junior 4	D.H.Saklofske & S.B.G. Eysenck	New Zealand	1978	644	672	.999	.999	.996	.994	.983	.993	.998	.997
Junior 5	S.B.G. Eysenck & J. Chan	Hong Kong	1982	698	629	.981	.985	.988	.993	.975	.975	.988	.959

of the test. Thus, to take but one or two examples, it was found that an item concerning locking doors at night lost its P loading completely in Greece; the explanation given was that the weather gets so hot that people leave their windows open, and with windows open there is no point in locking the door! Another item losing its loading on P in Greece was related to taking out insurance; apparently insurance is not well developed in Greece and there have been a number of scandals relating to insurance firms, hence hardly anyone in Greece takes out insurance, and so the item loses variance and necessarily is incapable of becoming correlated with other items. Items referring to punctuality are relatively meaningless in some Third World Countries, and lose their loadings, as do items relating to the suffering of animals, in countries where quite generally animals are regarded from the agricultural rather than the humane point of view. It is fortunate that such losses or shifts of loadings are relatively rare, as indicated by the robust nature of the indices of factor comparison; nevertheless, they make simple comparisons in terms of the original weight matrices doubtful when attempting to compare different nations or cultures. This warning applies particularly to the P and L scales, and rather less to the N and E scales, but even there the danger exists.

One further point may be made in relation to the problem of validity of the factors in different countries. Certain fairly robust invariances have been found in the original British studies, such as the fact that men have higher P scores than women, that females have higher N scores than males, that men have slightly higher E scores than women, and so forth. If such invariances were not found in other countries, we would have doubts about the validity of the tests in these countries; fortunately, the same invariances are practically universally found in the cultures studied so far.

Another source of validation is the comparison of normal, criminal, psychotic, neurotic and other groups known to differ with respect to one or more of the personality dimensions in question. Such studies have only been done in a small number of other countries, but where they have been done they have nearly always given results similar to those obtained in Great Britain (e.g. Eysenck, 1977; Dimitriou & Eysenck, 1978). An extension of this line of work would be of great value in further validation of the scales in question.

Cross-cultural differences in neuroticism, extraversion and psychoticism

Whereas, like Cattell, we have always insisted on the importance of empirically determined weight matrices being employed in different countries, and cross-cultural comparisons being made on the basis of reduced weight matrices, including only items identical in loading for the two countries, a great deal of work has been done by many authors using the original scoring system of the MPI, the EPI, and the EPQ in various countries. Lynn (1981) has listed these studies, and reports means and standard deviations of the thirty-eight publications surveyed by him, references are included in the list of references appended to this paper. This list contains a storehouse of information; is it possible to make use of it in spite of the failure in most of these publications to change the weight matrix? Lynn argues that this is possible, and has summarized the results in the form of giving mean scores of *P, E* and *N* for the various countries; these are reproduced in Table 3.4. This table also gives data for the national *per capita* incomes for the year 1970 for subsequent discussion of relationships between the mean personality characteristics and national wealth.

Lynn, in arriving at this table, excluded a number of studies too defective for use, on the grounds of too small numbers, failure to give separate data for males and females, and other defects. To obtain mean values from different scales

TABLE 3.4
Mean Scores for 24 Nations on Psychoticism, Extraversion and
Neuroticism Based on Eysenck Questionnaires
(From Lynn, 1981)

Country		Psychoticism	Extraversion	Neuroticism	Per cap. nat. income, 1970
Australia		58.99	51.53	50.56	2644
Canada		44.14	53.81	50.73	3214
Egypt		–	48.46	62.96	202
France		61.00	48.08	54.11	2550
Germany, West		66.12	49.10	51.84	2711
Ghana		–	42.29	53.07	238
Greece		65.94	52.50	54.47	1051
India		61.92	50.82	48.56	94
Iran		57.93	48.01	55.22	316
Italy		–	50.48	50.46	1591
Japan		73.01	46.56	53.85	1664
Jordan		–	57.11	56.27	260
Kuwait		–	54.25	60.81	3148
Lebanon		–	53.01	54.58	521
Nigeria		–	50.17	50.82	135
Poland		–	51.93	55.14	–
South Africa	black	–	51.63	55.05	728
	white	–	51.66	52.22	–
Sweden		–	50.81	41.71	3736
Syria		–	49.50	57.74	258
Turkey		67.96	49.44	44.60	344
Uganda		–	44.72	57.19	127
U.K.		50.00	50.00	50.00	1991
U.S.A.	Total	50.33	56.16	50.13	4274
	black	52.53	52.56	51.42	–
	white	50.09	56.56	49.99	–
Yugoslavia		66.96	47.63	49.21	–

(MPI, EPI, EPQ, etc.) he converted all means to T-scores based on a British mean of 50 and standard deviation of 15. He handles the difficulty that many studies have used students, others older samples, by using four different British sample means, one for the general population and one for students, both sub-divided into males and females for each questionnaire. The international data were converted to T-scores using the appropriate British means and standard deviations. Where there was more than one study from a country the means for different studies were first calculated and then an overall mean for each sex calculated by weighing each result by the size of the sample. Finally, the means for the two sexes were given equal weight in the derivation of a single overall mean for each country.

Lynn is of course aware of the difficulties presented by the fact that one or two items usually change loadings in different countries, but he argues that this does not necessarily invalidate the data, and that these can be regarded with a reasonable degree of confidence as broadly reliable and valid. Such a conclusion, of course, requires independent supporting evidence, and this can only be derived from comparison with other measures of the personality dimensions in question in the different countries concerned. These comparative results may be arrived at from two major sources. One of these, similar in nature to the personality questionnaires involved, is the use of other verbal self-rating scores, and these are dealt with in the remainder of this section. The alternative is the use of demographic indices, pioneered by Lynn (1971), and these form the major part of the next section.

Three major questionnaire studies are relevant to the validation of our own data, namely those of Cattell and Scheier (1961), of Hofstede (1976, 1980), and Lynn and Hampson (1975, 1977).

The study by Cattell and Scheier (1961) is an early pioneering study in which the Cattell Anxiety Questionnaire was administered to students in six countries; they found a rank order, from high to low anxiety, going from Poland through India, France, Italy, Britain to the United States. This rank order is broadly consistent with national differences shown in Table 3.4, with Poland and France having relatively high scores and Britain and the United States low scores on anxiety-neuroticism in both sets of data. Cattell and Scheier suggest that social factors generating high anxiety might be either a low standard of living (India), or politically authoritarian regimes (Poland). Lynn (1981) suggests that both the low standard of living and political totalitarianism can be looked upon as forms of stress, and since stress generates anxiety in individuals "it seems a sensible hypothesis that differences in stress might be responsible for differences in anxiety or neuroticism between nations." [P. 267.]

The Hofstede (1976, 1980) study is also concerned with neuroticism. Hofstede collected his data on approximately 70,000 subjects employed in a multinational organization in forty different nations. He required his subjects to answer on a five-point scale the questions: "How often do you feel nervous or tense at work?'', a question clearly related to neuroticism-anxiety. One question is of course a rather inadequate measure of a complex trait like this, but it has good face validity, high retest reliability, and the sample chosen is more closely equated for socio-economic status, academic ability, and other variables than are most samples in this field. Two separate surveys were carried out, embracing thirty two nations, and showing a rank correlation of +0.94, indicating a high retest reliability for national rankings. It is of course possible that subtle distortions in the meaning of the question would produce distorted results on both occasions, impuning the validity of the data.

TABLE 3.5
Mean Scores of a Five-Point Scale Answer to the Question
"How Often Do You Feel Nervous or Tense at Work?", Computed
from Seven Occupations in Each of 40 Countries, at Two
Points of Time. Total Number of Responses 70,895
(After Hofstede, 1976, 1980.)

Country	1967-69 total no. of resp. 30,310		1971-73 total no. of resp. 40,585		Mean of 1967-69 and 1971-73	
	Country mean score	Rank 32 countries	Country mean score	Rank 32 countries	Country score a	Rank 40 countries
Japan	2.64	1	2.45	1	2.55	1
Greece	2.74^a	3	2.52^a	2	2.63	2
Belgium	2.77	4	2.71	3	2.74	3
Argentina	2.69	2	2.81	6	2.75	4
Peru	2.85^a	5	2.78^a	5	2.82	5
Chile	2.88	–	n.s.	–	(2.84)	6
Columbia	2.86	6	2.84	7	2.85	7
Portugal	3.01^a	9	2.74	4	2.88	8
Yugoslavia^1	n.s.	–	2.92	–	2.92	9
Mexico	2.96	8	2.94	9	2.95	10
Venezuela	2.94	7	2.98	10	2.96	11.5
Taiwan	n.s.	–	2.92^a	–	(2.96)	11.5
Italy	3.03^a	–	n.s.	–	(2.99)	13
Spain	3.10^a	11	2.90	8	3.00	14
France	3.05	10	2.99	11	3.02	15
Switzerland	3.11	12.5	3.05	13.5	3.08	16
Brazil	3.11	12.5	3.06	15	3.09	17.5
Turkey	3.15^a	15	3.03^a	12	3.09	17.5
Israel	3.18^a	16	3.08	16.5	3.13	19
Germany	3.14^a	14	3.14	18.5	3.14	20
South Africa	3.29	20	3.05	13.5	3.17	21
Canada	3.26^a	19	3.16^a	20	3.21	22
Austria	3.30	21	3.14	18.5	3.22	24
Finland	3.36	24	3.08	16.5	3.22	24
Thailand	n.s.	–	3.18^a	–	(3.22)	24
Netherlands	3.22^a	17	3.23	22	3.23	26

(*Continued*)

TABLE 3.5 (*Continued*)

Country	1967-69 total no. of resp. 30,310		1971-73 total no. of resp. 40,585		Mean of 1967-69 and 1971-73	
	Country mean score	Rank 32 countries	Country mean score	Rank 32 countries	Country score a	Rank 40 countries
Philippines	3.25	18	3.26	24	3.26	27
Australia	3.37	25	3.24	23	3.31	28.5
U.S.A.	3.35^a	–	n.s.	–	(3.31)	28.5
Ireland	3.32^a	22.5	3.31	26	3.32	30
Great Britain	3.38	26	3.27	25	3.33	31
New Zealand	3.46	27	3.22	21	3.34	32.5
Hong Kong	3.32^a	22.5	3.36^a	27	3.34	32.5
Norway	3.57	29	3.39	28	3.48	34
Sweden	3.52	28	3.47	29	3.50	35
India	3.57^a	–	n.s.	–	(3.53)	36
Iran	3.63^a	30	3.59^a	30	3.61	37
Singapore	n.s.	–	3.59^a	–	(3.63)	38
Denmark	3.69	31	3.66	31	3.68	39
Pakistan	3.79^a	32	3.80^a	32	3.80	40
Mean of 32 countries surveyed 2 x	3.19		3.10		3.15	
Mean of 40 countries						
Spearman rank correlation 1967-1969 vs. 1971-1973	p = 0.94[+++]					

n.s. = not surveyed or insufficient responses.
^{a}= data for one or more occupational categories extrapolated.
Scores between parentheses are extrapolated from one survey only, assuming an average shift over time.
[1] Data from Yugoslav company in the same industry, surveyed in 1971.

Table 3.5 shows Hofstede's results, giving the results for the two separate studies, and the mean of the two studies in the case of the thirty two countries from which data were collected twice. For the remaining eight countries the figures are based on one study only.

As Lynn (1981) makes clear, Hofstede's work represents a major contribution to the data file on national differences in neuroticism; as he also makes clear, however, there may be some doubts about the accuracy of the data in view of the shortness of the questionnaire, and the difficulty in capturing the exact meaning of the question in translation into a large number of different languages. "If the words nervous or tense have slightly different strengths in different languages, the results could be quite seriously distorted." [P. 267.] Lynn also queries some of Hofstede's data in particular cases. "For instance, the very high score obtained by Belgium looks wrong. In general the nations of North West Europe have moderate or low means and it is difficult to believe that neuroticism levels in Belgium can be so much higher than in her European neighbours. Furthermore, this result is not consistent with the Belgian score obtained from demographic indices . . . hence the Belgium result is probably too high. There is also reason to believe that the Japanese mean is too high, since in the data from the Eysenck Questionnaires . . . Japan obtains about the same mean as the more neurotic of the advanced European nations such as France. This is also true in the results obtained from the demographic data. Finally, the mean for Iran is probably too low. However, in spite of the weaknesses in the case of results from one or two countries, the Hofstede results represent a major source of data in this field and are considered to be in general valid." [P. 269.]

What is the relationship between the Eysenck Questionnaire data (Table 3.4) and the Hofstede data (Table 3.5)? The correlation on countries included in both sets of studies is 0.36, which is a rather low value. However, it will be seen that the correlation is substantially lowered by the inconsistent results for Iran. Of the 15 countries for which there are scores on both measures, Iran comes out highest on N in the Eysenck series and lowest in the Hofstede series. Lynn (1981) prefers the Eysenck data "since they are based on three separate studies which all yield high neuroticism means for Iran. Thus if the Hofstede result for Iran is written off as an error we are left with a high degree of consistency between the rest of the Hofstede data and the Eysenck data." [P.272.] Data is adduced in the next section to show that both the Eysenck and the Hofstede data agree very substantially with a third and entirely independent method of evaluating cross-cultural differences, and that consequently Lynn's suggestion of leaving out Iran is almost certainly well taken.

The use of demographic indices for the measurement of national differences in personality

In this section we describe the very original and innovative work of Richard Lynn (Lynn, 1971, 1981; Lynn & Hampson, 1975, 1977). His approach consists of taking demographic phenomena such as national rates of suicide, alcoholism, accidents and so forth, and treating them as manifestations of the underlying trait of neuroticism or anxiety in the population (Lynn, 1981). "The phenomena taken are well known as correlates of neuroticism or anxiety among individuals and hence it seems a reasonable hypothesis that high prevalence rates in certain nations might reflect a large proportion of neurotic individuals and a high mean level of neuroticism for the total population." [p. 269.] The theory was first worked out and published in *Personality and National Character* (Lynn, 1971), using seven demographic manifestations of national anxiety level (rates of suicide, alcoholism, and accidents, as indices of high anxiety, and rates of chronic psychosis, coronary heart disease, the *per capita* calorie consumption and *per capita* cigarette consumption as low anxiety indices.) Eighteen advanced Western nations were used to collect the data, and it was found that the seven variables correlated reasonably well together, a factor analysis demonstrating a general factor which accounted for approximately 50% of the variance. Figure 3.1 shows the variables in question, and their factor loadings, and Fig. 3.2 shows the factor scores of the eighteen nations in question.

The logic of Lynn's approach requires first the discovery of a number of indirect demographic manifestations of national neuroticism level, and secondly an empirical demonstration that these are all intercorrelated over groups of nations. Furthermore, it would have to be shown by factor analysis that a general factor was present among the intercorrelations. As Lynn points out, the logic of the strategy is analogous to the establishment of the construct of general intelligence, where a number of people were given tests which appear to require intelligence, the tests are shown to intercorrelate and factor analysis demonstrates the existence of a general factor which is interpreted as general intelligence. In Lynn's study, the nations represent the subjects and the demographic

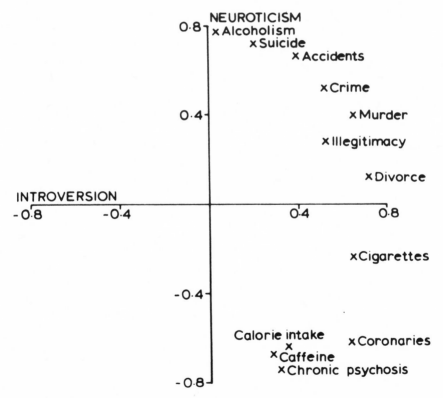

FIG. 3.1.   Principal components analysis of demographic data for seventeen countries. (From Lynn & Hampson, 1975.)

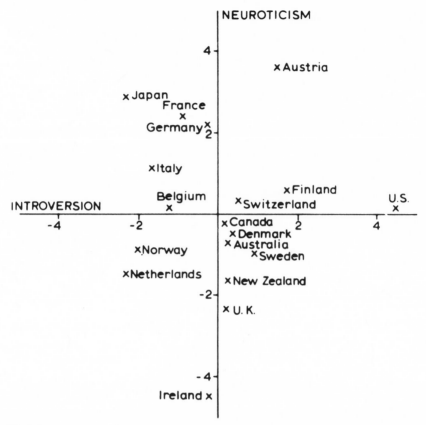

FIG. 3.2.   Factor scores of seventeen nations on demographic factors of neuroticism and extraversion-introversion. (From Lynn & Hampson, 1975).

indices are treated as scores on tests, which are then intercorrelated and factor analysed as in conventional psychometrics.

The existence of a sizeable general factor in this set of data is a matter of empirical fact; its interpretation as anxiety or neuroticism is a matter of inference and argument, and depends largely on the demonstration that the demographic phenomena in question are functions of anxiety or neuroticism among individuals. Such a demonstration has been undertaken by Lynn (1971) and there would be little point in repeating it here.

Later studies have succeeded in extending this theory by adding additional demographic measures, including indices of extraversion as well as neuroticism, and measuring mean levels of both personality dimensions at a number of points in time over the period 1935–1970 (Lynn & Hampson, 1975, 1977). Variables selected as measures of extraversion were rates of crime, murder, illegitimacy and divorce, and national *per capita* caffeine consumption. These five new variables, together with the previous seven, were factor analysed by principal component analysis which shows the presence of the two hypothesized factors, together accounting for 57.29% of the variance. Figure 3.1 shows the final results which are very much in line with prediction.

The factor scores of different nations on these two factors shown in Figure 3.2, indicate that high neuroticism scores are obtained by Austria and Japan, and low scores by Ireland and the United Kingdom. The highest extraversion scores are obtained by the United States and the lowest by Japan. These results are clearly similar to those obtained by questionnaire studies, and discussed in previous sections. This similarity can be quantified, and Lynn (1981) has shown that there is a correlation of .70 between these data and the Eysenck questionnaire data, and one of .75 between the Hofstede data and the demographic variables data. These results for the neuroticism variable are indicative of considerable agreement between the questionnaire and the demographic methods of measurement, and hence help in the mutual validation of these two methods.

Several criticisms have been made of Lynn's work. Thus it has been suggested that national differences in the prevalence rates of suicide, alcoholism, accident, and the other demographic phenomena may be due simply to local cultural and social factors specific to each nation, suicide for instance being determined by the strength of Roman Catholicism, the tendency of coroners to return accurate verdicts and so forth (Maher, 1975). Maher also suggests that rates of chronic psychosis, for instance, may merely reflect the numbers of mental hospital beds available; if the beds are available, patients will be found to fill them. Lynn has answered this point by stating that it does not deal with the fact of the intercorrelation of the measures and the presence of the two factors, very much as anticipated. "If the measures were simply functions of local cultural and social conditions there would be no intercorrelations among them and no factors." [P. 271.] Maher's criticism that the demographic measures might be entirely due to specific conditions overlooks the essential point, both of the empirical data and the theory, that factors can only be based on common variance.

A second criticism relates to the possibility of alternative explanations of the factors. Thus it is possible that it is *per capita* income which causes correlations between consumption of alcohol, and greater number of accidents; more affluent populations are likely to consume more alcohol, and have more accidents because of greater car ownership. Lynn (1981) has examined such possibilities, relating to *per capita* income, age structure of the population, and urbanization; "after detailed scrutiny it has been concluded that none of these possibilities will stand up as possible interpretations of the factors." [p. 272.]

As far as extraversion is concerned, comparisons are only possible between the Eysenck data and the Lynn data, Hofstede not having included any questions relating to extraversion. There are nine countries for which there are scores on both measures namely Australia, Canada, France, Germany, Italy, Japan, Sweden, the United Kingdom, and the United States; on both measures the United States score the most extraverted and Japan the most introverted. The product moment correlation between the two scores was 0.84, indicating a high degree of consistency.

We may summarise this section by saying that there is an astonishing amount of congruence between two methodologically entirely different and separate types of evidence. Questionnaire data, whether we use the Hofstede or the Eysenck data, and factors derived from demographic indices both agree to an extent indicated by correlations of between .7 and .8; this is a quite unexpectedly positive finding which will make it difficult for critics to maintain a negative attitude to either of these two sources of evidence. In science all sources of evidence are subject to error, and the best method of demonstrating the validity of a finding is to show that it can be replicated by reference to alternative methods of investigation. This Lynn (1981) has done, and we may conclude that there are important and replicable differences between nations affecting both their degree of neuroticism and their degree of extraversion. This is an important substantive finding; it may be expected with some degree of confidence that if the methods of collecting questionnaire data could be refined by using the methods outlined in previous sections, then possibly the correlations found with demographic variables might be even higher.

Causal factors in national differences

There is a good deal of speculation about the possible causes of hypothetical national differences, but little has been done to enable a scientific analysis to be made. Of particular difficulty in this field is the ancient question of whether such differences as are observed are due to genetic or environmental causes, or, rather, what proportion of the total variance would be accounted for by one or other of these factors. Eysenck (1977) has attempted to make a contribution to this field by showing that among European nations introversion is associated with the AB blood group (Angst & Maurer-Groeli, 1974) and that the introverted Japanese have a somewhat higher proportion of AB among the population than the British (approximately three times as many Japanese are AB as compared with British). These data are suggestive, but of course a great deal of work would have to be done before we can accept the Angst et al. data as presenting us with a replicable correlation, and before we can extend their findings to the international level of cross-cultural comparison. An attempt to do so on the basis of published data has been made by Eysenck (in press); the data for fairly large numbers of nations agree with prediction for E and N, and for P there are unpredicted but quite large differences in blood group antigens. Specific investigations involving identical samples tested for both blood group antigens and personality are needed before we can come to any final conclusion.

There is some suggestion of black–white differences; the negro nations of Ghana (42.29), Uganda (44,72) and Nigeria (50.17) on extraversion, which emerge from Lynn's summary of the Eysenck scale data (Table 3.4) are low compared with Caucasians (56.56), although in South Africa there is virtually no difference on *E* between blacks and whites. Obviously these data are at best suggestive, and cannot be taken in any sense as indicative of genetic causes. Here too blood group comparisons, and use of other genetic markers, might be invaluable.

Lynn's (1981) work has been more concerned with environmental factors, as these are much easier to quantify, to vary and to study. Turning first to neuroticism, he argues that the most obvious line of explanation of existing differences between cultures is that there are differences in *stress* in different countries, and that these are causal factors. He considers stresses arising from political, social and economic instability, such as are likely to occur with revolutions, *coups d'état*, rapid economic change involving the dislocation of traditional ways of living, and hyperinflation. Secondly he names the stress of war, military defeat and occupation. Thirdly he considers that some climates may be more stressful than others.

Looking at the data shown in Table 3.2 and 3.3, it is noteworthy that mean levels of neuroticism are generally low in the advanced Western democracies as compared with values elsewhere. Western countries, presumably, are less stressful to live in; they are politically stable, the economies are long-established, and free from the worst ravages of hyperinflation, and there are no violent revolutions or military coups. Lynn (1981) gives a table contrasting a group of advanced Western democracies on the one hand, and Arabic nations of the Near and Middle East on the other. (Table 3.6.) "It will be seen that means of the Arabic nations all lie between one third and two thirds of a standard deviation above the British mean, and indeed there is no overlap between the two groups of

TABLE 3.6
Mean Neuroticism Scores of Advanced Western Nations
Contrasted with Arabic Nations on Eysenck Questionnaire Data
(From Lynn, 1981.)

Advanced Western nations		Arabic nations	
Australia	50.56	Egypt	62.96
Canada	50.73	Iran	55.22
France	54.11	Jordan	56.27
Germany	51.84	Kuwait	60.81
Italy	50.46	Lebanon	54.58
Japan	53.85	Syria	57.74
Sweden	41.71		
U.K.	50.00		
U.S.A.	50.13		

nations. . . . It seems reasonable to explain the difference between the two sets of nations in terms of differences in stress.'' [p. 273.]

Other data consistent with the stress theory is the high level of neuroticism in Uganda (57.19), the elevated neuroticism mean in Greece (54.47) and Ghana (53.07); also consistent with the theory are the differences in levels of neuroticism between negro and caucasian populations in the United States and South Africa, negroes probably being subject to a certain degree of stress by virtue of their underprivileged position, and thus obtaining in both countries higher neuroticism means than caucasians. Contrary to prediction is the relatively low level of neuroticism in Nigeria (50.82), there having been some political instability in the civil war of the 1960s in this country.

The Hofstede data lends further support to the stress theory, in that data from countries in Latin America, have high anxiety means. These are notoriously turbulent societies characterised by considerable political conflict, revolutions and counter-revolutions, high rates of inflation, guerilla warfare and so forth, which together seem likely to generate high levels of neuroticism in the population. Table 3.7, taken from Lynn (1981) shows the contrast between advanced Western democracies and Latin American republics. In this table, Lynn has omitted the data for Japan and Belgium as erroneous, as discussed previously. Altogether the data may be taken to give some support to the theory, although by themselves they are of course incapable of establishing it on a firm basis.

Another line of argument altogether has been presented by Lynn and Hampson (1977). Arguing that military defeat and occupation would cause consider-

TABLE 3.7

Mean Scores for Advanced Western Democracies and for
Latin American Republics on Hofstede's Data
(From Lynn, 1981.)

Advanced Western democracies		Latin American republics	
Italy	101	Argentina	125
France	98	Peru	118
Switzerland	92	Chile	116
Germany	86	Columbia	115
Canada	79	Mexico	105
Austria	78	Venezuela	104
Finland	78	Brazil	91
Netherlands	77		
Australia	69		
U.S.A.	69		
Ireland	68		
Great Britain	67		
Norway	52		
Sweden	50		
Denmark	32		

able stress in those countries having suffered these catastrophies during the Second World War, they compared national levels of neuroticism of these nations with nine others which escaped this experience, using Lynn's demographic indices as measures. National neuroticism levels were measured for the year 1935, 1950, 1955, 1960, 1965, and 1970, and the results are shown in Fig. 3.3 and 3.4. The results show that in all nine defeated nations there is an increase in national neuroticism level from 1935 to 1950, followed by a decrease from 1950 to 1955–60. Among the control group of the remaining nine nations, no such general increase of this kind took place, and six of the nations actually experienced a decline in their neuroticism level, although small increases did take place in Sweden, Britain and Australia (Lynn 1981). "The different war experiences clearly distinguish the two groups of nations, and the changes in neuroticism level between the two groups from 1935 to 1960 are statistically significant." [p. 276.] These data would thus seem to confirm the validity of the stress hypothesis.

Poverty is a special type of stress which may have to be looked at critically. India, in the Eysenck data, obtained a mean on neuroticism which is about typical for the advanced Western democracies, and well below that of such countries as Greece, Poland, Uganda and the six Arab countries; India also obtains a low score on the Hofstede data. This seems to indicate that a low standard of living, and poverty in general, may not by itself constitute stress which raises the national level of neuroticism. Lynn has calculated correlations between neuroticism and national *per capita* income for 1970 for both the Eysenck and the Hofstede data, and in neither case is the correlation statistically significant, suggesting that poverty by itself may not be as likely to cause stress as are the other factors mentioned.

Lynn (1981) also considers the question of climate, but finds the data too contradictory to admit of any suggestive answer. "The most reasonable conclusion at this stage would appear to be that national differences in neuroticism are principally determined by differences in stresses on the populations. The most prevalent stresses are apparently military defeat and occupation, political instability and possibly the economic disruptions brought about by rapid economic development and industrialization. However, the low neuroticism means obtained by populations in India and Pakistan suggest that poverty as such does not constitute a stress generating high levels of neuroticism." [P. 278.]

We must next turn to national differences in extraversion, and the causal factors that may be involved. The first hypothesis examined by Lynn is that the high level of extraversion in the United States, and in other nations like Australia, Canada and white South Africa, may be due to the emigration of more extraverted people to these countries, extraverts being known to enjoy novelty, excitement and risk, such as would seem to be involved in immigration to a new country more than do introverts. It is indeed found, as originally suggested by Lynn and Gordon (1962) that the new nations have significantly higher extraver-

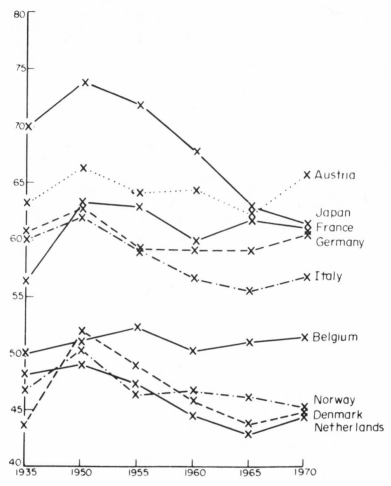

FIG. 3.3.   Rise and fall of national levels of neuroticism in nations suffering military defeat in the Second World War, as indexed by demographic indices. (From Lynn & Hampson, 1977)

sion scores on the Eysenck data, but while there is no overlap between France, Germany, Sweden and the U.K. on the one hand, and Australia, Canada, South Africa and U.S.A. on the other, the differences are not large, and cannot be taken to give strong confirmation to the hypothesis. A more likely hypothesis is economic affluence producing extraverted behaviour patterns. Lynn (1981) found significant positive associations between extraversion and affluence amongst the whole set of eighteen nations in his sample, the correlation for 1970 being 0.65. Furthermore, as he points out, over the period 1935–1970 all the eighteen national populations were growing more extraverted as measured by demographic indices, and at the same time were also growing more affluent (Lynn & Hampson, 1977.) For the Eysenck questionnaire data, the product moment correlation between these questionnaire means and *per capita* income in 1970, as shown in Table 3.4, is only 0.38, a value too low to give strong support to the hypothesis. No other hypothesis has as yet emerged which would be amenable to testing, and we must leave the topic with some doubts about the adequacy of causal explanations in this field.

A final word may be said about psychoticism, where the number of nations tested is very much smaller than it is for *N* and *E,* only amounting to twelve.

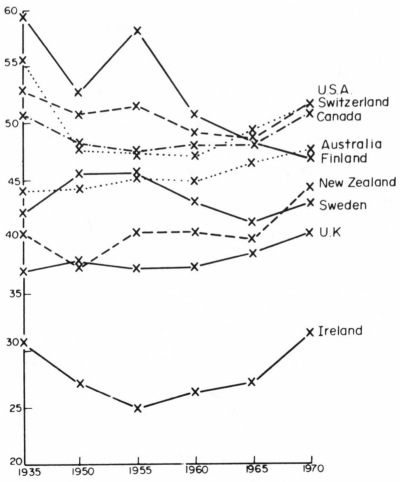

FIG. 3.4.   National Levels of neuroticism 1935–1970 in nine control nations, based on demographic indices. (From Lynn & Hampson, 1977.)

What is clear from the data is a low level of psychoticism in the economically advanced Western democracies compared with the underdeveloped and developing nations. A correlation between national means for psychoticism and national *per capita* income is -0.62, which is at the least suggestive. It is interesting to note that the variability of psychoticism, as far as national differences are concerned is much greater than that for neuroticism and extraversion.

Lynn (1981) has the final comment. ''It may be interesting to speculate on the causes of the strong association between national levels of psychoticism and *per capita* income. Considered historically it seems likely that the low levels of psychoticism among the advanced Western nations is a relatively recent phenomenon. The psychoticism scale is strongly associated with the factor of brutality and insensitivity to the feelings of others and it seems probable that the moral sensitivity of European peoples has increased markedly in fairly recent times. One only has to recall that as recently as a century and a half ago there was widespread popular enjoyment of public executions and approval for generally harsh treatment of criminals, children, the unemployed, and so forth, suggesting a level of psychoticism substantially higher than that present today. It remains to be seen whether the present high means for psychoticism in a number of countries will continue to fall over the next few decades as affluence increases.'' [P. 281.] This comment, and these findings, present us with a problem. *Per capita* income is of course an environmental variable, presumably related to socialization methods and other environmental factors. Yet evidence on individual differences is strongly suggestive of a marked genetic determination of psychoticism (Eaves & Eysenck, 1977; Eysenck & Eysenck, 1976.) It would clearly be premature to comment on this discrepancy. Possibly the development of demographic indices of psychoticism will enable us to discover further evidence on which to judge the value of Lynn's hypothesis.

SUMMARY AND CONCLUSIONS

The work reviewed here deals partly with methodological, partly with substantive findings and considerations. On the methodological side, it is suggested that cross-cultural comparisons require certain precautions for their investigation, and that a simple translation of questionnaires, and their administration to different cultural groups, is not adequate for the investigation of such differences. It is suggested that differential weight matrices must be constructed on the basis of factor analytic investigations of inter-item correlations in different samples, and that only in this way can we achieve a reliable and scientifically meaningful measurement on the basis of which to compare different cultures or nations.

Substantively it has been found that even using less adequate methods it can be shown that different types of questionnaire measurement give similar results for the comparison between many different nations, and perhaps, more surprisingly, that the results also correlate quite highly with the outcome of an analysis of demographic variables known to be associated with personality, and studied in an effort to compare different nations. The considerable amount of congruence discovered for both extraversion and neuroticism suggests that the data may give a fair and reasonable picture of national differences in personality at the present time; the evidence also suggests that fluctuations have taken place and presumably are taking place, over time.

The question of causation, as far as national differences in personality are concerned, is an exceptionally difficult one. The use of genetic markers, such as blood groups, has been suggested, but there is too little work done on this topic to justify any kind of conclusions. Environmental hypotheses have been advanced, such as that stress increases neuroticism/anxiety in given populations, or that high *per capita* income increases extraversion. The evidence for all these hypotheses is of course entirely statistical and correlational, but these two hypotheses do have some support which cannot be gainsaid. On the other hand, the support is inadequate to establish the hypotheses on a very firm basis. Essentially it must be concluded that the investigation of cross-cultural differences in personality is still at an early stage, and that it would be premature to come to very firm conclusions. All that can be said is that methods are now available for the proper study of such differences, at least on the descriptive level, and that the next few years are likely to see a rapid expansion of a research program along these lines.

One firm substantive finding can however be stated. It would appear that the three major dimensions of personality (*P, E* and *N*), as discovered by factor analysis on European and English-speaking populations. apply equally well to other cultures, such as those found in Japan, among Hong Kong Chinese, among African groups, and in various other cultures and nations. This is an important demonstration, as the strong genetic determination of these factors (Fulker, 1981) would suggest that such culture-transcendent constancies should indeed be found to characterise all human populations. This is a finding of fundamental interest in personality research, and it suggests that the possibility of comparisons between different races, cultures and nations can proceed adequately along dimensions of personality which they all share in common.

REFERENCES

Adcock, N. Testing the test: How adequate is the 16PF with a N.Z. student sample? *The New Zealand Psychologist*, 1974, 3, 11–15.

Adcock, N. & Adcock, C. The validity of the 16PF personality structure: a large New Zealand sample item analysis. *Journal of Behavioral Science*, 1977, 2, 227–237.

Adcock, N. & Adcock, C. *Cultural motivational and temporal problems with the 16PF test.* Munich: Paper presented at I.A.A.P. Congress, July 1978.

Amelang, M. & Borkenau, P. *Faktoren der Persönlichkeit.* I: Uber die faktorielle Struktur einiger Fragebogen-Skalen zur Erfassung von Merkmalen der Extraversion und emotionalen habilität. Zeitschrift für Differentielle und Diagnostische Psychologie, 1981.

Angst, J. & Maurer-Groeli, Y. A. Blutgruppen und Persönlichkeit. *Archiv für Psychiatrie und Nervenkrankheiten,* 1974, 218, 291–300.

Bederoff-Peterson, A., Jagtoft, K. and Astrom, J. *EPI - den svenska versionen.* Skandinaviska Testforlaget; Stockholm, 1968.

Berry, J. & Dasen, R. (Eds.) *Culture and cognition: Readings in crosscultural psychology.* London: Methuen. 1974.

Brislin, R., Lonner, W. & Thorndike, R. *Cross-cultural research methods.* London: Wiley, 1973.

Butcher, J. & Pancheri, P. *A handbook of cross-national MMPI research.* Minneapolis: University of Minnesota Press, 1976.

Carlier, M. Note sur la structure factorielle de la forme francaise du Questionnaire de Personalite d'Eysenck (E.P.I.). *Revue de Psychologie Appliqué, 1980, 30, 253–258.*

Cattell, R. B. *The isopodic and equipotent principles for comparing factor scores across different populations. The British Journal of Mathematical and Statistical Psychology,* 1970, 23, 23–41.

Cattell, R. B. & Scheier, I. N. *Measurement of neuroticism and anxiety.* New York: Ronald Press, 1961.

Cattell, R. B., Schmidt, L. & Pawlik, K. Cross cultural comparisons (U.S.A., Japan, Austria) of the personality factor structures of 10 to 14 year olds in objective tests. *Social Behavior and Personality,* 1973, 1, 182–211.

Choungourian, A. The Maudsley Personality Inventory: extraversion and neuroticism in the Middle East. *British Journal of Social and Clinical Psychology,* 1961, 8, 77–78.

Choynowski, M. The development of the Polish adaptation of Eysenck's Maudsley Personality Inventory. *Acta Psychologica,* 1969, 31, 45–65.

Comrey, A. & Duffy, K. Cattell and Eysenck's factor scores related to Comrey personality factors. *Multivariate Behavioral Research,* 1968, 3, 379–392.

Dawson, J. & Lonner, W. (Eds.) *Readings in cross-cultural psychology.* Hong Kong: University Press, 1974.

Dimitriou, E. C. & Eysenck, S. B. G. National differences in personality: Greece and England. *International Journal of Intercultural Relations,* 1978, 2, 3, 266–282.

Eaves, L. & Eysenck, H. J. Genotype-environmental model for psychoticism. *Advances in Behaviour Research and Therapy,* 1977, 1, 5–26.

Edwards, D. EPI profiles of Black and White South African university students. In: Van Der Spuy, H. I. J. & Shamler, D. A. F. (Eds.), *The psychology of apartheid.* Washington: University Press of America.

Eysenck, H. J. Primaries or second-order factors: A critical consideration of Cattell's 16 PF battery. *British Journal of Social and Clinical Psychology,* 1972, 11, 265–269.

Eysenck, H. J. Who needs a random sample? *Bulletin of the British Psychological Society,* 1975, 28, 195–198.

Eysenck, H. J. National differences in personality as related to ABO blood group polymorphism. *Psychological Reports,* 1977, 41, 1257–1258.

Eysenck, H. J. Personality factors in a random sample of the population. *Psychological Reports,* 1979, 44, 1023–1027.

Eysenck, H. J. *A model for personality.* London: Springer, 1981.

Eysenck, H. J. The biological basis of cross-cultural differences in personality: Blood group antigens. *Psychological Reports,* in press.

Eysenck, H. J. & Eysenck, S. B. G. *Personality structure and measurement.* London: Routledge & Kegan Paul, 1969.

Eysenck, H. J. & Eysenck, S. B. G. *Manual of the E.P.Q.* London: Hodder & Stoughton, 1975. San Diego: Edits, 1975.

Eysenck, H. J. & Eysenck, S. B. G. *Psychoticism as a dimension of personality.* London: Hodder & Stoughton, 1976.

Eysenck, H. J. & Eysenck, S. B. G. Culture and personality abnormalities. In: I. Al-Issa (Ed.), *Culture and psychopathology*. New York: University Park Press, 1981.

Eysenck, H. J., Eysenck, S. B. G., Gauquelin, M., Gauquelin, F., Pascal, C. & Pascal, D. La Structure de la Personnalité chez des Français confrontée a celle des Anglais comparaison "cross-culturelle". *La Personnalité*, 1980, No. 1–2, 7–29.

Eysenck, H. J., Gupta, B. S. & Eysenck, S. B. G. National differences in personality: India and England. To be published.

Eysenck, S. B. G. National differences in personality: Sicily and England. *Italian Journal of Psychology*. 1981, VIII, No. 2, 87–93.

Eysenck, S. B. G., Adelaja, O. & Eysenck, H. J. A comparative study of personality in Nigerian and English subjects. *The Journal of Social Psychology*, 1977, 102, 171–8.

Eysenck, S. B. G. & Chan, J. A Comparative Study of Personality in Adults and Children: Hong Kong and England. *Pers. & Ind. Diff.*, 1982, 3, 153–160.

Eysenck, S. B. G., Escolar, Victoria & Lobo, A. National differences in personality: Spain and England. Submitted to: *Revista de psiquiatria y psicologia Médica de Europa y America Latinas*.

Eysenck, S. B. G., Humphery, N. & Eysenck, H. J. The structure of personality in Australian as compared with English subjects. *The Journal of Social Psychology*, 1980, 112, 167–173.

Eysenck, S. B. G., Kozeki, Bela & Kalmanchey-Gelenne, Marta. Cross cultural comparison of personality: Hungarian children and English children. *Personality & Individual Differences*, 1980, 1, 347–353.

Eysenck, S. B. G. & Matolcsi, Agnes. National differences in personality: Hungary and England. Submitted to: *'Pszichologia'*.

Eysenck, S. B. G. & Seisdedos, N. Un estudio inter-naciones de la Personalidad. Revista de Psicologia General y Aplicada, Madrid, 1978.

Farley, F. H. American and British data on a three dimensional assessment of personality in college students. *Journal of Personality Assessment*, 1977, 41, 160–163.

Fulker, D. W. The genetic and environmental architecture of psychoticism, extraversion and neuroticism. In: H. J. Eysenck, (Ed.), *A model for personality*. New York: Springer, 1981.

Furnham, A. & Henry, J. Cross-cultural locus of control studies: Experimental and critique. *Psychological Reports*, 1980, 47, 23–29.

Götz, K. O. & Götz, K. Personality characteristics of professional artists. *Perceptual & Motor Skills*, 1979, 49, 327–334.

Greif, S. Untersuchungen zur deutschen Übersetzung des 16PF Fragebogens. *Psychologische Beiträge*, 1970, 12, 186–213.

Hannah, F., Storm, T. & Caird, W. K. Sex differences and relationships among neuroticism, extraversion and expressed fears. *Perceptual & Motor Skills*, 1965, 20, 1214–1216.

Hetzel, R., McMichael, A. J. & Kidson, M. The psychological health of university students as measured by a personality inventory. *Australian & New Zealand Journal of Psychiatry*, 1973, 7, 97–101.

Hofstede, G. *Nationality and organizational stress*. Brussels: European Institute for Research Management, 1976.

Hofstede, G. *Culture's consequences: International differences in work-related values*. London: Sage Publications, 1980.

Honess, T. & Kline, P. The use of the EPI and JEPI with a student population in Uganda. *British Journal of Social & Clinical Psychology*, 1974, 13, 96–98.

Howarth, E. & Browne, J. An item factor analysis of the 16PF. *Personality*, 1971, 2, 117–139.

Ibrahim, A. S. Extraversion and neuroticism across cultures. *Psychological Reports*, 1979, 44, 799–803.

Irfani, S. Eysenck's extraversion, neuroticism and psychoticism inventory in Turkey. *Psychological Reports*, 1977, 41, 1231–1234.

Irvine, S. The place of factor analysis in cross-cultural methodology and its contribution to cognitive theory. Munich: Paper read at International Association for Cross-cultural Psychology Conference, July 29–August 5, 1978.

Iwawaki, S., Eysenck, S. B. G. & Eysenck, H. J. Differences in personality between Japanese and English. *The Journal of Social Psychology,* 1977, 102, 27–33.

Iwawaki, S., Eysenck, S. B. G. & Eysenck, H. J. Japanese and English personality structure: A cross-cultural study. *Psychologia,* 1980, 23, 195–205.

Iwawaki, S., Eysenck, S. B. G. & Eysenck, H. J. The universality of typology: A comparison between English and Japanese schoolchildren. *The Journal of Social Psychology,* 1980, 112, 3–9.

Iwawaki, S., Sujiyama, Y. & Nanri, R. Maudsley Personality Inventory. *Japanese Manual,* 1964.

Jensen, A. The Maudsley Personality Inventory. *Acta Psychologica,* 1958, 14, 314–325.

Kaiser, H., Hunka, S., Bianchini, J. Relating factors between studies based upon different individuals. P. 333–343. In: H. J. Eysenck & S. B. G. Eysenck, (Eds.), *Personality structure and measurement.* London: Routledge & Kegan Paul, 1969.

Kline, P. Extraversion, neuroticism and academic performance among Ghanian university students. *British Journal of Educational Psychology,* 1966, 36, 92–94.

Laungani, P. A cross cultural study of personality and conformity. Ph.D. thesis, University of London, 1981.

Levinson, D. (Ed.) *A guide to social theory: Worldwide cross-cultural tests,* Vol. 1–5. New Haven: Human Relations Files, 1977.

Levonian, E. A statistical analysis of the 16-personality factor questionnaire. *Educational and Psychological Measurement,* 1961, 21, 589–596.

Lojk, L., Eysenck, S. B. G. & Eysenck, H. J. National differences in personality: Yugoslavia and England. *British Journal of Psychology,* 1979, 70, 381–387.

Loo, R. A psychometric investigation of the Eysenck Personality Questionnaire. *Journal of Personality Assessment,* 1979, 43, 54–58.

Lovegrove, M. Personality, conservatism and ability in a non-Western culture. *West African Journal of Educational and Vocational Measurement,* 1977, 4, 40–46.

Lowe, J. D. & Hildman, L. K. EPI scores as a function of race. *British Journal of Social & Clinical Psychology,* 1972, 11, 191–192.

Lynn, R. *Personality and national character.* London: Pergamon, 1971.

Lynn, R. Cross-cultural differences in neuroticism, extraversion and psychoticism. In: R. Lynn (Ed.), *Dimensions of personality.* London: Pergamon, 1981.

Lynn, R. & Gordon, I. E. Maternal attitudes to child socialization: some social and national differences. *British Journal of Social and Clinical Psychology,* 1962, 1, 52–55.

Lynn, R. & Hampson, S. National differences in extraversion and neuroticism. *British Journal of Social and Clinical Psychology,* 1975, 14, 223–240.

Lynn, R. & Hampson, S. Fluctuation in national levels of neuroticism and extraversion, 1935–1970. *British Journal of Social and Clinical Psychology,* 1977, 16, 131–137.

Maher, B. Neurosis is small potatoes. *Contemporary Psychology,* 1975, 20, 360–361.

Malpass, R. Theory and method in cross-cultural psychology. *American Psychologist,* 1977, 32, 1069–1079.

Marsella, A., Tharp R., Ciborowski, R. (Ed.) *Perspectives on cross-cultural psychology.* London: Academic Press, 1979.

Matesanz, A. & Hampel, R. Eine interkulturelle Vergleichsstudie mit den FPI an deutschen und spanischen Probanden. *Zeitschrift für experimentelle und angewandte Psychologie,* 1978, 25, 218–229.

Mehryar, A. H. Some data on the Persian translation of the EPI. *British Journal of Social & Clinical Psychology,* 1970, 9, 257–263.

Nikjoo, N. A standardisation of the EPQ in Iran. Unpublished D.Phil. thesis. Coleraine: New University of Ulster, 1980.

Rahman, M. A. & Eysenck, S. B. G. National differences in personality: Bangladesh and England. *Bangladesh Journal of Psychology*, 1980, 6, 113–119.

Rao, S. Occupational role and personality—a comparative study of a few occupational groups in India. *Indian Journal of Psychology*, 1966, 41, 59–64.

Royce, J. R. The conceptual framework for a multi-factor theory of individuality. In: J. R. Royce (Ed.), *Multivariate analysis and psychological theory*. 1973 Pp. 305–407.

Rump, E. E. & Court, J. The EPI and social desirability response set with student and clinical groups. *British Journal of Social & Clinical Psychology*, 1971, 10, 42–54.

Saklofske, D. H. & Eysenck, S. B. G. Cross-cultural comparison of personality: New Zealand children and English children. *Psychological Reports*, 1978, 42, 1111–1116.

Schneewind, K. A. Entwichlung einer deutschsprachigen Version des 16PF Tests von Cattell. *Diagnostica*, 1977, 23, 188–191.

Sells, S., Demaree, R. & Will, D. A taxonomic investigation of personality. Texas Christian Institute of Behavioral Research, 1968.

Sells, S., Demaree, R. & Will, D. Dimensions of personality: 1. Conjoint factor structure of Guilford and Cattell trait markers. *Multivariate Behavioral Research*, 1970, 5, 391–422.

Sibour, F., Amerio, P. & Jona, G. Adattamento italiano del MPI. Bollettino di Psicologia Applicana, 1963, pp. 59–60.

Spielberger, C. & Diaz-Guerrero, R. *Cross-cultural anxiety*. London: Wiley, 1976.

Steiner, W. Personal communication. Bonn: IBM, 1970.

Studenski, R. Effect of information about success and failure on neuroticism and extraversion-introversion measurements. *Polish Psychological Bulletin*, 1977, 8, 91–94.

Tarrier, N., Eysenck, S. B. G. & Eysenck, H. J. National differences in personality: Brazil and England. *Personality and Individual Differences*, 1980, 1, 164–171.

Timm, U. Reliabilität und Faktorenstruktur von Cattell's 16PF Test bei einer deutschen Stichprobe. *Zeitschrift für experimentelle und angewandte Psychologie*, 1968, 15, 354–373.

Triandis, H. et al. (Eds.) *Handbook of cross-cultural psychology* (6 vols.) London: Allyn & Bacon, 1980.

Tyson, G. A. Some South African student scores on the MAS and MPI. In: Van der Spuy, H. I. J. and Shamley, D. A. F. (Eds.), *The psychology of apartheid*. Washington: University Press of America 1978.

Vohra, H. B. L., An investigation of the relationship among intelligence, aptitude, personality, academic achievement and vocational choice of polytechnic students. Ph.D. thesis, Panjab University, India, 1977.

Warren, N. (Ed.) *Studies in Cross-cultural Psychology*. Vols. 1, 2. London: Academic Press, 1977; 1980.

Wundt, W. Volkerpsychologie (9 vols.). Leipzig: Engelmann, 1904–1919.

4 The Eysenck Psychoticism Scale

Gordon Claridge
Magdalen College, Oxford

Several converging lines of research now strongly indicate that the psychotic states, especially schizophrenia, have associated with them personality and other characteristics which can be observed in normal individuals and which almost certainly help to define the predisposing features of such disorders. The recently developed Eysenck *P*-scales - both adult and junior versions - purport to tap such characteristics and therefore to provide a questionnaire instrument for measuring the third dimension of psychoticism which Eysenck's personality theory has always contained. In reviewing the current status of the adult *P*-scale a number of problems with the validity of the new questionnaire are noted. These include the failure of the 'criterion groups' of diagnosed psychotics to achieve particularly high scores on the scale, the intrusion of Lie scale responding on *P*-scale performance, and the questionable face validity of the latest version of the scale (the EPQ), the items of which focus more on general anti-social traits than on obviously psychotic characteristics. Doubts are also raised about the feasibility of capturing within a single scale the characteristics associated with *all* forms of psychotic disorder. Despite such reservations, it is concluded that the Eysenck scale probably does tap part of the variance of psychotic traits to be seen in normal people. This is illustrated by reference to work on "psychoticism" carried out by the author and his colleagues. Historically, that work started from a slightly different viewpoint, attempting to isolate psychophysiological characteristics in psychotic patients and then searching for evidence of these in normal people. Appearance of the *P*-scale caused a convergence with Eysenck's work and several experiments reported here help, in the author's view, to strengthen the validity of his questionnaire. Thus, high *P* scorers have been found to resemble psychotic patients in a number of psychophysiological characteristics and to behave in a way which is consistent with the author's theory that schizophrenia involves a curious form of central nervous "imbalance." Recent observations suggest, however, that this resemblance may be confined to certain high P scorers, namely *introverts;* the finding confirms an unsatisfactory feature of the scale—the heterogeneity of groups scoring highly on it—but at the same time suggests that when used in combination with other personality measures the P-scale may be capable of identifying at least some individuals predisposed to particular forms of psychosis. Pursuing the latter line of reasoning, further work in the author's laboratory is now attempting to develop a "borderline schizophrenia" questionnaire, judged to have better face validity than the P-scale, but intended to be used alongside it in future psychological and psychophysiological studies. Results so far look promising, especially some findings relating the new questionnaire to hemisphere differences in information processing. It is concluded that the concept of dimensionality as applied to the psychotic states is eminently viable and that, although many problems of theory and measurement remain, Eysenck can, on both counts, be considered a major pioneer in the field.

The possibility that psychotic characteristics may form part of normal variation, though an old idea, is one which is now beginning to receive increasingly formal attention from workers in the field of personality. As we shall see later, there are several historical and theoretical reasons for this upsurge of interest, but one of its prime movers, in psychology at least, is certainly Eysenck—or, to be more correct, the Eysencks; for the current revival of Hans Eysenck's original notion of psychoticism as a third dimension of personality has been very much a husband and wife venture, with Sybil Eysenck playing a prominent role. Together the Eysencks, with characteristic energy and single-mindedness, are now rapidly pushing forward work on their new dimension; equally characteristically, the P-scale, which is the pivot of their research, has generated considerable controversy.

The present chapter is in no sense a comprehensive review of work on the P-scale. Rather, at the editor's suggestion, it is a description of research inspired by and making use of the scale, which my colleagues and I have been conducting in recent years. The chapter is effectively divided into two parts. The first part rests heavily on a recently published essay (Claridge, 1981) in which I discussed "psychoticism," both as a concept in psychopathology, and with reference to the Eysencks' particular contribution to its measurement. From that more general account I shall try to extract my main conclusions about the current status, as I see it, of the Eysenck psychoticism scale; this will provide a background against which to assess the particular experimental studies described later in the chapter.

As mentioned a moment ago, the view that there is some continuity between normal and psychotic behavior has been with us for a long time. In the psychiatric literature its popularity has waxed and waned, varying according to the prevailing climate of opinion about the nature of psychosis itself; and here I am referring mainly to schizophrenia, because it is about that disorder (or set of disorders) that most of the argument has raged. Certainly, Eugen Bleuler (1911), in first coining the term "schizophrenia" did not appear to believe that a sharp distinction could be made between the recognizably mad and the marginally abnormal or latently psychotic individual; while Jung (1907), influenced, of course, by Bleuler, wrote extensively (and perceptively) about the understandable, and therefore potentially "normal," quality of the psychotic state. Except where kept alive in certain quarters, especially in the psychoanalytic literature, such ideas fell out of favour as the emphasis shifted to more purely organic disease explanations of schizophrenia. Those explanations were themselves again widely challenged with the upsurge, in the 1960's, of the radical psychiatry or anti-psychiatry movement, when writers like Laing (1959) and Szasz (1961) upset the complacency of the more rigid disease theorists and in their own way, though perhaps for the wrong reasons, brought the attempt to understand schizophrenia more into the domain of normal psychology. The wilder excesses of the radicalists have now been spent and, on the psychiatric front, views about the nature of schizophrenia seem to have settled down to a more guarded disease position, several features of which are relevant to the continuity-discontinuity issue. Thus, genetic studies (see, Gottesman & Shields, 1976) suggest that schizophrenia, like many diseases, may be inherited as a graded, perhaps polygenically determined, predisposition, widely found in the general population; this therefore leaves open the possibility that many of its characteristics might, in muted form, contribute to personality variation observed in psychiatrically normal people. An offshoot of that development has been the search for, and claim that one can demonstrate, such characteristics in some individuals who, while genetically at "high-risk" for schizophrenia, are neither clinically psychotic nor necessarily likely to become so (Mednick, Schulsinger, Higgins & Bell, 1974). Then recently, and continuing a long-standing theme in the psychiatric literature of North America, if not of Western Europe, interest has intensified in the description and classification of the so-called "borderline syndromes," states which seem to fall halfway between neurosis and psychosis and some of which will almost certainly prove to form a clinical spectrum with true schizophrenia (Gunderson, 1979). Within the sphere of psychopathological variation, and in some psychiatric thinking, the notion of a certain "dimensionality" to the psychotic states is therefore finding increasing experimental and clinical support.

In the personality theory of academic psychology continuity between the normal and the abnormal has always been an acceptable idea, though descriptions of personality differences have more often drawn upon observations of clinical characteristics that are considered to be neurotic rather than psychotic. Nevertheless, it is thirty years since Hans Eysenck (1952b) first suggested that psychoticism may be a major source of personality variation, additional to the dimensions of introversion-extraversion and neuroticism which, until recently, formed the main focus of his work. In contemplating psychoticism, Eysenck was undoubtedly influenced by Kretschmer (1925) whose much earlier, but purely descriptive, schema postulated that psychotic states—both schizophrenia and manic-depressive psychosis—do indeed merely represent extreme variations in normal behavior. Eysenck's novel contribution was to test the idea experimentally (Eysenck, 1952a); in doing so he also examined Kretschmer's particular suggestion that schizophrenics and manic-depressives occupy opposite ends of a biopolar dimension, the "normal" counterparts of which give rise to the now familiar descriptions of "schizothymia" and "cyclothymia." In contrast, Eysenck's hypothesis called for a *single* dimension of psychoticism, variations between individuals equally high in that characteristic being referrable to other dimensions of personality. Eysenck attempted to decide empirically between those two alternatives by carrying out "criterion analysis" of a battery of objective tests administered to groups of normal and clinically psychotic subjects. Details of that experiment and its shortcomings, which I have dealt with elsewhere (Claridge, 1981), need not concern us here. Suffice it to say that, given the primitive state of personality study at that time, the results did demonstrate a certain continuity between the test performance of normal subjects and that of psychotic patients on a factor which Eysenck identified as "psychoticism." Subsequently, Trouton and Maxwell (1956), using the rather different strategy of factor analyzing symptom items in psychiatric patients, demonstrated that two factors, named by them "neuroticism" and "psychoticism," were necessary to describe the observed variation. However, it was not until a questionnaire measure of the new dimension had been developed that the latter took its place in Eysenck's theory, alongside the other two, already well-established, dimensions of extraversion and neuroticism. The measurement of psychoticism by questionnaire itself went through a long gestation period, traced in detail by Eysenck and Eysenck (1976). Several prototypical "*P*-scales" were developed, differing somewhat in item content, a point I shall return to later, until a final published version appeared in the new three-factor inventory, the Eysenck Personality Questionnaire, or EPQ (Eysenck and Eysenck, 1975). Paralleling Eysenck's earlier attempts to measure personality over a wide age range, the new questionnaire comes in both adult and junior versions. They effectively replace the earlier two-factor EPI and JEPI, though it is perhaps worth noting that revision of the Eysenck questionnaires involved more than merely adding a third (psychoticism) scale. As inspection of the item content of the new EPQ (and JEPQ) will reveal, isolating a third dimension of personality evidently entailed realigning the other two dimensions, especially extraversion. The latter now emerges as a more pure factor of sociability, rather than as a composite of sociability and impulsivity, the other component previously considered by Eysenck to be an important defining feature of extraversion (Eysenck and Eysenck, 1969). Put another way, it could be said that the Eysencks partly discovered psychoticism by replacing a two-factor with a three-factor description of questionnaire items, some of which, those concerned with impulsivity, were already present in their existing scales. Having said this, it is also important to note that the *P*-scale is considered to embrace more than just impulsive behavior; the intention is to measure additional traits such as aggressiveness, lack of warmth or empathy, cruelty, sensation-seeking, insensitivity, and liking for odd and unusual things. As envisaged by the

Eysencks, the high *P* scorer is therefore someone who is unconventional and does not fit in socially, a person in conflict, both within himself, and with others.

This pen-picture of the high *P* scorer clearly captures a facet of personality noticeably missing from Eysenck's original two-dimensional description; psychobiographically, as well as literally, it expands the potential explanatory value of his personality theory into three dimensions. At the same time, obvious questions are raised about the psychometric status of the new scale. At one extreme some critics (e.g., Bishop, 1977) would appear to doubt whether it is even theoretically sensible to construe psychosis dimensionally, in the way that this has been done for the neurotic disorders. However, on that score, for the reasons already briefly referred to, I would declare my support for the Eysencks in their search for personality characteristics that describe the predisposition to psychotic illness. A more constructive question, I believe, is whether, notwithstanding the Eysencks' own interpretation of their *P*-scale, they have as yet achieved their objective. Put more formally, what indeed is the validity of the present *P*-scale as a true measure of psychotic personality traits?

Perhaps understandably, most critics of the validity of the *P*-scale have, as their first line of attack, assaulted Eysenck on his home ground; that is to say, they have pursued his own argument that a test of the validity of a personality dimension purporting to measure abnormal traits is to examine the position on that dimension of appropriate "criterion groups" of psychiatric patients. When this is done the *P*-scale fares badly, as judged by the published norms for the EPQ (Eysenck and Eysenck, 1975). Three facts stand out here: first, psychotic patients, while having greater than average scores on the *P*-scale, are by no means the highest scoring group; secondly, their scores are regularly surpassed by those of criminals and various other anti-social or deviant groups, such as drug addicts; and, thirdly, psychotics characteristically have high Lie scores. These three findings have formed the nub of a set of arguments and counterarguments about the validity of the *P*-scale, the essence of the dispute being contained in a series of published exchanges between the Eysencks and Block, one of their main critics (Eysenck, 1977; Eysenck and Eysenck, 1977; Block, 1977a, b). Briefly, the case against the Eysencks is that, because of the relatively modest scores obtained by the psychotic criterion groups, the *P*-scale cannot be considered a true measure of psychoticism, though it is generally admitted that the scale does reliably tap antisocial personality traits; the slightly raised *P* scores obtained by psychotics can, according to Block (op. cit.) be put down to the fact that such patients, due to their impaired mental state, probably respond in a random fashion when completing the questionnaire.

The Eysencks' own interpretation of their normative data is, of course, different. Regarding the fact that deviant but non-psychotic individuals obtain high *P*-scores, higher than psychotics themselves, they make two points. One is that the *P*-scores found in psychotic patients must be taken in conjunction with their performance on the Lie scale; the latter, the Eysencks argue (and they provide some evidence for this), tends artificially to depress the average P score for the psychotic sample, allowing it to be surpassed by that of psychopaths, whose Lie scores are low. The second point they make is that the high psychoticism rating of psychopaths, far from negating the validity of the P-scale, actually confirms it. In reaching that conclusion they are relying on clinical and genetic evidence that muted forms of psychosis may manifest themselves as various forms of anti-social personality disorder.

Each side of the dispute on the P-scale performance of clinical samples has some merit. It is indeed embarassing for the Eysencks that attempts to validate the scale by reference to criterion groups has not worked as well as it has, for example, in the case of the neuroticism scale. The finding that psychotics simultaneously have high Lie scores and the possibility that this somehow distorts their performance on the P-scale are interesting observations in their own right and would be consistent with the fact that the P and L scales of the EPQ are, in some respects, the obverse of each other; the former measures unconventionality and the latter partly reflects conforming traits of personality[1]. However the Eysencks' attempt to link the two together in order to explain why the mean P scores of criterion groups are as low as they are is unconvincing; even in psychotics with low Lie scores the average P score is only marginally greater (Eysenck and Eysenck, 1976).

In rebutting the charge that psychotics merely respond randomly on the EPQ the Eysencks quote a study by Thompson (1975) indicating that this is not so. That evidence, being based on the performance of normal subjects, is weak, though others (e.g., McPherson, Presly, Armstrong & Curtis, 1974), working with psychiatric samples, have noted that the psychotic patients they observed completing the EPQ did not appear to be answering randomly. Personally I believe that the Eysencks are right in rejecting *random* responding as the sole explanation of their data, though I suspect that psychotics do present a special problem as criterion groups for psychoticism, not encountered when using psychiatric samples to try and validate other personality dimensions. By the very nature of their illness, many psychotics are distractible, ambivalent in attitude, and highly variable in their performance of psychological tasks. It seems inconceivable that such factors are without influence on questionnaire responding, though the exact way in which these may intrude into performance on the EPQ has yet to be determined. In the meantime, it seems fair to suspend judgement on that particular dispute about the P-scale and to bear in mind that there are unique

[1]Another observation that might be made about this inverse relationship between the P and L scales, of course, is that it is therefore surprising that psychotics manage to get *relatively* high P scores despite having high scores on the Lie scale. Thus, they seem to be expressing a rejection of social conventions while at the same time claiming to conform to them! Very tentatively, and pursuing an idea I put forward elsewhere (Claridge, 1981), and which I will return to again, it could be argued that this "ambivalence" of personality structure is an essential quality of psychoticism.

and peculiar difficulties about using psychotic patients to validate any self-rating scale of psychoticism.

Turning now to the much more consistently raised P scores found in various forms of personality disorder, whether these data are considered as evidence for, or against, the validity of the P scale as a measure of psychoticism depends essentially on how firmly one espouses the view that such disorders are biologically and psychologically related to full-blown psychosis, that is that clinically they are *formes frustes* of the latter. In adopting such a position to justify their P-scale data the Eysencks are in fact supported by a considerable amount of evidence, though a word of caution is in order. It concerns the interpretation of genetic studies (e.g. Heston, 1966) which, in demonstrating a raised incidence of psychopathic individuals in the families of schizophrenics, have been taken as evidence for a 'spectrum' model of psychosis. As Gottesman and Shields (1976), in evaluating that evidence, point out, present data do not unambiguously rule out the possibility that psychopathy and schizophrenia are genetically distinct and merely appear to co-exist in the same families because of assortative mating, the tendency for schizophrenics frequently to choose spouses who are of unstable personality and who have a history of anti-social behavior, such as alcoholism or criminality. The moderately raised P-scores of schizophrenics might therefore simply reflect some shared tendency to anti-social behavior and not psychotic traits *per se*.

A further complication here is the heterogeneity both of the psychoses themselves and of the personality disorders that are thought to relate to them. In formulating his views about psychoticism Eysenck has followed the *Einheitpsychose* theory, namely that there is a *general* vulnerability to psychotic breakdown, the affective illnesses and the various forms of schizophrenia sharing a common genetic tendency. The evidence is by no means unequivocal on this point, however. Gottesman and Shields (1976) reach the uncontroversial conclusion that different varieties of psychosis seem neither to breed true to type in families nor to show complete lack of differentiation; in other words, these authors neither fully reject nor fully accept the *Einheitpsychose* theory. However, reviewing the same evidence Stone (1980) comes down more forcibly in favour of the schizophrenias and the affective psychoses being manifestations of two distinct sets of genetic influence. His discussion is in the context of a (masterly) review of the literature on the "borderline syndromes" which, as I have implied, are prime candidates for the description of disorders that are *formes frustes* of the major psychoses. But if, as Stone suggests, the latter are genetically distinct, and given that the borderline syndromes are themselves clinically very heterogeneous, it may be illogical to try and discover fundamental personality traits which they have in common.

Eysenck, however, being committed to the *Einheitpsychose* theory believes that the clinical heterogeneity of the psychoses (and he would presumably argue similarly for the borderline syndromes) can be put down to a blending of, or interaction between, a genetically determined loading on his general factor of psychoticism and genetically determined variations in other characteristics. He suggests that introversion-extraversion is especially important, proposing specifically that schizophrenia and manic-depression are, respectively, introverted and extraverted forms of psychosis. Although an attractive hypothesis, evidence utilizing the P-scale supports it only weakly. The norms for the EPQ are of little help since no scores for manic-depressives are given, the term "psychotic" being used synonymously with "schizophrenic"; the only affective disorders represented are a small group of endogenous depressives who had a mean extraversion score slightly *lower* than that of schizophrenics. More convincing were the results of a special test of the hypothesis by Verma and Eysenck (1973) who factor analysed a large battery of measures, including scores from the PEN inventory, an early version of the EPQ. On a third-order factor, identified as extraversion, affective disorders, including manic-depressives, did emerge as more extraverted than schizophrenics, though the relatively modest loading of the factor on the E-scale (-0.31) leaves some room for doubting whether the factor was correctly identified.

Looked at from the standpoint of Eysenck's theory, certain other results from the study just quoted were also rather puzzling. Thus on a "psychoticism" factor which was also identified, and which loaded on the P-scale, schizophrenics had lower scores than other psychotics, paranoids being highest of all. This observation was very like that made by McPherson et al. (1974) who, also using an early form of the P-scale, found that scores were highest in patients with a diagnosis of mania and paranoia, schizophrenics again having rather low scores.

What seems to emerge from this last set of results, and it is supported by other facts to be mentioned in a moment, is that the Eysencks do not yet appear to have succeeded in capturing (if indeed that is possible) the full range of psychoticism traits that are common to *all* forms of psychosis. Schizophrenics, who after all should be one of the major criterion groups for the dimension, do not load particularly highly on it. Of course, it could be argued that schizophrenics are especially susceptible to whatever effects (random responding, Lie scale bias and so on) which have been said to distort the questionnaire scores of psychotics. But some of our own recent results would appear to rule that out; for we have found that even if tested in remission, when the distracting effects of acute illness should have been minimized, patients clearly diagnosable as schizophrenic often have very low, sometimes zero, P scores.

Another way to approach this general question of heterogeneity and the precise alignment of the P-scale with respect to psychotic traits would be to examine individuals suffering from various forms of spectrum disorder which, according to dimensional theory, should border on the major psychoses. Unfortunately, this does not yet appear to have been done, the Eysencks themselves looking more towards criminal populations for samples of individuals assumed to manifest muted psychotic disorder. Thus, they consider that different forms of criminal activity may be associated with different combinations of the three dimensions of extraversion, neuroticism, and psychoticism (Eysenck and Eysenck, 1976). However, in my view such evidence, apart from moving away from the main question at issue, runs into the danger of circular argument, given the still uncertain relationship between psychosis and criminality. More relevant would be the study of individuals selected on *clinical* grounds as falling into one or other subgroup of the "borderline syndromes." The reason this still remains to be done is perhaps that the latter concept is largely confined to North American psychiatry, where Eysenck's ideas have scarcely penetrated. Admittedly, Stone (1980) in his recent book on the borderline syndromes does make reference to Eysenck's personality theory, but he confines himself largely to its earlier, two-dimensional, form, comparing it with other typological models to try and account for the different varieties of personality structure to be found in the borderline syndromes. In the absence of any direct reference to the P-scale as such it would take us beyond the scope of this chapter to consider Stone's discussion in detail, though his conclusions deserve brief comment. Given, as we have seen, that he believes the evidence points towards genetic distinctiveness of schizophrenia and affective disorders, Stone argues for the borderline syndromes associated with them also being fundamentally different. He leans, if anything, towards a typology similar to that originally proposed by Kretschmer, with borderline syndromes related, respectively, to schizophrenia and affective psychosis being opposed to each other, the two forms having in common only a variation along some general "severity" dimension. In other words, Stone appears to conclude that the different varieties of borderline syndrome are too unalike to have any *intrinsic* qualities in common which could be labelled "psychoticism." If he is right then we might be led to predict that higher P scores would be found to be associated with syndromes bordering on affective psychosis rather than on schizophrenia.

A not dissimilar conclusion could be drawn from a recent study by Tyrer and Alexander (1979). Being British in origin the study was not concerned with borderline syndromes as such but with their nearest equivalent in British psychiatry, the so-called "personality disorders." Tyrer and Alexander applied cluster and factor analysis to behavioral ratings obtained on a group of such patients and identified two types of individual. One they labelled "passive-dependent." The other they described as "sociopathic," characterized by traits such as callousness, aggressiveness, and impulsivity; in other words, features almost identical to those used by the Eysencks to describe psychoticism. Again we see evidence that the P-scale, by itself, may not be capable of capturing the entire range of psychotic traits but only those associated with some particular forms of psychosis.

Certain features of the P-scale itself also bear on this general question. One is its item content and the other is the form of the score distribution on the scale. These two factors are linked in the sense that through successive versions of the

P-scale there have been attempts to improve the latter by making changes in the former. Early versions of the scale for example, that contained in the PEN inventory, showed a heavily skewed distribution of scores, indeed a clear reversed J distribution; so much so that some critics, including myself (Claridge and Chappa, 1973), were led to complain that the scale seemed to be tapping only paranoid, affect-laden forms of psychoticism and did not cover more passive, retarded, or autistic traits, a conclusion, incidentally, supported by the results of the clinical studies, described above, by Verma and Eysenck (1973) and by McPherson et al. (1974), both of whom used the PEN inventory. Ironically perhaps, the latter contained a number of items with a distinctly "psychotic" content. These, presumably because of their low endorsement rate, were subsequently removed in forming the EPQ, which now shows a rather less skewed distribution. However, it is not at all clear that the way in which this psychometric improvement was brought about actually solved the basic problem concerning the comprehensiveness and power of the scale as a measure of general psychoticism. Thus, the published scale is now diluted by a preponderance of items referring to mildly unconventional behavior; it is something of a compromise between the demands of psychometric purity and the requirements of face validity. On the latter score it seems, if anything, to have retreated slightly from its original purpose and, for some, runs the danger of being a 'catch-all' for any kind of vaguely irresponsible behavior.

In reaching similar conclusions elsewhere (Claridge, 1981) I was nevertheless led to comment that it would be unlikely if the *P*-scale proved to be merely a measure of anti-social traits, having no connection with the predisposition to at least some forms of psychotic breakdown, including some variations of schizophrenia. In the latter regard it is, in my view, extremely interesting that the traits apparently tapped by the *P*-scale are remarkably similar to some of those observed in the pre-morbid personalities of schizophrenics, as revealed in follow-back and other "high-risk" studies (Garmezy, 1974). Furthermore, the nature of such personalities, often a curious mixture of shy introversion and aggressive impulsivity, perhaps highlights the peculiar difficulty of capturing in a single scale or questionnaire the essence of "psychoticism." At the very least it would seem profitable to pursue empirical studies of the *P*-scale and to defer for the moment more fundamental decisions about its status within a general theory of "psychoticism: for example, whether Eysenck is right and psychoticism can be construed as a common dimension describing the predisposition to *all* forms of psychosis, with heterogeneity being referrable to other dimensions; or whether a bipolar dimension similar to Kretschmer's is nearer to reality; or whether these are merely alternative, not mutually exclusive, ways of conceptualizing slightly different kinds of experimental and clinical data.

It is on that note that I would like to turn to the second part of this chapter, an appropriate point to do so, as it happens, since the research my colleagues and I have been conducting on the *P*-scale in recent years actually emanated from a view of "psychoticism" rather different from that preferred by Eysenck; starting before work on the *P*-scale had begun, its convergence, nevertheless, with the latter serves to reinforce the remarks made at the end of the last paragraph.

While eschewing, for the moment, detailed arguments about the relative merits of different theoretical conceptions of psychoticism, it is nevertheless necessary, in order to explain the direction of our later work on the *P*-scale, to present some early thoughts I had on the topic. This can best be done by considering again a suggested model of psychoticism, arrived at some years ago, following an extensive study of normal and psychiatric subjects, including psychotic patients (Claridge, 1967). The model, which is reproduced in Fig. 4.1, was essentially a *post hoc* attempt to account for a large body of experimental data; these included personality and clinical characteristics, as well as variations on a number of psychophysiological measures and tests of psychological functions, such as attention, perception, and psychomotor performance. Many of the latter were chosen out of consideration for Eysenck's causal theory of introversion–extraversion and neuroticism; indeed, the original aim of the study was to test the viability of that theory when applied to neurotic samples, psychotic patients being included simply as a comparison group. Figure 4.1 summarizes the main conclusion drawn from the work, the results of which seemed to point to the existence of two major personality dimensions—psychoticism and neuroticism—each of which was defined, at its extremes, by different varieties of

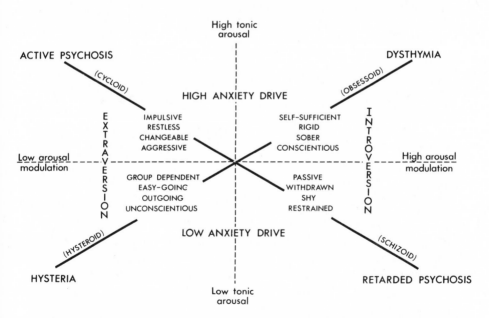

FIG. 4.1.   Diagram illustrating the author's 1967 model of personality and psychiatric disorder, reproduced from Claridge (1967).

psychosis and neurosis. It was considered that these descriptive continua reflected differences, at a biological level, in the organizational properties of the central nervous system. Specifically, it was suggested that there were individual variations in the activity level of, and homeostatic relationship between, two hypothetical brain circuits: a "tonic arousal system," concerned with general activation, and an "arousal modulating system," having excitatory and inhibitory properties, and concerned with the suppression and facilitation of sensory input.

The biological features of the model depended on two sets of empirical data. One was the observation, based partly on factor analysis of the experimental measures, that two separable components of psychophysiological variation could be reliably identified; these components looked as though they may represent the two underlying central nervous mechanisms emphasized in the model. Secondly, in psychotics it was found that measures which seemed to tap the two components differed, not so much in their overall *level,* as in the manner in which they *covaried,* when compared with neurotics. In other words, on neither component, taken by itself, did psychotics as a whole appear to differ from neurotics; rather it was the way in which the components were inter-related that differentiated the two samples. In terms of the model, this was taken to mean that the two hypothetical mechanisms—tonic arousal and arousal modulation—could operate in either of two homeostatic modes: negative feedback corresponding to a neuroticism dimension (dysthymia-hysteria) or positive feedback corresponding to "psychoticism." Variations *within* psychosis were considered to reflect the direction in which tonic arousal and arousal modulation became, through positive feedback between them, effectively "dissociated." As shown in Fig. 4.1, low tonic arousal coupled with excessive inhibitory regulation of sensory input was associated with retarded, introverted, withdrawn forms of psychosis; paranoid, emotionally active psychotic reactions were characterized by high tonic arousal and weak inhibition, manifest in excessive attentional overload.

It is instructive here to compare this theoretical approach with that of Eysenck, for there are a number of important differences. One difference lies in the empirical data from which the model illustrated in Fig. 4.1 was derived. Thus, its starting-point was, as Eysenck would put it, the "causal" level of analysis or, in Pavlovian terminology, that of "nervous typology." In other words, the model was constructed on the basis of observed *biological* variations, on to which descriptive personality and clinical characteristics were subsequently mapped. Eysenck, however, has tended more often to proceed in the opposite direction, that is to arrive at descriptive dimensions through factor analysis of superficial traits and then to postulate possible causal determinants of such dimensions.

From this flows a further difference between the two approaches. Eysenck, having isolated his descriptive dimensions, has then characteristically assigned to each of them a separate neurophysiological substrate. Thus, in his earlier writings on extraversion and neuroticism (Eysenck, 1955) he proposed that those dimensions reflected cortical excitation–inhibition balance and autonomic reactivity, respectively; while his later revision (Eysenck, 1967) identified them individually with the respective activities of the ascending reticular formation and the limbic system. So far he has not formally made a comparable proposal for psychoticism, though a similar theoretical strategy is evident in a tentative suggestion, following Gray (1973), that it may have something to do with the neurophysiology of aggression (Eysenck and Eysenck, 1976).

Eysenck's thinking in this general regard has important consequences for the way in which he conceptualizes dimensions like psychoticism. Thus, according to him all individuals high on such a dimension should share a common biological feature—in the form of, say, an increased level of activity in some neural structure or brain circuit. This requirement is, of course, necessary in order for him to maintain the position that psychoticism, and neuroticism, are unipolar and independent dimensions each having a separate neurophysiological substrate and each capable of describing all individuals who are labelled either psychotic or neurotic. It is clear from the model shown in Fig. 4.1 that my own conclusions from our 1967 work were somewhat different. Following that model the only biological characteristic common to all types of psychotic, or their normal variants, would be the tendency towards a particular kind of central nervous imbalance. The individual circuits involved would simply, depending on the form this imbalance took, be at different levels of activity; furthermore they would be the very same circuits as those implicated in the physiological substrate of neuroticism. It is also clear that this model, and the empirical data supporting it, virtually demanded a view of psychoticism closer to that proposed originally by Kretschmer, namely a bipolar continuum of psychotic characteristics running from what he described as cycloid traits, at one end, to schizoid traits, at the other, and which I identified, in clinical terminology, as active and retarded psychosis, respectively.

In comparing the conclusions drawn from this early study with those of Eysenck another difference between our respective approaches must also be borne in mind. Constructing the model just described depended heavily on data obtained from psychiatric patients. This had both advantages and disadvantages. On the one hand, it allowed important sources of individual variation to be drawn out in magnified form; these were then interpolated to describe possible normal personality dimensions. On the other hand, actually identifying such dimensions rested very much on general theoretical considerations; the only direct evidence we had at that time that we may be tapping a normal dimension of "psychoticism" was the finding that, in the group of non-psychiatric subjects tested, both modes of interaction between tonic arousal and arousal modulation could be detected, suggesting that some normal individuals did, as dimensional theory demanded, show psychotic nervous system "styles." Eysenck, on the other hand, has concentrated his main search for psychoticism on the study of normal populations, proceeding into the clinical sphere in order to try and find validity for his new dimension. That, too, has its advantages, in tackling the problem at source, as it were. But it also, as we have seen, carries its drawbacks, raising doubts about the ability of the *P*-scale to capture the full essence and range of psychotic traits. In practice, the two approaches, starting from normal populations and moving outwards or from clinical samples and moving inwards, are complementary. Of the two strategies Eysenck's is perhaps the more difficult, as witness the long interval that elapsed between his proposal for psychoticism as a third dimension and his introduction of a questionnaire instrument for measuring it. When the new scale did eventually appear the event proved, for us, to be something of a minor breakthrough; prior to that it had been difficult to find methods for selecting from normal populations individuals who putatively might show psychotic traits and on whom hypotheses about the nature of psychoticism could be tested. Even if only as a first approximation to a measure of psychotic traits the *P*-scale is, therefore, in my view, a major advance in personality description.

In using the new scale my colleagues and I have tried to conduct research on a broad front; especially crucial has been our attempt to maintain continuity between work on patient samples and work on normal subjects. Because of the results of the earlier study, already referred to, we have been particularly interested in the possible biological basis of psychoticism. As I have mentioned, Eysenck himself has so far confined his own speculations on this score to the suggestion that psychoticism may be equated with aggressiveness, its biological basis being sought in hormonal differences, particularly with respect to the sex hormones (Eysenck, 1976). The fact that males have consistently higher *P* scores than females (Eysenck and Eysenck, 1975) would certainly support that view, though the data are open to other interpretations. They might for example simply reflect sex differences in the early conditioning of the expression of aggressive behavior. Or, even if representing true biological differences, they could refer to that part of the variance in *P* score which appears to measure criminality and which, as we have seen, has not yet convincingly been shown to be uniquely "psychotic." For, as I have argued elsewhere (Claridge, 1981), while aggressiveness certainly does form part of the clinical picture in some psychotics, this is by no means always the case and it seems intuitively unlikely that aggressiveness *per se* provides the clue to the fundamental biological nature of psychoticism. What that feature is, is still a mystery and likely to remain so until the investigation of clinical psychosis, combined with the study of appropriately selected individuals "at risk," have together identified a unique set of biological "markers" which are more than merely non-specific indicators of general abnormality; recent examples of that flaw are the much vaunted "dopamine hypothesis" (Meltzer and Stahl, 1976) and claims for an eye-scanning defect in psychosis (Březinová and Kendell, 1977).

Our own efforts in this direction, rightly or wrongly, though naturally, have been to follow through our earlier supposition that the essence of psychosis, and therefore of psychoticism, may be a relative "dissociative" tendency in the nervous systems of some individuals. Empirically this could be examined, we argued, using a simple "covariation strategy," that is, to compare suitably selected individuals, not for their deviation on a single measure or along some single parameter, but with respect to the correlation between pairs of measures or parameters of central nervous function. This approach, we felt, might help us to capture what our 1967 experiments had led us to conclude, namely that psychosis is a defect of central nervous *organization,* rather than a simple unidirectional deviation of function. An obvious next question was whether the tendency to such dissociation was a possible biological substrate of psychoticism as a normal personality trait. The opportunity to investiage this hypothesis properly first arose with the appearance of an early version of the *P*-scale, that contained in the unpublished PEN inventory. In order to explain the origins of that work it is again necessary to backtrack slightly and refer to some earlier findings which provided the empirical springboard for our first investigations of the *P*-scale.

Coincidentally, working in parallel though more narrowly concerned with the psychophysiology of schizophrenia, Venables (1963) had also observed that it was the *covariation* between psychophysiological variables which uniquely seem to distinguish psychotics from other individuals. His measures of choice were two-flash threshold discrimination and an index of electrodermal activity (skin potential level), venables demonstrating that schizophrenics differed from normal subjects in showing a significant reversal in the sign of the correlation between the two variables. Inspired by Venables' result, the ease of measuring the two-flash threshold and electrodermal activity, and the theoretical significance of these indices for the possible understanding of the neurophysiology of schizophrenia, my colleagues and I then embarked upon a series of investigations using a similar strategy. Three different types of experiment, partly overlapping in time, were undertaken.

The first, a single study of LSD-25, compared the effects of that drug and a placebo on the skin potential and two-flash threshold performance of a group of normal subjects (Claridge, 1972). A second, more recent, experiment, this time using skin conductance, also examined two-flash threshold and electrodermal level in a group of drug-free schizophrenics (Claridge, 1978; Claridge and Clark, 1982). And thirdly, data have been collected over a period of time on skin conductance and two-flash threshold in normal samples selected for high *P* scores (Claridge and Chappa, 1973; Claridge and Birchall, 1973, 1978). The comparisons there have been with individuals low in *P* but high in neuroticism, the reason being that in the early PEN inventory used in those studies the *P* and *N* scales tended to be positively correlated.

The results of all of these experiments have, in some form or other, already been published elsewhere and here I shall confine myself to presenting a summary of the findings and drawing some general conclusions from them. As mentioned above, the focus of our attention has been the nature of the covariation between two-flash threshold and the electrodermal measure. In fact, in all three types of experiment the results have been remarkably similar, their general form being shown, diagrammatically, in Fig. 4.2. What I have denoted there the "non-psychotic relationship" describes the manner in which two-flash threshold and electrodermal level would normally be expected to covary; that is, it describes a conventional inverted-U function, two-flash threshold discrimination improving up to an optimum and then declining thereafter. This kind of relationship was observed under the placebo condition of the LSD experiment and in subjects low in psychoticism. The so-called "psychotic relationship" which we have observed, however, is of quite the opposite form, perceptual discrimination being very acute at either end of the electrodermal range and at its worst at moderate levels of skin conductance or potential; as seen in the figure, the data as a whole form a curious U-shaped function.

Although the "psychotic" data from the three types of experiment all agree in following the trend illustrated in Fig. 4.2, several comments are necessary about the actual results. One strangely consistent feature of the data has been the tendency for subjects frequently to cluster in the lower half of the electrodermal range. This has meant that the lower arm of the observed U-function has been much more easily definable than its upper arm. There, as shown in Table 4.1, the agreement between the three different sets of results has been extremely good. Under LSD, in the high P subjects studied by Claridge and Chappa (1973), and in drug-free schizophrenics tested immediately on admission to hospital by Clar-

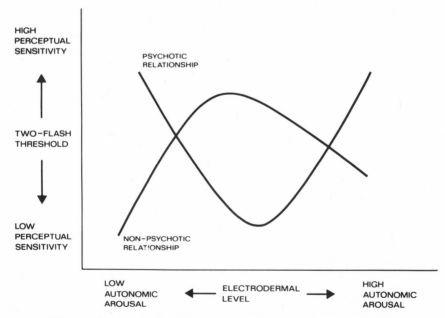

FIG. 4.2.   Diagrammatic representation of two hypothesized forms of relationship between perceptual discrimination (two-flash threshold) and autonomic arousal (electrodermal level).

idge and Clark (1982), low range individuals showed a consistently high, negative correlation between the two experimental measures. In contrast, subjects under placebo in the drug experiment and low P subjects showed equally substantial correlations, but in the opposite, positive, direction[2]. The comparable upper range results for the data shown in Table 4.1 were less clear-cut, however. The drug study again yielded relationships of opposite sign, the direction now being positive for LSD and negative for placebo; but the upper range data were more scattered and the actual correlations lower, being $+0.11$ and -0.32, respectively. In normal subjects selected for psychoticism Claridge and Chappa actually found few people in the upper range of skin conductance, though they did note that individuals who were high in electrodermal level tended to fall in a zone of improved perceptual discrimination; in other words their performance was consistent with the U-function. The latter has in any case now been more clearly confirmed by Claridge and Birchall (1978) who have recently reported the results for a rather larger group of high P subjects, covering the full range of electrodermal level. Their data showed a significant curvilinear regression of the hypothesized U form, consistent with the "psychotic relationship" illustrated in Fig. 4.2. Low P/high N subjects also followed a curvilinear regression but of the opposite, inverted-U, shape.

Before commenting further on these results as they relate to psychoticism, some additional remarks are necessary about the data we have obtained on psychotic patients. It is important to note that the results from the Claridge and Clark study contained in Table 4.1 concern the *first* occasion of testing only. The patients in that experiment were actually tested on three consecutive days after admission and when all three sets of two-flash threshold and skin conductance data were examined a rather complex picture emerged. On the first day the form of the data almost exactly replicated that found by Claridge and Chappa in their small group of normal high P scorers: a high negative correlation in the low skin conductance range (as shown in Table 4.1) but, in the upper range, very few patients, who nevertheless fell in the zone of improved perceptual discrimination. On subsequent days, however, patients showed a gradual shift towards increasing skin conductance levels, with the result that by the third occasion of testing very few patients fell in the *low* range of electrodermal activity. The relationship between skin conductance and perceptual discrimination then became, weakly, positive. In other words, when taken together the data for psychotics did appear to conform overall to a U-shaped function, but the individual measures were clearly somewhat unstable and subject to considerable change over time. Our guess is that this reflects the highly fluctuant nature of the mental

---

[2]It should be noted that in reporting results on the relationship between two-flash threshold and electrodermal activity we have always followed the convention of reflecting the signs of the correlations between them. Thus, a positive correlation indicates that as electrodermal level increases there is an *improvement* in perceptual discrimination.

TABLE 4.1
Comparison of "Low Range" Correlations between
Two-Flash Threshold (Perceptual Discrimination)
and Electrodermal Level in Three Experiments

LSD study (Claridge)	Normal subjects (Claridge and Chappa)	Schizophrenic patients (Claridge and Clark)
LSD condition -0.82	High P subjects -0.78	Tested on admission -0.80
Placebo condition +.074	Low P subjects +0.64	

state associated with clinical psychosis; indeed it may represent precisely that tendency towards "dissociated" central nervous function which we have argued is the hallmark of psychotic disorder.

Despite some reservations about the firmness of this last set of data, we nevertheless feel that there is a convincing degree of consistency in the results. The same pattern of relationships emerges from three quite different types of experiment in which some form of "psychoticism" is implicated: in schizophrenic patients, in normal subjects under the influence of a psychotomimetic drug, and in individuals selected on the basis of the P-scale. Furthermore, in all three instances the form of the relationship between two-flash threshold and electrodermal activity is highly unusual. Counterintuitively, in such individuals perceptual acuity seems to be very good when autonomic arousal is very low or, alternatively, when it is very high, beyond the point where normally it would, according to the usual inverted-U principle, have begun to decline. We would argue, therefore, that the data provide further evidence that some individuals, possibly predisposed to psychosis, show an "unbalanced style" of central nervous organization, as postulated in our original model.

At this juncture reference should be made to the results of other workers who have examined two-flash threshold and electrodermal activity from a similar point of view. Because of its origins in the schizophrenia literature, most research has been concerned with patient samples (Lykken and Maley, 1968; Gruzelier, Venables & Lykken, 1972; Gruzelier and Venables, 1975). The results have, frankly, been disappointing, but, unfortunately, all of the experiments subsequent to Venables' original report have, unlike our own, been conducted on medicated patients. For this reason they can probably be dismissed. Thus, Claridge and Clark, in the study referred to above, actually examined the influence of medication on the patients whom they had earlier tested prior to treatment. The effects were massive and totally eliminated any systematic relationship between two-flash threshold and electrodermal activity. Independent confirmation of our findings in drug-free schizophrenics must therefore await further research.

Regarding normal subjects, as far as I know only one other group of workers has examined two-flash threshold and electrodermal activity in relation to the *P*-scale. Recently Robinson and Zahn (1979), reporting such a study, confirmed that the two measures did indeed covary in opposite directions in high and low *P* scorers. However, their results were rather weaker than our own, a fact which has prompted some correspondence with Robinson about the possible reasons for the discrepancy between our respective sets of data. One reason may be the different versions of the *P*-scale used by Robinson and Zahn and by ourselves. Robinson and Zahn used the EPQ scale, whereas all of our results were based on the *P*-scale from the earlier PEN inventory. As noted earlier, the latter contained many more "psychotic" items and was perhaps more discriminating of truly deviant individuals, a fact Birchall and I touched upon elsewhere in discussing the validity of the Eysenck scales (Claridge and Brichall, 1978).

The correspondence with Robinson has, however, since unearthed another possible, and interesting, source of variation in these data. Several theoretical and empirical considerations had led me to suspect that the "psychotic" reversal of covariation between two-flash threshold and electrodermal activity may be particularly, perhaps mainly, evident in one subgroup of high *P* scorers, namely introverts. One reason for making this suggestion was that recently, when re-examining the Claridge and Clark data for psychotic patients, we discovered that the appearance of a U-shaped relationship between two-flash threshold and skin conductance was entirely due to the performance of a subset of schizophrenics, who clinically were more retarded and affectively flattened and who were significantly more introverted on a combined measure from the Eysenck and Cattell scales. There was no evidence of a U function in the data of more extraverted, affectively disturbed patients. Partly on the basis of this observation I proposed to Robinson that he might re-examine his own data on normal subjects from a similar point of view. This he kindly did and recently reported (personal communication) that the reversal of covariation which he and Zahn had found in high *P* scorers on the EPQ did indeed seem to be confined mainly to the introverts in the sample.

When our own data on two-flash threshold and skin conductance in normal subjects were also considered from this point of view, we found the same sort of picture emerging. This is illustrated in Fig. 4.3, which is a modified version of a figure published by Claridge and Birchall (1978) in their paper reporting their final set of data on two-flash threshold and skin conductance in high *P* subjects. What I have done there is to indicate the plotted scores for the relatively more introverted subjects in that group, chosen according to the rather lenient criterion of having an E score (on the PEN inventory) of 10 or less. It can be seen that the postulated U-function is even more evident in this subgroup than in the high *P* subjects as a whole. The most dramatic effect of removing the relatively more extraverted subjects is observed in the upper skin conductance range, defined as in our original report, *viz* readings beyond about 7 micromhos. This unfortunate-

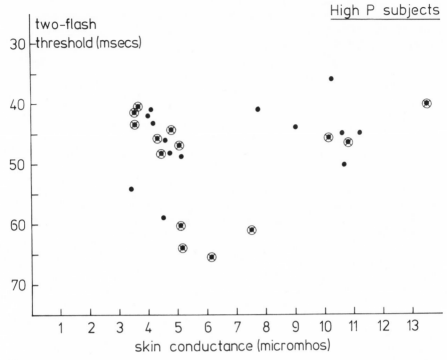

FIG. 4.3. Plotted two-flash threshold and skin conductance readings for high P subjects, taken from Claridge and Birchall (1978) and modified as explained in the text. Crossed circles represent the more introverted subjects.

ly does reduce the number of upper range individuals—a familiar problem I have already referred to—and makes formal statistical analysis somewhat unrealistic. However, it is worth noting that the correlation between two-flash threshold and skin conductance in these upper range introverts reached a very high value (+0.94), compared with +0.42 if all high range subjects are included.

Clearly a quite complicated picture is beginning to emerge here but if we consider together these findings, Robinson's re-analysis of his own data, and our own results with schizophrenic patients, some general conclusions can be reached. It appears that at least some individuals who are high in psychoticism, as judged by the Eysenck *P*-scales, show a distinct pattern of psychophysiological response, as measured by two-flash threshold and electrodermal activity. Furthermore, the response pattern observed closely resembles that to be found in some psychotic states, to that extent providing some validity for the *P*-scale, as well as offering some clues about the possible biological basis of psychoticism as a dimension of personality. In the latter respect the results are consistent with the view expressed earlier that ''psychoticism'' may represent a particular ''style'' of nervous system functioning in which the mechanism regulating sensory responsiveness, as reflected here in two-flash threshold discriminability, are capable of becoming relatively dissociated from those controlling tonic arousal. Certainly, at a purely empirical level, the results obtained with two-flash threshold and electrodermal measures would seem to confirm the value of using a "covariation strategy" to analyze such data, since neither measure alone would have discriminated between the various groups studied.

For this reason we have continued to use the same strategy in some of our more recent research on the psychophysiological correlates of psychoticism. Most of these later studies are still in progress and here I shall confine myself to describing their general direction and presenting some preliminary findings and observations. Following the series of studies of the two-flash threshold we were led to consider a change in experimental technique and decided to investigate the use of visual evoked response procedures. There were several reasons for this decision. First, we felt it important to try and get closer to the possible neurophysiological mechanisms that might underly the variations in sensory responsiveness measured by the two-flash threshold. Secondly, EEG techniques provide relatively greater objectivity of measurement than psychophysical methods; this could be especially crucial in patient investigations. Thirdly, we had become increasingly impressed by the need for more detailed studies of intra-individual variations in psychophysiological status. Techniques like the two-flash threshold are rather coarse-grained procedures for that purpose and, although the method had sufficed for making comparisons across groups of subjects, we felt that the study of the evoked response would be more suited to examining individuals.

The particular application of the visual evoked response which we are currently investigating is its use in the determination of individual differences in the so-called "augmenting-reducing" phenomenon, the tendency for the amplitude of the evoked response to increase, or alternatively decrease, as a function of changing intensity of stimulation. Augmenting-reducing has been, and continues to be, the subject of a considerable amount of research, in relation to both normal personality and psychiatric disorder (Callaway, 1975; Landau, Buchsbaum, Carpenter, Strauss & Sacks, 1975; Shagass, Straumamanis & Overton, 1975; Zuckerman, 1979). Its particular interest to us was the possibility that it may directly reflect variations in those central nervous mechanisms concerned with what earlier I labelled "arousal modulation." Thus, several investigators, though especially Buchsbaum (1976), have explicitly considered that the tendency for individuals to amplify or to damp down their response as stimulus intensity increases represents the operation of a central excitatory-inhibitory mechanism regulating sensory input; the parallel with our own notion of arousal modulation was therefore fairly self-evident.

The technique we have routinely adopted for measuring augmenting-reducing is that followed by most other workers using the visual evoked response for that purpose; namely, it involves determining the linear slope of the function relating

VER amplitude across four intensities of light flash, increasing in logarithmic fashion. So far we have limited our analyses of the evoked response amplitudes to peak-to-peak measurements of the P100/N135 component occurring after flash onset. In applying this or similar techniques of augmenting-reducing measurement to the problem of individual differences all previous workers have confined themselves to a simple classification of subjects. That is to say, they have been content to label individuals as either "augmenters" or "reducers," usually on the basis of a single determination of augmenting-reducing slope. However, our interest in the procedure has been to use it as a measure of *change* in "arousal modulation" within the individual and, furthermore, to examine to what extent, and in what way, such changes are related to alterations in tonic arousal, again as indicated by skin conductance. Thus, following our previous general strategy, we have been concerned, not so much with augmenting-reducing differences as such, but with the *covariation* between augmenting-reducing slope and skin conductance, focusing in this case more on within-subject relationships. Our general prediction is that such relationships will themselves vary as a function of personality, especially psychoticism.

The initial step in this research programme was to determine, first, whether augmenting-reducing is, as some workers have maintained, a fixed characteristic of the individual and, secondly, if not, whether it does indeed vary systematically as a function of arousal level. This question was answered in a recent study by Birchall and Claridge (1979) who conducted two replicated experiments on a group of randomly selected normal subjects. In each subject four estimations of augmenting-reducing slope were determined within a single session, skin conductance level being monitored throughout. Several important findings emerged. First, it was clear that an individual's augmenting-reducing slope could change considerably during the course of the testing session, sometimes even shifting from an augmenting to a reducing mode of response or vice versa. Secondly, within subjects these changes *were* related to fluctuations in skin conductance level, though the direction of covariation differed across individuals; in some the response shifted towards greater augmenting as skin conductance increased while in others the shift was towards greater reducing. Thirdly, the form of covariation between augmenting-reducing change and skin conductance change itself depended on the level of electrodermal activity over which the subject was operating during the experiment.

This rather complex, but systematic, pattern of relationships is illustrated in Fig. 4.4, taken from the Birchall and Claridge paper, which gives full details of the experiment. The abscissa in the figure represents skin conductance level and the ordinate the within-subject correlation between skin conductance and augmenting-reducing slope. Each data point therefore represents an individual, plotted according to his mean skin conductance level during the experiment and the manner in which his augmenting-reducing response varied as a function of electrodermal activity over the testing session. It can be seen that over the group as a

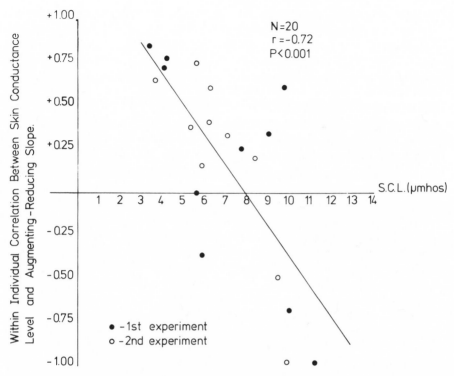

FIG. 4.4.   Change in augmenting-reducing slope with varying intra-subject skin conductance level for individuals operating over different ranges of electrodermal level; the results of two experiments are shown. Reproduced from Birchall and Claridge (1979).

whole there is a strong negative regression. This means that individuals whose general skin conductance level fell in the lower range tended to show a positive relationship between skin conductance and augmenting-reducing; that is to say, if, for example, a subject's skin conductance increased during testing he tended to move towards greater augmenting. The opposite was true of subjects who operated over the upper range of electrodermal activity; in these cases further increases in skin conductance were associated with a shift towards relatively greater reducing.

Our interpretation of these data is that, although individually very different, all of the subjects in the experiment were operating according to a similar psychophysiological principle, one which can be construed as a "balanced" mode of sensory regulation. Thus, individuals on the right side of Fig. 4.4 could be viewed as necessarily, and adaptively, damping down their sensory responses under the combined influence of increasing arousal and stimulus intensity; such effects would be more tolerable to the poorly aroused individuals on the *left* side of the diagram who could continue, without sensory overload, to amplify their responses to the increasingly intense stimuli.

There is a clear parallel here with our original formulation of "arousal modulation" and "tonic arousal" operating, in some individuals, in a homeostatic mode characterized by negative feedback. Such individuals should, according to the model, be of a non-psychotic nervous type. By the same token, there should be other individuals—high in "psychoticism" who fall along a line cutting diagonally across that drawn in Fig. 4.4, and showing a *positive* regression between the two measures plotted there.

We have recently conducted an experiment to test out this hypothesis, using the same augmenting-reducing and skin conductance procedures as previously to examine differences between normal individuals selected according to their scores on the EPQ. The results of that experiment have not yet been fully analyzed, but some preliminary findings can be reported here.

Considering the data in the same form as that shown in Fig. 4.4, we have found that the correlation for a group of 44 low P subjects was -0.45 (p < 0.01). In other words, they followed the same pattern as our original, randomly selected, subjects, showing what we described as a "balanced" mode of augmenting-reducing change as a function of arousal. Within this low P group, subjects both high and low in N were represented. When considered separately both subgroups showed a similar negative regression, though the correlation was greater for low N than for high N subjects, the respective values for r being -0.74 (p < 0.001, df = 20) and -0.43 (p < 0.05, df = 20).

On first analysis the results for our group of high P subjects seem rather more complicated. In the group as a whole the correlation was virtually zero, r being -0.09 (NS, df = 28); to that extent, therefore, these individuals did appear to be behaving in a different fashion from low P scoring subjects. However, the complete lack of association between the two experimental measures in the high P sample suggests that they were a very heterogenous group and currently we are examining the data further to see whether we can define subsets of high P individuals who might confirm our hypothesis more clearly. One possibility we have considered follows our hunch, discussed already, that the "unbalanced" mode which we have postulated may be confined to certain high P subjects only, most likely introverts. To test this idea we selected out the more introverted subjects in the high P sample. Unfortunately, even using the lenient cut-off point of an E score of 10 or less there were only eight individuals, but in this group the correlation between the two experimental variables was very high and in the predicted opposite direction from that found in low P subjects; r was $+0.87$ (p < 0.01). Interestingly, in a comparable group of *extraverted* high P subjects (with E scores of 16 or above) the correlation, although not significant ($r = -0.44$, N = 10), was negative, as in the two low P groups. These results are clearly consistent with those observed for the two-flash threshold/skin conductance data and again suggest that, insofar as "psychotic" forms of central nervous responding can be inferred from such relationships, these appear to be confined to individuals showing the particular combination of introversion and high psychoticism.

Regarding the "covariation strategy" itself as a method for analyzing data of this kind, its potential value has, I think, been further demonstrated in the results of a recent study reported by Haier, Buchsbaum, Murphy, Gottesman & Coursey, (1980). They conducted a similar exercise using a visual evoked response measure of augmenting-reducing and a biochemical index of central nervous "arousal", namely the level of platelet MAO activity. Their covariation strategy differed slightly from ours, being more like our earlier comparisons of two-flash threshold and electrodermal activity. That is to say, they plotted the scores of a group of normal subjects along two axes, representing the biochemical index and a *single* measure of augmenting-reducing; four combinations of scores were therefore possible. Assessing the degree of psychopathology in their subjects Haier and his associates reported that the more deviant individuals tended to show one of two combinations on their experimental measures. Subjects either showed evoked response augmenting together with high CNS arousal or tended to be reducers with low CNS arousal, as judged by MAO levels. Both of these combinations, they argued, are relatively "unbalanced" central nervous states which may form an important biological substrate for the predisposition to mental illness. Although Haier and his colleagues did not themselves use the P-scale there is nevertheless here a satisfying convergence of theory and empirical evidence.

I would now like to turn to a slightly different, though theoretically closely linked, approach to the possible biological basis of psychoticism, recently developed by my colleague, Dr. David Robinson. He has been more concerned with Eysenck's other two dimensions of extraversion and neuroticism, but in the course of his work he has also had occasion to consider how individual differences on the P-scale may relate to the physiological variables in which he has been interested. It would not be possible here to do justice to the full scope of Robinson's ideas and experimental results, but he has described these in detail himself in his own writings (Robinson, 1980, 1982).

Drawing on neurophysiological data, and taking account of the dynamics of EEG activity, Robinson has constructed a model which, he suggests, offers a physiological basis for the Pavlovian hypothetical excitatory and inhibitory processes; the latter he identifies with cortical and thalamic elements of the diffuse thalamocortical system. Constants reflecting the transmission characteristics of these elements, and corresponding to the Pavlovian notion of "strength", have been derived from a mathematical analysis of averaged evoked responses to systematically varied frequencies of sinusoidally modulated light stimuli. Robinson has shown that individual differences in the values of these constants relate to personality in normal subjects. One dimension describes some individuals in whom the constants increase and decrease together; in Pavlovian terms these subjects would be described as "balanced" but differing in overall "strength". At a behavioral level the dimension corresponds closely to a personality continuum running from neurotic introversion, at one end, to stable extraversion, at the other. Cutting, as it does, across Eysenck's own dimensions of extraversion and neuroticism, the continuum identified by Robinson can clearly be aligned with Gray's similar "anxiety" dimension (Gray, 1970); it also corresponds to my own "dysthymia-hysteria" dimension, described earlier[3].

Robinson has also demonstrated a second dimension which describes other individuals in whom the constants take different, rather than similar, values; in Pavlovian terms these subjects woud be considered "*unbalanced.*" On general theoretical grounds it might have been expected that these individuals would be high in psychoticism but, in fact, a more complex picture emerged. In his particular sample the highest P scores were actually found in subjects who fell in the middle of the two dimensions; that is to say, individuals having intermediate and similar values of the two EEG constants. Paradoxically, they were the most "balanced" subjects of all.

In order to appreciate the significance of this last finding it is first necessary to consider another observation which Robinson made at the same time. Having access to a very large set of EPQ data he was led to examine the distribution of P scores across the sample, particularly with reference to differences in extraversion. The results of his analysis are shown in Fig. 4.5; plotted there are the mean P scores for subsets of individuals at different points on the E-scale, males and females being considered separately and as a combined group. It is clear from the diagram that P scores are not evenly distributed over the whole range of extraversion. Instead, in males at least, there is a high peak at middle values of E; then, in both sexes, there are two further peaks, at either end of the extraversion dimension. In other words, there appear to be three variants of high psychoticism. One, where the highest P scores seem to cluster, is associated with moderate degrees of introversion-extraversion; this group coincides exactly with that identified by Robinson in his own, smaller, sample. The other two variants show high P scores, but in association with either extreme introversion or extreme extraversion.

An interesting question is whether the P-scale only taps "true" psychoticism in these last two variants; or, indeed, that it only does so where the combination of high P and *low* E occurs. The results described earlier suggest that the latter may be the case; at least they suggest that the two variants may be psychophysiologically distinct. Unfortunately, Robinson's data do not throw light on this particular question, since the requisite combinations of high P with extreme

---

[3]Recently (Claridge, Donald, & Birchall, 1981), in discussing some data relating drug response to personality, we have drawn a more explicit comparison between my own and Gray's suggested modification to Eysenck's theory of extraversion and neuroticism, as well as also considering the relevance of the data to psychoticism.

values of E, in either direction, were poorly represented in his sample. He was therefore restricted to analysis of psychoticism found in subjects with *moderate* E scores, the third subgroup shown in Fig. 4.5.

In conducting his analysis, Robinson again drew on a Pavlovian concept, that of "concentration-irradiation." For reasons he has argued in detail elsewhere (Robinson, 1980) it is possible to derive the prediction that individuals with intermediate and similar values of the constants referred to earlier (i.e. the very

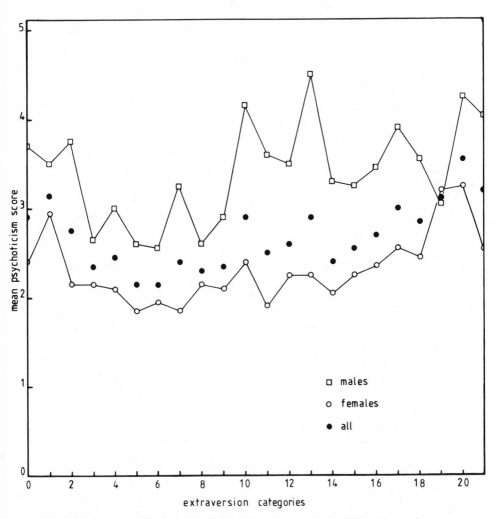

FIG. 4.5.   Mean scores for males, females, and both sexes combined at different levels of extraversion in a large heterogeneous sample of 3240 individuals. Note the peaking of psychoticism scores at both ends of the extraversion scale and, in males, in the mid-range of E.

high P scorers in his sample) should also be characterized by excessive "concentration." In Pavlovian terms this implies a tendency to highly circumscribed excitation of cortical areas after stimulation; in psychological terms it suggests extreme narrowing of attention; and in neurophysiological terms, Robinson supposes, it is paralleled by the role in selective responding to sensory input played by the diffuse thalamocortical system which, as I mentioned earlier, is the neural circuit he considers important.

Pursuing these ideas, Robinson has suggested that individuals with greater Pavlovian "concentration" should also be predisposed to develop particular kinds of cognitive style. Here he perceived a link with Witkin's notion of field dependence–independence, a dimension of cognitive style that has previously been used to try and explain differences between various forms of psychosis (Witkin, Faterson, Goodenough & Karp, 1962; Witkin, Oltman, Raskin, & Karp, 1971; Silverman, 1964). Part of his research involved the administration of the embedded figures test of field dependence. This, together with the subtests of the WAIS and the EPQ scales were subjected to factor analysis; also included was an index of deviation from intermediate and similar values of the EEG constants. A fairly complex pattern of relationships emerged but one factor, which could be clearly identified with the P-scale, had a substantial loading on the embedded figures test. The EEG variables had only a moderate loading on the factor but the association was in the expected direction: high P scores, the proposed EEG measure of "concentration", and field independence tended to go together. Bearing in mind that Robinson's high P scorers corresponded mainly to individuals falling in the middle of the distribution shown in Fig. 4.5, these results would support the view that that form of psychoticism is, as he predicted, associated with greater "concentration" in the Pavlovian sense. It is worth noting, too, that the factor just described was also highly loaded on the Lie scale of the EPQ— though, of course, in the opposite direction from P. This led Robinson to suggest that in that particular subgroup of high P scorers the P and L scales are essentially inversely related measures of the same set of traits; though this may not be the case in other variants of psychoticism, such as those associated with extreme values of extraversion where, paradoxically, P and L scores appear to covary in the same direction.

Considering Robinson's data from a clinical viewpoint, and hence its implications for the validity of the P-scale, there seems a strong possibility that the "middle" group of high P scorers identified in his research refers mainly to that part of the scale's variance which encloses psychopathic or antisocial behavior and that it may, in itself, have little to do with psychotic traits *per se*. I have already discussed other evidence that the P-scale may be partly serving such a function. Certainly, it seems to be extremely good at picking out criminal or other socially deviant individuals in whom there is no *independent* evidence of psychotic traits; the simultaneously low Lie scores found in such people would also be consistent with that interpretation, as would the sex differences evident for the "middle" high P scorers shown in Fig. 4.5. Furthermore, Robinson has suggested a way in which the neurophysiological organization of this variant of high P scorer might account for psychopathic behavior. To put it briefly, he has speculated that the excessively focused attention and circumscribed cortical activation associated with Pavlovian "concentration" could lead to "here and now," situationally specific, behaviors conducted without reference to any easily accessible or previously generalized framework of reference.

However, Robinson has also tentatively suggested that "middle" high P scorers *may* be individuals prone to psychosis, but of a particular form, namely paranoid reactions. As Robinson notes, Pavlov himself surmised that paranoia may be associated with "increased concentration," while Witkin suggested a relationship with field independence. Robinson also draws attention to the fact that, in the Verma and Eysenck (1973) study referred to earlier, paranoid patients emerged with the highest rating on the psychoticism factor and in a middle position on a factor identified by the authors as extraversion. An important consideration here, perhaps, is the well-recognized distinction between paranoid schizophrenia and paranoia, where the patient shows a highly encapsulated delusional system which could be seen as developing on the basis of the highly articulated cognitive style which Robinson would associate with excessive "concentration." It is also interesting to note that his emphasis on the apparent extreme "normality" of these individuals finds support in Venables' (1963) demonstration some years ago that paranoid patients with "coherent delusions" are quite different from other psychotics, including other paranoid schizophrenics: psychophysiologically such patients were remarkably normal.

Our excursion a moment ago into the cognitive aspects of psychoticism brings us neatly to the final part of this chapter, which is concerned with elaborating on that theme. The idea that variations in psychoticism, however that might be measured, ought to be manifest in cognitive differences between individuals needs no introduction here. The abnormalities of thinking, language, attention, and other cognitive functions in clinical psychosis are so profound, and so central to the disorder, that they could scarcely fail to be represented in muted form should a dimension, or dimensions, of psychoticism exist. However, in the narrower context of the P-scale and of our particular research on the problem it is again necessary to sketch in a certain amount of background detail.

Although the main emphasis in our 1967 study was psychophysiological, cognitive variables played an important part in helping to define the dimensions reproduced earlier in Fig. 4.1. That was especially true of "psychoticism," where the model attempted to combine features of Eysenck's theory and certain views, current at that time, about the nature of attentional and thinking disorder in schizophrenia (Payne, 1960). The evidence, incorporated in the model and partly used to define the concept of "arousal modulation," suggested that the psychophysiological variations found among different types of clinical psychosis were paralleled in the kind of cognitive disorder they displayed. The postulated dimension of psychoticism seemed roughly to correspond to a continuum of broadened and narrowed attention and, in terms of thinking, to that of overinclusion-underinclusion. Conceptually it was a very easy step to consider that among normal subjects such variations may represent differences in "cognitive style," especially as other workers, such as Silverman (1964), McConaghy (1960) and others had reached a similar conclusion. In our own data direct evidence for such a link was sparse because the study had concentrated more on psychiatric than on normal subjects. However, one tiny finding was encouraging. As mentioned earlier, in our normal sample both "neurotic" and "psychotic" nervous types were represented, as defined by our measures of "arousal modulation" and "tonic arousal." Interestingly, in the, rather small, group of subjects who resembled psychotics psychophysiologically there was evidence of unusual cognitive performance as shown in behavior on an object sorting test of overinclusive thinking. This suggested that, just as among psychotic patients psychophysiological differences may be reflected in particular kinds of thought *disorder,* so among normal individuals resembling them biologically, such differences may also be reflected in particular kinds of cognitive *style.*

In some later research I was able to test out this hunch more systematically (Claridge, 1973). The experiment in question formed part of a larger study of normal adult twins on whom we took psychophysiological measures derived from the earlier work on psychiatric patients and aimed at trying to define again the two hypothetical parameters of tonic arousal and arousal modulation; the measures included sedation threshold and various indices of autonomic and EEG activity. Factor analysis of the data revealed two factors which did seem to correspond to these two psychophysiological components: "arousal modulation," defined mainly by EEG variables, such as alpha frequency and "tonic arousal," defined by sedation threshold and autonomic measures. Using factor scores, the subjects were then classified into "neurotic" nervous types, on the one hand, and "psychotic" nervous types, on the other, according to the direction in which their scores on the two components covaried; thus "psychotic" nervous types showed apparent dissociation between tonic arousal and arousal modulation, as found previously in psychotic patients.

The two nervous types were then compared on a number of cognitive tests which had also been administered to the twins; these included several commonly used tests of divergent thinking, such as Unusual Uses and Object Drawing. Although alike in general intelligence, the two groups were found to differ significantly in their performance on the so-called "creativity" tests, "psychotic" nervous types being significantly more divergent. These results helped to confirm the earlier supposition that we may have been tapping a "psychoticism" dimension which was not only psychophysiologically measurable, but also recognizable as variations in cognitive style. Subsequently (Claridge, 1972), I elaborated upon that idea in the context of a discussion about the genetics of schizophrenia and its possible links with creativity. This "great wits and madness" argument is one which had intrigued me, as it has numerous other writers, for many years and it now seems to be gaining increasing support. It would take me beyond the scope of the present discussion to consider the argument in detail. I have done so elsewhere in my previous essay on psychoticism (Claridge, 1981); while Prentky (1980) has recently brought together a good deal of biographical and experimental evidence linking creativity to psychopathology. Suffice it to say here that the general inspiration of our work on psychoticism has been that, if not creativity, at least cognitive style differences almost certainly represent an important way in which the dimensional aspects of psychosis should manifest themselves.

As with our psychophysiological research, the opportunity to test that idea out further was eased by the advent of the *P*-scale. Apart from David Robinson's work, which I have already mentioned, two studies have been carried out by my colleagues, aimed at investigating the correlation between the *P*-scale and cognitive test performance. The first, by Woody (1976) was a relatively straightforward examination of the hypothesis that high *P* scorers should show greater divergence of thinking on ''creativity'' tests. His results, which have been summarized by Woody and Claridge (1977), convincingly demonstrated that in a group of university students there were very high positive correlations—averaging around +0.65—between EPQ *P* scores and a measure of originality, obtained from all five of the divergent thinking tests used; a simple count of the number of responses subjects generated on the tests was also consistently related to *P,* though to a lesser degree. Woody's results are in general agreement with other studies, reviewed by Eysenck and Eysenck (1976), aimed at testing the same hypothesis. Indeed, his findings were especially clear-cut, compared with those of other workers, a fact which Woody put down to the use of an untimed procedure and to the administration of the tests in a relaxed atmosphere; restriction of the range of general intelligence represented in his sample, imposed by his use of university students, was probably also an important factor. Although the latter limits the generality of his results, within the sample studied by Woody there was little doubt that high *P* scorers were much more likely to generate unusual associations. However, before uncritically accepting this, or other similar, evidence as support for true cognitive style differences in high *P* scorers, another possibility has to be considered. As Woody readily admitted himself, it is perfectly feasible, given the manner in which responses are demanded of the subjects in most open-ended tests, that high *P* scorers are simply more willing to *verbalize* unusual associations; in other words, the common variance being tapped may be a tendency, on both the *P*-scale and divergent thinking tasks, to express unconventional attitudes. Such an interpretation would somewhat weaken the argument that results of the kind reported by Woody provide validity for the *P*-scale as a measure of true psychoticism. Against this, however, must be set the evidence reported above, namely that when individuals are selected on the basis of *psychophysiological* differences, which are better underpinned theoretically, the same pattern of relationships with divergent thinking appeared.

Woody's research has recently been followed up with a much more elaborate series of investigations by my colleague, David Rawlings, whose results, because they have not yet been fully analyzed, can only be presented here in outline. Rawlings has utilized a variety of experimental procedures, referring to several theoretical models which he has considered relevant to the general question of cognitive style differences as they relate to personality. He has also not confined himself to the P-scale but, instead, has also examined other questionnaires which may be tapping similar traits. This is therefore an appropriate point to digress for a moment and mention briefly another offshoot of our research programme on psychoticism, namely the attempt to develop an alternative questionnaire instrument for measuring psychotic characteristics in normal subjects. The reason stems partly from general dissatisfaction with the face validity of the P-scale and partly from the feeling that a scale more closely aligned with the clinical features of psychosis may be better at isolating specifically psychotic traits in the general population.

Our first effort in this direction was a test devised some years ago by Reichenstein (1976) who took various self-reported symptoms of schizophrenia, such as difficulties in attention and thinking, perceptual abnormalities, and so on, and cast them in the form of a questionnaire. Administering the questionnaire to a group of normal subjects, she found a surprisingly normal distribution of scores. She also demonstrated a significant, though by no means perfect, correlation with the Eysenck P-scale, providing some validity for the latter but also suggesting that the search for an alternative instrument may be worthwhile. Encouraged by Reichenstein's study we have since continued to develop a similar questionnaire, the latest version, on which we are still collecting data, being designed around recent attempts to devise systematic rating scales for defining the borderline syndromes. In particular, we have been influenced by the work of Spitzer and his colleagues (Spitzer, Endicott & Gibbon, 1979). Spitzer has, usefully in my view, distinguished between "schizotypal personality," defined by such rated items as magical thinking, suspiciousness, social isolation and so on, and "unstable personality," defined by items like impulsivity, aggressiveness, and poor interpersonal relationships. Although not uncorrelated in Spitzer's studies, the two clusters he describes do seem to represent different varieties of borderline state and, in devising the latest version of a self-rating questionnaire based on them, we have kept the two types of items separate. For convenience we have temporarily labelled them BS (borderline schizophrenia) items and BP (borderline personality disorder) items.

Although a proper validation study of this questionnaire remains to be done, Rawlings' inclusion of it, together with the P-scale, in his research has provided some preliminary data on normal subjects. One factor analysis recently completed by him included our new questionnaire, together with the P-scales from both the EPQ and the earlier PEN inventory[4]. Also entered into the factor analysis were several tests of "creativity." Two particular findings of interest here emerged. One concerns the pattern of relationships for the personality questionnaire. There two separate factors were found, a factor loaded substantially with the EPQ *P*-scale and another with high loadings on both the BS and BP components of our "borderline" questionnaire; the latter factor also loaded on neuroticism and on the PEN inventory *P*-scale. This finding was in line with our earlier suggestion that the older *P*-scale may have been a better measure of strictly "psychotic" traits and was confirmed by the individual correlations between the different scales. Thus, although BS and BP did correlate significantly with the EPQ *P*-scale, the correlations were fairly low, the values for *r* being $+0.26$ ($p < 0.02$) and $+0.25$, ($p < 0.02$), respectively; the comparable correlations with the PEN *P*-scale were $+0.47$ ($p < 0.001$) and $+0.40$ ($p < 0.001$).

The second finding of interest that emerged from this part of Rawlings' research concerned differences in creativity test performance. Relationships here tended to be spread over several factors, including one identifiable as general intelligence, but their association with "psychoticism" was confined to the factor loaded highly with the EPQ scale; the PEN/borderline factor showed no loadings on creativity test performance. This last result was slightly contradicted by the fact that the individual correlations between borderline questionnaire scores and scores on particular creativity tests did occasionally reach significance, though on the whole the relationships were rather weak. Indeed, in general, compared with Woody's earlier, very clear-cut results, there is much less evidence in Rawlings' data for a straightforward association between psychoticism and creativity test performance. The remainder of his research was therefore directed to various other facets of the problem.

One concerned the role of "perceptual defense" as a possible mediator of observed relationships between *P* and divergent thinking test performance. Thus, Rawlings had noticed that *P* correlated significantly with the frequency with which, on such tests, aggressive and sexual responses were elicited from subjects. A formal study confirmed that high scorers on the PEN, but not on the EPQ, did show less perceptual defense in responding to emotive and neutral words, a finding which is in line with the suggestion made earlier that part of the common variance between psychoticism and divergent thinking may reflect the threshold different subjects have for verbalizing unusual or socially unacceptable associations.

Another area explored by Rawlings was the relationship between creativity, psychoticism, and performance on tests of divided attention, an approach having

---

[4]It should be noted here that, since the earlier and later scales contained some common items, the PEN "P-scale" used by Rawlings strictly referred to only those items unique to the PEN.

its remoter origins in the early work of McGhie (1969) on attention in psychotic patients and a recent antecedent in a study by Dykes and McGhie (1976) who showed some similarities between schizophrenic and highly creative normals on dichotic listening tasks. A series of studies by Rawlings yielded some results which, although on first analysis rather variable, contain some interesting trends. In one experiment, using a procedure similar to that employed by Dykes and McGhie, subjects were simply asked to shadow words presented to one ear while ignoring those presented to the other. Creativity test score did not relate consistently to performance; indeed the results were, if anything, in the opposite direction to those of Dykes and McGhie. However, there was an association, in the predicted direction and almost significant, between PEN, but not EPQ, *P* score: high *P* subjects tended to show more total instrusions from the irrelevant channel. In a second experiment rather different results emerged, however. Here subjects had to shadow as before, but also to try and recall words from the irrelevant channel, a method previously shown by Wishner and Wahl (1974) to differentiate schizophrenics from normal subjects. Using this modified procedure Rawlings found that the EPQ *P* scale correlated significantly with the total instrusions score; in this case, however, the PEN scale showed no association. Creativity performance also showed a relationship, the more divergent subjects being more distracted by the additional task. As Rawlings concludes, the results obtained in this field seem to depend on the instructions given to the subjects. His own findings suggest that under some conditions high *P* scorers do show poor ability to divide attention; but his results also again point to some differences in the traits measured by the EPQ and PEN scales of psychoticism.

Of Rawlings' remaining studies one other is worth particular mention here because the strategy he employed looks, in my view, to be very promising. It involved the examination of differences in hemispheric function as a possible basis for cognitive style variations which relate to personality. Studies in the general area of hemisphere function proliferate daily and promise to become yet another psychological bandwagon. However, such research has a special relevance in the present context because of its particular application in the study of the psychotic disorders (Gruzelier and Flor-Henry, 1979). Admittedly, as the latter compendium of research on the topic demonstrates, psychotic patients have yet again proved elusive, in showing sometimes gross asymmetry of hemispheric function, yet little that is consistent from one study to the next. Nevertheless, the value of the approach cannot yet be gainsaid, especially as there have been, as far as I know, no previous experiments comparable to that reported by Rawlings. He looked at hemisphere differences with respect to the distinction between "local" and "global" modes of perceptual processing. He based his experiment on a method reported by Martin (1979) who was concerned with the general question of hemispheric specialization for local and global processing of visually presented linguistic stimuli; she in turn had developed the procedure from those described originally by Navon (1977). The stimulus material consisted of large letters, made up of smaller letters, subjects being instructed to report the local or global shape after presentation to either the right or the left hemisphere. Briefly, Martin had shown that, in an unselected group of subjects, local processing for this kind of stimulus was clearly localized in the left hemisphere, whereas global processing did not appear to be strongly lateralized.

In his experiment Rawlings examined subjects selected on the basis of the Eysenck scales and on an early version of the ''borderline'' questionnaire referred to above. This version did not attempt to separate out two item clusters and was closer in content to the ''schizotypal'' component of the later questionnaire. His results for the P scales showed no association with performance on the task of hemispheric function, but significant differences did emerge when high and low scorers on the ''borderline'' questionnaire were compared. His results are

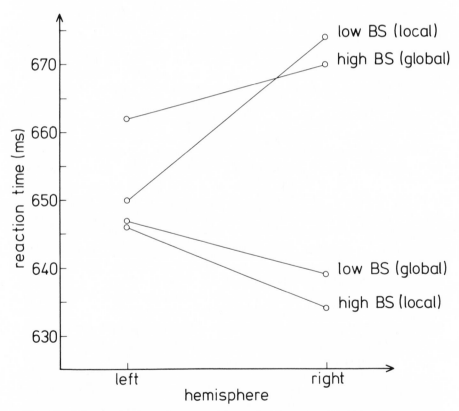

FIG. 4.6.   Mean reaction times of two groups of normal subjects selected for high and low scores on the 'borderline schizophrenia' questionnaire referred to in the text. Performance is compared for 'local' and 'global' processing of visual stimuli presented either to the left or to the right hemisphere. Note particularly the difference in reaction times for 'local' processing: low BS subjects were fastest in the left, and high BS subjects fastest in the right, hemisphere.

shown, in diagrammatic form, in Fig. 4.6. Considering, first, subjects with low "borderline" scores, it can be seen that they behaved as Martin's unselected sample: "local" judgements were made quickest when the stimuli were presented to the left hemisphere; "global" judgements showed little difference across hemispheres. High scorers on the "borderline" questionnaire, however, showed quite the reverse pattern of performance. They performed as rapidly as low scorers in making "local" judgements, but did so best with the *right* hemisphere. This rather clear demonstration of a difference in cerebral lateralization was supported by the results of a second experiment conducted by Rawlings using a discriminative reaction time procedure in which subjects had to respond with their right or left hands to letter stimuli presented randomly to the right or left visual fields. As with the previous task, he found no association with either PEN or EPQ scores. However, there was a significant interaction between visual field and "borderline" questionnaire performance, high scorers showing evidence of poor verbal processing in the left hemisphere. On this occasion Rawlings used the later version of our questionnaire and it is interesting to note that the relationships he observed with hemisphere function were confined to its BS (borderline schizophrenia) component; they were *not* found for the BP (borderline personality disorder) component, which probably taps traits closer to those measured by the Eysenck scales. The finding confirms, and provides some objective validity for, Spitzer's view that the two components refer to different forms of "borderline" personality structure. It also suggests that, insofar as hemisphere differences are relevant, they are only evident in certain varieties of "psychoticism," a conclusion which of course generally agrees with that reached earlier from other studies of the *P*-scale itself. In the latter respect it will be of interest to see whether Rawlings, with further analysis of his data, can find evidence for an association between hemisphere function and particular combinations of EPQ scores.

In concluding this chapter let me try to draw together the various threads that have run through the discussion. One fact which emerges and which is highlighted by the results just described is the variable performance of the Eysenck *P*-scale when used to pick out people high in supposed psychotic traits. Admittedly, differences in hemispheric organization are only one of a myriad of predictions one might be led to make from existing theory and from evidence about the nature of the psychoses themselves; which is the source to which we must look for ideas and experimental techniques for validating questionnaire measures of "psychoticism." But the prediction, if no stronger, is no weaker than others that might be chosen from a vast and varied store of different approaches to psychotic disorder. The point I am making is that, although the *P*-scale, in some experiments, has shown results theoretically consistent with its purpose, its item content, and therefore its specificity, still leaves cause for worry. The EPQ, in particular and compared with the earlier PEN inventory, seems, if anything, to have retreated away from being a measure of psychotic traits and it may be that more powerful psychometric instruments could be developed by staying closer to the clinical characteristics of psychosis, attempting to translate these into questionnaire form. The "borderline" questionnaire I have described here is an attempt to do that; others of a similar type have also been described (Neilsen & Petersen, 1976; Chapman, Edell, & Chapman, 1980; Launay & Slade, 1981).

Having said this, it must also be borne in mind that the Eysenck P-scale has, in a sense, a special kind of status, having been developed from an orderly and highly systematic theory of personality which virtually demanded, and which could scarcely avoid, ultimately demonstrating a third dimension of psychoticism; for all of the evidence points to the existence of psychotic traits in the normal population. Eysenck's preference, in constructing the P-scale, for items taken from the personality, rather than from the clinical, domain is therefore deliberate. And he may be right that the anti-social traits mainly tapped by the scale *are* the essence of psychoticism. Or it may be that the P-scale only indirectly taps "true" psychoticism, by virtue of the fact that some individuals high in the latter superficially display anti-social or unconventional characteristics. Certainly, as many of the results described here show, high P scorers are a widely differing collection of individuals and, while Eysenck's theoretical position would predict this, it is by no means obvious that such heterogeneity can be explained solely by reference to other dimensions, like extraversion. However, on present evidence it does look as though particular combinations of E and P, for example introversion and psychoticism, may be selecting out individuals truly predisposed to psychotic breakdown. At least, that would be my current guess; even if wrong it would seem wise for future studies of the P-scale to proceed in a piecemeal fashion, that is to examine variations in psychoticism alongside variations on Eysenck's other dimensions, especially introversion-extraversion. It might then be possible to define precise biological and other characteristics of particular variants of psychoticism. In doing so, it may also be useful to carry alongside the Eysenck questionnaire other scales having a more clinically relevant item content.

Eysenck's theoretical position demands, of course, that ultimately it should be possible to discover some, genetically determined, biological feature which *all* high P scorers have in common. From the studies reviewed here it is difficult at present to visualize what that might be, though one theme runs through the evidence and has influenced the thinking of my colleagues and myself. There is some convergence of view that what may characterize clinical psychosis (and by the same token, its muted variants) is a certain *imbalance* of central nervous organization. This idea was fundamental to my own early "dissociation" model of psychosis, from which stemmed our later "covariation" studies of the P-scale; it is echoed in the conclusions drawn by Robinson from his analysis of EEG variations; and it is implicit in Rawlings' results on hemispheric function differences among "borderline" personalities. The notion of imbalance is, of course, a very general one, arrived at as an interpretation for very different kinds of experimental data, which are difficult to relate to each other. For example, conceptually it is virtually impossible at the moment to see how one can graft on to a "vertical" model of central nervous imbalance, from which my own thinking originally proceeded, a "horizontal" one contained in the evidence for hemispheric dissociation. But probably that is where part of the task lies. Already some slight points of contact can be discerned in our own work. Thus, it is interesting that the differences thrown up by Rawlings refer particularly to the manner in which individuals, "locally" or "globally," process sensory information; Robinson, from another theoretical perspective altogether has emphasized the importance of Pavlovian "concentration," and its consequences for cognitive style variations, as a possible correlate of psychoticism; in the same vein, evidence relating attentional strategies to psychophysiological "dissociation" has formed an important part of my own ideas on the problem.

Even if it is accepted that the notion of CNS imbalance is a useful concept for integrating certain evidence about psychosis and psychoticism, the problem of individual differences still remains. One solution would be to map directly on to Eysenck's descriptive framework. This is essentially what I tried to do in my 1967 model by proposing "active" and "retarded" types of psychosis; in the personality domain these types were seen to correspond roughly to extraversion and introversion; in the cognitive sphere they were considered to parallel variations in broadening and narrowing of attention and overinclusiveness and overexclusiveness of thinking. David Robinson has followed a similar line of reasoning, with the interesting addition that he would construe extreme CNS *balance* as no less abnormal than extreme imbalance, associating it with a very particular form of paranoid reaction; according to his interpretation it would be the latter who would show very narrowed attention, both of my "unbalanced" active and retarded psychotics showing broadening of attention.

All of these speculations are highly satisfying! Apart from other considerations they allow one to gain on both the Kretshmerian swings and on the Eysenckian roundabouts: a single dimension of psychoticism representing deviations in central nervous balance and a bipolar dimension of schizothymia-cyclothymia reflecting the various forms such deviations take. But I can see at least two difficulties here. One is that, because individual differences are still the most obvious and important fact about psychosis and psychoticism, a unitary view of the latter becomes, in practice, unuseable; as a single unifying descriptive dimension psychoticism almost becomes an artifact of the factor analytic method used to produce it, perhaps capturing some of the very superficial qualities common to different forms of psychotic predisposition, but unable, by itself, to lead to discoveries about their different biological bases. Another difficulty stems from the nature of the psychoses themselves. Clinically they are highly variable states. Looked at longitudinally individual patients may pass through various psychotic "types," presenting with different patterns of symptomatology at different times. Considered in terms of the theoretical models used to explain their behavior they may, on different, occasions, show extreme narrowing or extreme broadening of attention, poverty or over-extensiveness of thinking, physiological underresponsiveness or overresponsiveness, and so on. The psychoses can be likened, as I have suggested on other occasions, to quicksilver, basically invariant but somehow constantly subject to fluctuation. It occurs to me that this quality may be intrinsic to the very notion of central nervous imbalance and that the ultimately successful models of psychosis and therefore of psychoticism, are likely to be those that can take such variability into account. So far no such models have been achieved.

Closing this chapter I would like to return to one further speculation which, in passing, I indulged in earlier and which, in a sense, flows from my last remark. It concerns the measurement of psychoticism by questionnaire. I have several times expressed doubts about the ability of the *P*-scale to capture the full essence of psychotic personality. This doubt arises not just from a worry about the item content of that particular inventory, but also from a feeling that "psychoticism" consists of a peculiar alignment of traits which it may be difficult with any questionnaire procedure to collect together into a single scale. It is peculiar, I would suggest in representing the association in the individual of characteristics which are normally considered incongruent. Evidence for this abnormal clustering of traits is found even in the EPQ itself. I am referring to the fact that, although in the majority of subjects the Lie and *P* scales appear to be strongly negatively correlated, quite the opposite is true in those individuals in whom the *P* scale seems most likely to be tapping "true" psychoticism. The fact that the latter often seem to show *introversion* associated with high *P* is also contradictory, given the generally "extraverted" nature of the scale's items. Yet the feature *is* consistent with clinical observations which I have had occasion to refer to earlier, namely the ambivalence of the borderline personality and the odd mixture of traits seen in prepsychotic children. I suspect that this is a facet of personality description which those of us interested in the pursuit of psychoticism would be ill-advised to ignore.

POSTSCRIPT

As with my previous essay on psychoticism, I feel it is necessary to insert a postscript to this chapter, in order to incorporate some comments made by Hans Eysenck himself, who saw the chapter in manuscript form after it had been submitted to the editor. Eysenck quite fairly recognized that I was especially concerned in the chapter to expose some weaknesses in his theory and consider some alternative views of psychoticism. It seems equally proper to include here the points which Eysenck raised; some of these were briefly touched upon in the earlier essay.

The first point concerns the validity of the P-scale as revealed in its correlations with other measures that can be considered either empirically or theoretically relevant to clinical psychosis. On the biological front Eysenck draws attention to two sets of evidence, including some data recently collected by Schalling. She has apparently shown that P-scale scores correlate highly with levels of the metabolite of serotonin, 5-HIAA, determined from analysis of CSF in normal and psychiatric subjects. This is especially interesting in view of the fact that serotonin has, of course, long been suspected as an important neurotransmitter involved in the psychotic state; it also provides further rationale for our own results, reported here, drawing a parallel between P-scale variations and the effects of LSD-25, which is known to have its main effect on serotonin neurons (Jacobs and Trulson, 1979).

A further piece of biological evidence which appears to support Eysenck's claim for the validity of the P-scale as a measure of psychoticism comes from a study he refers to by Gattaz (1981) who recently reported the results of testing for human leucocyte antigens (HLA) in a group of chronic paranoid schizophrenics. He showed that one particular antigen (HLA-B27) was present in certain patients, namely those with high P scores, though it was absent in others. Referring to his previous work along similar lines Gattaz comments that the finding would be consistent with an earlier result showing the presence of the antigen in schizophrenic patients with poor prognosis; it would also agree with the observation by Verma and Eysenck (1973) that P correlated with the severity of psychotic illness. The fact that only some diagnosed schizophrenics show HLA-B27 is, of course, a double-edged result for Eysenck. On the one hand, it suggests that the P-scale is indeed tapping a significant fraction of "psychoticism," for which the antigen may prove to be an important genetic marker. On the other hand, the result points to the genetic heterogeneity of schizophrenia; taken together with the evidence that other forms of psychosis, such as affective disorder, are genetically distinct, this still leaves open to question the comprehensiveness of the P-scale. Nevertheless, it would be churlish to deny that Gattaz's finding considerably strengthens the validity of the P-scale.

A conclusion in rather similar vein could be reached from the results of the recently reported study by Launay and Slade (1981) whose current attempts to construct a questionnaire of "psychotic predisposition" was referred to briefly in the main text. The Launay and Slade questionnaire is actually an "hallucination scale," validated on patients suffering from persistent auditory hallucinations. As Eysenck rightly pointed out, this scale has also been shown to correlate significantly with the P-scale in an unselected group of prisoners, suggesting that both measures are tapping a genuine feature of psychoticism and are capable of doing so in individuals who are not clinically psychotic. Launay and Slade also report that the association between the two scales appears to involve some covariation with paranoid/aggressive tendencies, an observation which, taken together with the Gattaz result, the item content of the P-scale, and the fact that hallucinations are found in only some psychotic patients, may again emphasize the specificity of what the Eysenck questionnaire measures. But again that specificity appears to be clearly relevant to the personality and cognitive traits predisposing to psychosis.

Another observation made by Eysenck concerns the attempt to validate the *P*-scale by giving the EPQ to psychotic patients. The disappointing results obtained could, Eysenck now suggests, be partly due to the fact that all of the psychotics tested so far have been in institutions. According to him, hospitalization, for whatever reasons, tends to be associated with high Lie scores which, in the case of psychotics, could help to depress *P* scores in the way in which he has previously argued. I think this is a fair point, introducing an additional factor which would compound the other difficulties, already mentioned, of measuring questionnaire psychoticism in clinically disturbed patients. Actually, I believe that the failure of prediction here is the least worrying of the EPQ's weaknesses, preoccupying the Eysencks' critics far too much. I would agree with Eysenck that what really matters when judging the validity of an instrument like the *P*-scale is whether the total weight of evidence is convincing; whether, to borrow from his own comments on this chapter, "there are many individual facts which point in the same direction, even though each of them may not be very powerful." Viewed in this way, and even ignoring the additional evidence just referred to, there is, I think, no doubt about the narrow validity of the *P*-scale. Whether it is as powerful as Eysenck claims is a matter of opinion. Eysenck himself, understandably, has reached that conclusion. I have been more cautious. The difference is one which will hopefully be resolved by continued research on the *P*-scale and through the kind of exchange of ideas that prompted this postscript.

REFERENCES

Birchall, P. M. A., & Claridge, G. S. Augmenting-reducing of the visual evoked potential as a function of changes in skin conductance level. *Psychophysiology* 1979, *16*, 482–490.

Bishop, D. V. M. The P scale and psychosis. *J. abn. Psychol.*, 1977, *86*, 127–134.

Bleuler, E. *Dementia Praecox or the Group of Schizophrenias* (Translated, 1950, by J. Zinkin) International Universities Press, New York, 1911.

Block, J. P scale and psychosis: continued concerns. *J. abn. Psychol.*, 1977a, *86*, 431–434.

Block, J. The Eysencks and psychoticism. *J. abn. Psychol.*, 1977b, *86*, 653–654.

Březinová, V., & Kendell, R. E. Smooth pursuit eye movements of schizophrenics and normal people under stress. *British Journal of Psychiatry*, 1977, *130*, 59–63.

Buchsbaum, M. Self-regulation of stimulus intensity: augmenting/reducing and the average evoked response. In Schwartz, G. E. and Shapiro, R. (Eds.) *Consciousness and Self-Regulation.* London: Wiley, 1976.

Callaway, E. *Brain Electrical Potentials and Individual Psychological Differences.* New York: Grune and Stratton, 1975.

Chapman, L. J., Edell, W. S., & Chapman, J. P. Physical anhedonia, perceptual aberration, and psychosis proneness. *Schiz. Bull.* 1980, *6*, 639–653.

Claridge, G. S. *Personality and Arousal.* Oxford; Pergamon, 1967.

Claridge, G. S. The schizophrenias as nervous types. *Brit. J. Psychiat.* 1972, *112*, 1–17.

Claridge, G. S. A nervous typological analysis of personality variation in normal twins. In Claridge, G. S. et al., (Eds.) *Personality Differences and Biological Variations: A Study of Twins.* Oxford: Pergamon, 1973.

Claridge, G. S. Animal models of schizophrenia: the case for LSD-25. *Schiz. Bull.* 1978, *4*, 187–209.

Claridge, G. S. Psychoticism. In Lynn, R. (Ed.) *Dimensions of Personality. Papers in Honour of H. J. Eysenck.* Oxford: Pergamon, 1981.

Claridge, G. S., & Birchall, P. M. A. The biological basis of psychoticism: a study of individual differences in response to dexamphetamine. *Biol. Psychol.* 1973, *1*, 123–137.

Claridge, G. S., & Birchall, P. M. A. Bishop, Eysenck, Block and psychoticism. *J. abn. Psychol.* 1978, *87*, 664–668.

Claridge, G. S., & Chappa, H. J. Psychoticism: a study of its biological basis in normal subjects. *Brit. J. soc. clin. Psychol.* 1973, *12*, 175–187.

Claridge, G. S., & Clark, K. Covariation between two-flash threshold and skin conductance level in first-breakdown schizophrenics: relationships in drug-free patients and effects of treatment. *Psychiatry Research*, 1982, *6*, 371–380.

Claridge, G. S., Donald, J. R., & Birchall, P. M. A. Drug tolerance and personality: some implications for Eysenck's theory. *Person. and Individ. Diffs.* 1981, *2*, 153–166.

Dykes, M., & McGhie, A. A comparative study of attentional strategies of schizophrenic and highly creative normal subjects. *Brit. J. Psychiat.* 1976, *128*, 50–56.

Eysenck, H. J. Schizothymia-cylcothymia as a dimension of personality. II. Experimental. *J. Person.* 1952a, *20*, 345–384.

Eysenck, H. J. *The scientific study of personality.* Routledge and Kegan London: Paul, 1952b.

Eysenck, H. J. A dynamic theory of anxiety and hysteria. *J. ment. Sci.* 1955, *101*, 28–51.

Eysenck, H. J. *The biological basis of personality.* Charles C. Thomas, Ill: Springfield, 1967.

Eysenck, H. J. *Sex and personality.* London: Open Books, 1976.

Eysenck, H. J. Psychosis and psychoticism: a reply to Bishop. *J. abn. Psychol.* 1977, *86*, 427–430.

Eysenck, H. J., & Eysenck, S. B. G. *Personality structure and measurement.* London: Routledge and Kegan Paul, 1969.

Eysenck, H. J., & Eysenck, S. B. G. *Manual of the Eysenck Personality Questionnaire.* London: Hodder and Stoughton, 1975.

Eysenck, H. J., & Eysenck, S. B. G. *Psychoticism as a dimension of personality.* London: Hodder and Stoughton, 1976.

Eysenck, H. J., & Eysenck, S. B. G. Block and psychoticism. *J. abn. Psychol.* 1977, *86*, 651–652.

Garmezy, N. Children at risk: the search for the antecedents of schizophrenia. Part I: Conceptual models and research methods. *Schiz. Bull.* 1974, No 8, 14–90.

Gattaz, W. F. HLA-B27 as a possible genetic marker of psychoticism. *Person. and Individ. Diffs.* 1981, *2*, 57–60.

Gottesman, I. I., & Shields, J. A critical review of recent adoption, twin, and family studies of schizophrenia: behavioural genetics perspectives. *Schiz. Bull.* 1976, *2*, 360–398.

Gray, J. A. The psychophysiological basis of introversion-extraversion. *Behav. Res. Therap.* 1970, *8*, 249–266.

Gray, J. A. Causal theories of personality and how to test them. In Royce, F. R. (Ed.) *Mulitvariate analysis and psychological theory.* London: Academic Press, 1973.

Gruzelier, J. H., & Venables, P. H. Relations between two-flash discrimination and electrodermal activity, re-examined in schizophrenics and normals. *J. psychiat. Res.* 1975, *12*, 73–85.

Gruzelier, J., & Flor-Henry, P. (Eds.) *Hemisphere asymmetries of function in psychopathology.* Amsterdam. Elsevier/North Holland, 1979.

Gruzelier, J., Venables, P., & Lykken, D. Schizophrenia and arousal revisited. *Arch gen. Psychiat.* 1972, *26*, 427–432.

Gunderson, J. G. The relatedness of borderline and schizophrenic disorders. *Schiz. Bull.* 1979, *5*, 17–22.

Haier, R. J., Buchsbaum, M. S., Murphy, D. L., Gottesman, I. I., & Coursey, R. D. Psychiatric vulnerability, monoamine oxidase, and the averaged evoked potential. *Arch. gen Psychiat.* 1980, *37*, 340–345.

Heston, L. L. Psychiatric disorders in foster home reared children of schizophrenic mothers. *Brit. J. Psychiat.* 1966, *112*, 819–825.

Jacobs, B. L., & Trulson, M. E. Mechanisms of action of LSD. *American Scientist.* 1979, *67*, 396–404.

Jung, C. G. The psychology of dementia praecox. In: *The collected works of C. G. Jung*, Vol. 3 *The psychogenesis of mental disease* (Translated, 1960, by R. F. C. Hull). London: Routledge and Kegan Paul, 1907.

Kretschmer, E. *Physique and character* (Translated by W. J. H. Sprott). London: Kegan, Trench and Trubner, 1925.

Laing, R. D. *The Divided Self.* London: Tavistock, 1959.

Landau, S. G., Buchsbaum, M. S., Carpenter, W., Strauss, J., & Sacks, M. Schizophrenia and stimulus intensity control. *Arch. gen. Psychiat.* 1975, *32*, 1239–1245.

Launay, G., & Slade, P. The measurement of hallucinatory predisposition in male and female prisoners. *Person. and Individ. Diffs.* 1981, *2*, 221–234.

Lykken, D., & Maley, M. Autonomic versus cortical arousal in schizophrenics and non-psychotics. *J. psychiat. Res.* 1968, *6*, 21–32.

McConaghy, N. Modes of abstract thinking and psychosis. *Amer. J. Psychiat.* 1960, *117*, 106–110.

McGhie, A. *Pathology of attention.* London: Penguin, 1969.

McPherson, F. M., Presly, A. S., Armstrong, J., & Curtis, R. H. 'Psychoticism' and psychotic illness. *Brit. J. Psychiat.* 1974, *125*, 152–160.

Martin, M. Hemispheric specialization for local and global processing. *Neuropsychologia.* 1979, *17*, 33–40.

Mednick, S. A., Schulsinger, R., Higgins, J., & Bell, B. (Eds.) *Genetics, environment, and psychopathology.* Amsterdam: Elsevier/North-Holland, 1979.

Meltzer, H. Y., & Stahl, S. M. The dopamine hypothesis of schizophrenia: a review. *Schiz. Bull.* 1976, *2*, 19–76.

Navon, D. Forest before trees: The precedence of global features in visual perception. *Cognitive Psychology,* 1977, *19*, 353–383.

Neilson, T. C., & Petersen, N. E. Electrodermal correlates of extraversion, trait anxiety and schizophrenism. *Scand. J. Psychol.* 1976, *17*, 73–80.

Payne, R. W. Cognitive abnormalities. In Eysenck, H. J. (Ed.) *Handbook of Abnormal Psychology* (1st Edition). London: Pitman, 1960.

Prentky, R. A. *Creativity and psychopathology. A neurocognitive perspective.* New York: Praeger, 1980.

Reichenstein, S. A pilot study into the incidence of schizophrenic symptoms in a normal population. Unpublished dissertation, University of Oxford. 1976.

Robinson, D. L. Properties of the diffuse thalamocortical system and human personality: a direct test of Pavlovian/Eysenckian theory. *Person. and Individ. Diff.* 1982, *3*, 1–16.

Robinson, D. L. Relationship between human personality, human intelligence and properties of the diffuse thalamocortical system. D. Phil. thesis, University of Oxford. 1980.

Robinson, T. N., & Zahn, T. P. Covariation of two-flash threshold and autonomic arousal for high and low scorers on a measure of psychoticism. *Brit. J. soc. clin. Psychol.* 1979, *18*, 431–441.

Shagass, C., Straumanis, J. J., & Overton, D. A. Psychiatric diagnosis and EEG-evoked response relationships. *Neuropsychobiol.* 1975, *1*, 1–15.

Silverman, J. The problem of attention in research and theory in schizophrenia. *Psychol. Rev.* 1964, *71*, 352–379.

Spitzer, R. L., Endicott, J., & Gibbon, M. Crossing the border into borderline personality and borderline schizophrenia. *Arch. gen. Psychiat.* 1979, *36*, 17–24.

Stone, M. H. *The borderline syndromes.* New York: McGraw-Hill, 1980.

Szasz, T. S. *The Myth of mental illness.* New York: Hoeber-Harper, 1961.

Thompson, A. H. Random responding and the questionnaire measurement of psychoticism. *Soc. Behav. Pers.* 1975, *3*, 111–115.

Trouton, D. S., & Maxwell, A. E. The relation between neurosis and psychosis. *J. ment. Sci.* 1975, *102*, 1–21.

Tyrer, P., & Alexander, J. Classification of personality disorder. *Brit. J. Psychiat.* 1979, *135*, 163–167.

Venables, P. H. The relationship between level of skin potential and fusion of paired light flashes in schizophrenic and normal subjects. *J. psychiat. Res.* 1963, *1*, 279–287.

Verma, R. M., & Eysenck, H. J. Severity and type of psychotic illness as a function of personality. *Brit. J. Psychiat.* 1973, *122*, 573–585.

Wishner, J., & Wahl, O. Dichotic listening in schizophrenia. *J. consult. clin. Psychol.* 1974, *42*, 538–546.

Witkin, H. A., Dyk, R. B., Faterson, H. F., Goodenough, D. R., & Karp, S. A. *Psychological differentiation: Studies of development.* New York: Wiley, 1962.

Witkin, H. A., Oltman, P. K., Raskin, E., & Karp, S. *A manual for the embedded figures test.* Palo Alto: Consulting Psychologists Press. 1971.

Woody, E. Z. Psychoticism and thinking abilities. MSc thesis, University of Oxford. 1976.

Woody, E. Z., & Claridge, G. S. Psychoticism and thinking. *Brit. J. soc. clin. Psychol.* 1977, *16*, 241–248.

Zuckerman, M. *Sensation Seeking.* New Jersey: Lawrence Erlbaum Assoc, 1979.

5 Are Subtle MMPI Items Expendable?

Malcolm D. Gynther and Barry R. Burkhart
Auburn University

Thirty-six years ago Meehl argued, in his classic article entitled "The Dynamics of 'Structured' Personality Tests" (1945), that the construction of items and their assembly into scales on an a priori basis is fallacious inasmuch as this procedure assumes that "the psychologist building the test has sufficient insight into the dynamics of verbal behavior and its relation to the inner core of personality that he is able to predict beforehand what certain sorts of people will say about themselves when asked certain sorts of questions [p. 297]." Meehl (1945) asserted that a response to a questionnaire item was an intrinsically interesting and significant bit of verbal behavior, "the nontest correlates of which must be discovered by empirical means [p. 297]."

According to Meehl (1945), once we grant that what people say about themselves is important—whether or not it agrees with others' views—we may admit "powerful items to personality scales regardless of whether the rationale of their appearance can be made clear at present [p. 300]." In other words, the relation between the behavior dynamics of a subject and the tendency to respond verbally in a certain way does not have to be psychologically obvious, given the state of the science of behavior. Thus, mysterious relationships such as that between "I sometimes tease animals" (answered false) and depression may and do occur.

REVIEW OF EMPIRICAL AND THEORETICAL STUDIES

This spirited defense of the contrasted group methodology and the utility of subtle as well as obvious items has led to numerous lines of research. For our purposes, we can trace that segment concerned with item obviousness and subtlety. Wiener and Harmon (1946) were stimulated by Meehl's article to develop subtle and obvious keys for the Minnesota Multiphasic Personality Inventory (MMPI). As Wiener (1948) pointed out, the responses to obvious items probably can distinguish seriously disturbed individuals, but a more subtle test is necessary to differentiate among the characteristics of a normal population that might be seen by the college counselor. Keys were developed by rationally dividing all MMPI items into two groups: (1) those to which significant responses as indicating emotional disturbance were relatively easy to detect; and (2) those to which they were relatively difficult to detect. Although Wiener and Harmon attempted to develop keys for all clinical scales, they were only able to do so for scales 2(D), 3(Hy), 4(Pd), 6(Pa), and 9(Ma). They found that scales 1(Hs), 7(Pt), and 8(Sc) consisted almost entirely of obvious items and concluded that scale 5(Mf) probably has a validity too low as a scale to yield positive results. (Scale 0(Si) was not published when they were conducting their study.) A series of analyses showed that: (1) high L scale scores are associated with higher subtle (S) rather than obvious (0) scores, whereas the converse is true for low L scores; (2) individuals of high ability have equal 0 and S scores, whereas those of low ability have higher 0 than S scores; (3) psychologically sophisticated individuals almost completely avoid significant 0 responses and have much higher S scores; (4) elevated MMPI profiles from individuals without psychiatric diagnoses show higher S scores and lower 0 scores than high profiles from those with psychiatric diagnoses; and (5) when successful and unsuccessful students and on-the-job trainees were tested, 0 scores were found to be significantly higher than S scores for the unsuccessful group.

Cofer, Chance, and Judson (1949) studied the relationship between malingering and Wiener's keys. College sophomores were instructed to fake bad and fake good, as well as to complete the MMPI under standard conditions. Subtle items tended to be unaffected by the malingering instructions, whereas usage of obvious items varied as a function of instructions.

Another early investigator of the subtle–obvious dimension (Seeman, 1952) designed an experiment to test whether psychologically trained individuals would be able to classify which MMPI scale subtle items belonged to with the same accuracy as obvious items. A "none" category was also available if the item appeared to be of no value for any of the diagnostic categories listed. Obvious items were correctly classified far more frequently than subtle items, and the latter were assigned the none category 43% of the time, whereas the comparable figure for obvious items was 11%. Seeman (1953) also had students attempt this task again after having had an MMPI course. Although the none category was used markedly less on this occasion, clinical psychology students were still unable to identify the subtle items.

Shortly thereafter, Berg (1957) advanced his deviation hypothesis, which did not focus on MMPI item analysis but led to results that are definitely relevant. Berg proposed than any item content, no matter how irrelevant, can be used to construct a personality inventory. This hypothesis, which could be seen as taking subtlety to and beyond the limits of reason, was shown to be false by Goldberg and Slovic (1967) among others. These investigators had subjects rate the face validity of items related to achievement, items related to affiliation, and irrelevant items. The validity of an item was determined by examining its correlation with external criteria reflecting achievement and affiliation. Goldberg and Slovik (1967) concluded that: "only scales built from items of the highest face validity had significant cross validity [p. 466–467]."

McCall (1958) compared the obvious and subtle scale 2 items. He found that items discriminated diagnosed depressives from nondepressive psychotics in proportion to their face validity. Apparently the inclusion of subtle items does not enhance the discriminating power of certain scales. Duff (1965) investigated the relationship between discriminating power and subtlety of items in MMPI scales 3(Hy), 4(Pd), and 8(Sc). Item subtlety was determined by judgments of advanced doctoral students in clinical and counseling psychology. Item discrimination was based on differentiation between a normal group and three hospitalized clinical groups. Results showed that only about 40% of the most subtle scale 3 and scale 4 items discriminated (scale 8 contained very few subtle items) as contrasted to over 90% of the most obvious items in each of the three scales.

Although numerous other studies (Anthony, 1971; Stone, 1965; Vesprani & Seeman, 1974; Wales & Seeman, 1968, 1969) concerned themselves with the subtle–obvious dimension or some variant of it, the next major development appeared in an article by Jackson (1971), which challenged Meehl's (1945) original presentation. Although Jackson's argument is too complex to summarize readily, certain points stand out: (1) empirical derivation of scales is justified only under circumstances of complete or almost totally complete ignorance, but "the ignorance about personality to which Meehl alluded a quarter of a century ago hardly seems a suitable defense at the present time [p. 232]"; (2) a substantive basis for item selection lessens the chances of failure when the items are administered to a new sample; (3) "most subtle items have been shown to correlate negatively with the rest of the items contained in a particular MMPI scale, raising the suspicion that they did not belong there in the first place [p. 234]"; and (4) "a sample of item content most directly relevant to a particular trait will be the most efficient way of going about measuring it [p. 234]."

Meehl (1972) did not attempt to refute Jackson's argument, recognizing that "such a monolithically 'criterion-statistical' view on item-analysis as that of my 1945 paper is too strong [p. 150]." Further, he (1972) stated that: "I now believe . . . that an item ought to make theoretical sense, and without too much *ad hoc* 'explaining' of its content and properties [p. 155]." More specifically, Meehl (1972) said: "Ideally, we would like an item to reflect as 'directly as possible' the psychological factor after which the scale is named [p. 169]." "if an item has really stable psychometric . . . properties . . . it is the business of a decent theory to 'explain' its possession of those properties in the light of its verbal content [p. 155]." To summarize, obvious items should be the best discriminators, but subtle items having certain characteristics may also have predictive power.

Recent studies addressing this issue seem to indicate that, for the most part, items can be viewed as behavior samples rather than as signs as originally proposed by Meehl (1945). For example, Koss and Butcher (1973) identified six crises in terms of the behavior and complaints of patients. They then asked experienced psychologists to select MMPI items directly relevant to each crisis. Newly admitted patients who fit the definitions of the behaviors and complaints of each of the six groups were then compared with a noncrisis control group. The investigators found that 76% of the items judged to have content relevance to one of the crisis situations differentiated each of the crisis groups from the control group. In other words, most obvious items are valid discriminators. However, this relationship clearly cannot be taken for granted, as the 24% that did not work indicates. (Koss, Butcher, & Hoffman, 1976 and Lachar & Wrobel, 1979 obtained very similar valid–invalid ratios in their studies of critical items that are typically face valid, i.e., obvious.)

The bulk of the literature, both empirical and theoretical, seems to indicate that obvious items are the wheat and subtle items are the chaff. However, it should not be forgotten that obvious items are vulnerable to faking. An individual who wishes to fake good when being evaluated for a job or an individual who wishes to fake bad to avoid military service can, in either case, readily manipulate his or her responses to obvious items (cf. Cofer et al., 1949). On the other hand, the endorsement of subtle items under these two conditions is in the opposite direction to that intended, as Burkhart, Christian, and Gynther (1978) have shown.

Second, another recent study (Burkhart, Gynther, & Christian, 1978) showed that psychologically minded subjects endorse more subtle and fewer obvious items under standard and fake-good instructions than less psychologically minded subjects. This finding not only confirms Wiener's (1948) early observation about the relationship between psychological mindedness and subtle–obvious item endorsement but is also consistent with the suggestion by Wales and Seeman (1968) that endorsement of zero items is related to social astuteness. If this is the case, then endorsement of subtle items could yield a useful, unobtrusive measure of this dimension.

Third, despite Cronbach's (1970) plea for separate scoring of subtle and transparent MMPI items, no comprehensive scaling of all these items on this dimension had been performed. The three previous efforts in this direction— Meehl and Hathaway's (1946) X and 0 items, Wiener's (1948) subtle–obvious distinctions for certain scales, and Duff's (1965) subtle-intermediate-obvious ratings for scales 3, 4, and 8—have usually relied on experts' judgments, have not accounted for most of the items, and have classified the items into two or three gross categories. Hence, no standard has been available for the development of subtle–obvious keys or the confirmation or disconfirmation of the discriminating power of subtle items.

DERIVATION OF SUBTLE–OBVIOUS RATINGS FOR MMPI ITEMS

Christian, Burkhart, and Gynther (1978), however, have recently obtained mean subtle–obvious ratings of all MMPI items answered true and false. In this study, such ratings (ranging from 1 [very subtle] to 5 [very obvious] with regard to psychopathology) were obtained from individuals relatively naive with respect to psychological inventories. Comparison of these values with those obtained by previous investigators shows that the earlier work yielded values that clustered in the neutral or obvious categories. Very obvious and very subtle items, in particular, were strikingly underrepresented. The relationship between obviousness ratings and Messick and Jackson's (1961) desirability ratings was also examined, with a product-moment correlation of .78, which suggests that these two dimensions have much in common. However, the relationship is not high enough to substitute one for the other.

Table 5.1 shows the percentage of items in five subtle–obvious categories for the clinical scales of the MMPI. Scale 6*(Pa)* contains the most "very obvious" items, and scale 5*(Mf)* contains the most "very subtle" items. If one combines the two obvious categories, scale 8*(Sc)* and scale 7*(Pt)* have the highest totals, 66% and 64%, respectively. Scale 5*(Mf)* has by far the highest percentage of very subtle and somewhat subtle items, and scale *O(Si)* is second in this regard. It is noteworthy that more than half of scale 1's *(Hs)* items are classified as "neither subtle nor obvious," as Wiener (1948) considered this scale a marker

TABLE 5.1
Percentage of Items in Subtle-Obvious
Categories for MMPI Clinical Scales

Scale	Very Subtle	Somewhat Subtle	Neither Subtle Nor Obvious	Somewhat Obvious	Very Obvious
Hs	03	09	58	30	00
D	08	28	33	25	05
Hy	08	30	32	30	00
Pd	04	20	38	26	12
Mf	42	28	26	05	00
Pa	02	20	20	27	30
Pt	00	04	31	58	06
Sc	01	00	32	46	20
Ma	06	30	39	15	08
Si	12	34	35	17	00

variable for obviousness. As far as validity scales *L, F,* and *K* are concerned, mean obviousness ratings show that *F* ranks first on this dimension, just ahead of scale 8, whereas *L* ranks 11th and *K* 12th, just ahead of scale 5, which has the lowest mean obviousness rating.

Given the availability of subtle–obvious ratings, analyses of the comparative predictive power of each type of item are now possible. Although certain scales (e.g., 8) cannot be examined because of a lack of subtle items, those scales with a relatively balanced number of obvious, neutral, and subtle items have, with the exception of scale 6, been investigated by us and our colleagues. These studies all tested Jackson's (1971) hypothesis, which in its most explicit form states that endorsement of obvious items will be related to external criteria. Subsidiary issues such as the presumed negative relationship between subtle and obvious items were also examined. It should be pointed out that, if Jackson's position is confirmed, revision of tests developed by contrasted group methodology would be in order.

The *Pd* Scale Study

The first study (Gynther, Burkhart, & Hovanitz, 1979) examined scale 4 *(Pd)*. The external criterion was a modification of the nonconformity scale used by Elion and Megargee (1975). Twenty-two items were added to this eight-item scale to achieve a more comprehensive range of nonconforming behavior. Some items were relatively innocuous (e.g., "Have you ever ignored fines for overdue books?"), whereas others involved serious offenses (e.g., "Have you ever sold narcotic drugs [e.g., heroin]?"). This new scale appears to have sound psychometric properties. Coefficient alpha was .83, and the split-half reliability was .86. Test–retest correlation for a 2 week period was .94 using a new sample of 80 subjects, equally divided by gender. These values are not surprising, given the biographical nature of the questions.

For the purposes of this study (and the others to be reported), Christian et al.'s (1978) ratings were categorized as subtle if they fell between 1.00 and 2.59,

TABLE 5.2
Correlations Among Non-Conformity Scores
and *Pd* Subscales for Males and Females

| | Non-Conformity Scores | |
	Males	Females
Pd-O	.33***	.40***
Pd-N	.18	.21*
Pd-S	.26**	.16

*p <.05
**p <.01
***p <.001

neutral if they fell between 2.60 and 3.39, and obvious if they fell between 3.40 and 5.00. The theoretical range for the nonconformity scale was 0–90. In actuality, the scores ranged from 2–41 for males and from 1–27 for females for the 100 men and 110 women from introductory psychology classes who served as subjects.

The relationships between *Pd* scores and nonconformity scale scores are shown in Table 5.2. For males, *Pd-0* and *Pd-S* scores were significantly related to the criterion. These results are not consistent with the hypothesis that obvious items will account for all of the discriminative power in a predictor-criterion relationship. However, in the case of females, only obvious and neutral scores were related to the criterion. Furthermore, statistical analysis showed a significant difference in the predictive power of obvious and subtle scores, $t(107) = 1.68, p < .05$, one tailed. These results for females are consistent with Jackson's hypothesis.

Multiple correlations were run to determine the relative contributions of the separate subscales with the others controlled. For males, the multiple correlation of the subtle and obvious items with the nonconformity score was .41. If one considers this finding in conjunction with the zero-order correlations, it is clear that the obvious items contributed a substantial amount over and above the subtle items $(.41^2 - .26^2 = .10)$, $F(1, 97) = 11.72, p < .001$. The subtle items, on the other hand, added a statistically significant, although relatively small, contribution over and above the obvious items $(.41^2 - .33^2 = .06)$, $F(1, 97) = 6.88$, $p < .05$. For females, the same general pattern was found. In this case, the multiple correlation between subtle and obvious items and nonconformity scores was .44.

The relationships we have just described show that obvious items have more predictive power than subtle items and, further, that neutral items contribute little, if anything, to an understanding of the predictor-criterion relationship. What were the correlations among the various *Pd* subscores? The correlation between *Pd-0* and *Pd-N* was .45 ($p < .001$); the correlation between *Pd-0* and *Pd-S* was −.01(ns)—note that it is not significantly negative as Jackson has claimed; and the correlation between *Pd-N* and *Pd-S* was .21 ($p < .01$). Inasmuch as *Pd-0* and *Pd-S* are independent, in combination they could make for good prediction.

To sum up these data, the obvious *Pd* subscale is the most powerful predictor, but the subtle *Pd* subscale has a unique contribution to make. Neutral *Pd* items have no contribution to make not already included in *Pd-0* items and could be excluded with no loss of power.

The *D* Scale Study

The next set of data to be considered has to do with the MMPI scale 2*(D)*. The same college students who served as subjects for the *Pd* study were also data sources for this investigation. In fact, *Pd* and *D* results were collected at the same time. The investigators (Burkhart, Gynther, & Fromuth, 1980) used three criteria: (1) the depression subscale from the Profile of Mood States (POMS) (McNair, Lorr & Droppleman, 1971); (2) the Beck Depression Inventory (BDI) (Beck, 1967); and (3) an abbreviated version of the Pleasant Events Schedule (PES) (MacPhillamy & Lewinsohn, 1974). These tests were selected because each appeared to assess different facets of the construct of depression. The POMS-D is a reliable measure of depressed mood, whereas the BDI appears to focus on the cognitive aspect of depression. The PES was selected to provide a behaviorally based measure of depression.

The data were initially analyzed separately by gender. However, because no important differences were observed, only combined analyses are reported here. Table 5.3 contains the zero-order correlations among the D scale, the three D subscales, and the BDI, POMS, and PES. Some of these correlations are higher than those found for the Pd subscales. The total D scale is moderately correlated with BDI and the POMS-D scale and somewhat less correlated with the PES. The correlation between D-0 and BDI is significantly greater than the correlation between the total D scale and BDI ($t[206] = 2.63, p < .01$). This same pattern also was found between D and D-0 correlations with the POMS-D. D-S had a significant negative correlation with BDI and POMS-D scores.

The multiple correlation of the three subscales with BDI was .63. Further analyses showed that D-0 significantly increased the correlation and that D-N produced a small, but significant, increment in predictive ability. However, D-S did not provide a unique contribution over and above D-0 and D-N. Similar findings were obtained when relationships with the other two criteria were examined.

A correlational analysis of the D subscales shows that D-0 and D-N display considerable overlap (i.e., $r = .66, p < .001$). D-S, on the other hand, had a significant negative relation with D-0 ($r = -.28, p < .001$) and D-N ($r = -.17$,

TABLE 5.3
Correlations Among Depression Measures,
D Scale and D Subscales

	BDI	POMS-D	PES[a]
D-total	.49***	.37***	-.26**
D-O	.60***	.55***	-.20*
D-N	.55***	.44***	-.22*
D-S	-.22*	-.27**	-.06

[a]High scores on PES indicate less depression, thus the negative correlation with the other depression scales on which high scores signify more depression.
    *$p < .01$
   **$p < .001$
  ***$p < .0001$

$p < .05$). These relationships are more in line with Jackson's remarks about subtle items than those found for the Pd subscales.

In the construction of the D scale, correction items were included to differentiate nondepressed patients who scored high on the preliminary depression scale from a depressed group. Eight of these correction items occur on the D-S subscale, but only one appears on D-0 and two on the D-N subscale. We hypothesized that perhaps the negative correlation of the D-S subscale with BDI and POMS-D might be attributed to the inclusion of these correction items, which were not supposed to be measures of depression. To test this, the correction items from D-S were removed, and the data reanalyzed. The adjusted D-S scale correlated $-.20$ and $-.27$ with BDI and POMS-D, respectively. These values are very similar to those obtained with the uncorrected D-S scale. So, with or without the correction items, subtle items do not add to the predictive power of the D scale.

To sum up, face-valid items were the best predictors of depression as measured by the BDI, POMS-D, and the PES. Practitioners may want to give more weight to D-0 than to the standard D scores because the former predicts these criteria more powerfully than the latter. Considering the content overlap, it was hardly surprising that the MMPI D scale and the BDI correlated positively. One might have expected that the correlation would be even higher than .49.

The *Ma* Scale Study

The next set of data deals with scale 9*(Ma)*. Hovanitz and Gynther (1980) used 86 male undergraduates at Auburn University as subjects for this study. Obtaining suitable criteria for this scale was more difficult than for the D scale. We were also concerned about the fact that both previous studies had compared self-report inventories as predictors with self-report inventories as criteria, although one might argue that the biographical nonconformity questionnaire operates at a different level than the depression measures. In any case, the following were selected as criteria: Zuckerman's (1977) Sensation Seeking Scale as the questionnaire measure; an Activity-Level Biographic Data form as the life-history measure; and the Porteus Maze as the objective test measure following Cattell, Eber, and Tatsuoka's (1970) descriptions of Q, L, and T data. Cattell believes that the latter procedure, which typically involves the use of miniature situation tests, can overcome the vulnerabilities to role distortion (i.e., faking) inherent in self-description and ratings by others.

Zuckerman's scale is made up of four factors: thrill and adventure seeking, experience seeking, disinhibition, and boredom susceptibility. Internal reliabilities for each factor range from .56 to .82. Test–retest estimates for the different factors range from .70 to .94.

The 40-item activity-level measure was constructed to assess purposeful activity, independence, and social interests, as well as behaviors that indicate a lack of foresight and judgment. Examples of items are: "How many different jobs have you held since beginning high school?" "How many different people have you dated?" "How many times have you run out of gas while driving your car?" "How long do you spend eating breakfast?" A score was obtained by assigning a value of 0 (low in activity) to 4 (high in activity) to each response. With 80 subjects, coefficient alpha for this biographic questionnaire was .82; split-half reliability was .84.

The Porteus Maze test has been around for many years. It is considered a reliable and valid measure of the constructs of foresight, planning ability, judgment, impulsiveness, and ability to delay gratification (Riddle & Roberts, 1977). A score was obtained from this test by summing the following errors: cutting across corners, lifting the pen contrary to instructions, and bumping into lines along the maze pathway. Time to complete these tests was also recorded to provide another criterion measure.

Table 5.4 summarizes the zero-order correlations among the *Ma* subscales and the various criteria. The interesting thing about these findings in terms of the obvious, neutral, and subtle subscales is that there were about as many fairly strong relationships associated with subtle items as there were with obvious items. Whereas the *Pd* and *D* studies indicated that subtle items have limited or no predictive power, here they seem to play a distinct predictive role. *Ma-S*, for example, is the only score that predicts the biographical data; it is also the only score that predicts thrill and adventure seeking. *Ma-O*, on the other hand, predicts experience seeking and errors and time taken on the mazes. *Ma-N* was not significantly associated with any of the criteria.

The relative predictive validity of the *Ma* subscales with all hypomania criteria was assessed by a canonical correlational analysis. The three subscales served as one set of variables, and the other was composed of the seven criteria (i.e., SSS factors, etc.). The canonical correlation for the first pair of variates was .58 ($p < .001$). The *Ma-O*, *Ma-N*, and *Ma-S* subscales correlated .93, .09, and $-.19$, respectively, with the predictor canonical variate. Thus, the variate is defined best by the *Ma-O* subscale. The second canonical correlation was not significant.

The *Ma* subscales were also compared with Harris and Lingoes' (1955/1968) rationally derived *Ma* subscales. Inspection of Table 5.5 reveals some interesting relationships. *Ma-S*, for example, was strongly associated with the imperturbability factor, but only weakly or not at all with any of the other factors. *Ma-O* and *Ma-N*, it may be noted, had a significant negative association with imperturbability, a term that means self-possessed, calm, impassive—hardly what one ordinarily thinks of in the context of hypomania. Those features that do seem reflective of hypomania (e.g., psychomotor acceleration) were strongly associated with *Ma-O* and *Ma-N*.

Multiple correlations between all criteria and each item of the *Ma* scale were also performed. The highest correlation, .55, was found for "I am afraid when I

TABLE 5.4
Correlations Among *Ma + .2k, Ma* Subscales
and Hypomania Criteria

Criteria		Ma + .2K	Ma-O	Ma-N	Ma-S
SSS:	TAS	.14	-.01	.00	.30**
	ES	.28**	.29**	.15	.09
	Dis	.24*	.11	.14	.17
	BS	.05	.01	.08	-.01
Biographic Data		.18	-.06	.05	.29**
Mazes:	Errors	.18	.41***	.00	.00
	Time	-.11	-.21*	.06	-.06

*p < .05
**p < .01
***p < .001

look down from a high place,'' keyed false, classified as subtle. The second highest correlation, .50, was found for ''I have had blank spells in which my activities were interrupted and I did not know what was going on around me,'' keyed true, classified as obvious. The next three highest correlations, all .42 or .43, were for items categorized as subtle. These were: ''It makes me uncomfortable to put on a stunt at a party even when others are doing the same sort of thing'' (keyed false); ''When in a group of people I have trouble thinking of the right things to talk about'' (keyed false); and ''I have been inspired to a program of life based on duty which I have since carefully followed'' (keyed true). It is curious that four of the five most predictive items are subtle when the canonical analysis indicated that *Ma-0* had the greatest predictive power among the subscales.

Intercorrelations among these subscales show less overlap than for the *D* subscales. *Ma-0* and *Ma-N* were significantly related (*r* = .42, *p* < .001), but *Ma-0* and *Ma-S* were not (*r* = −.11, ns) and neither were *Ma-N* and *Ma-S* (*r* =

TABLE 5.5
Correlations Among Harris & Lingoes'
Ma Subscales, *Ma-O, Ma-N,* and *Ma-S*

	Ma-O	Ma-N	Ma-S
Amorality	.35***	.40***	.15
Psychomotor Acceleration	.54***	.66***	.22*
Imperturbability	-.44***	-.22*	.63***
Ego Inflation	.46***	.51***	-.03

*p < .05
**p < .01
***p < .001

−.03, ns). Here is another instance where Jackson's prediction of a significant negative relation between obvious and subtle items did not get support.

Results for *Ma* did not duplicate the results for either *Pd* or *D*. In the former study, obvious items were the most powerful predictors, but subtle items did have a small but unique contribution to make. In the *D* study, obvious items were overwhelmingly the best predictors, so much so that *D-0* probably should replace the standard *D* scale. In this study, obvious items predicted some hypomania criteria, but subtle items were equally predictive of other hypomania criteria. The differences in the results of the three studies may be partly a function of the complexity of the various constructs. Our impression is that scale 9 is more heterogeneous than either scale 2 or 4.

The *Hy* Scale Study

The fourth study (Wilson, 1980) of the relative predictive power of obvious and subtle items deals with scale 3*(Hy)*. Selection of suitable criteria posed a considerable problem due to the many differing definitions of what has been called the "elusive neurosis." Some researchers emphasize psychophysiological factors, some psychosocial factors, others familial relationships, and still others perceptual-cognitive processes.

To measure psychophysiological aspects of the construct, a modification of the Perley-Guze Hysteria Symptom Checklist (Guze, Woodruff, & Clayton, 1972; Perley & Guze, 1962) was used. This checklist contains 59 separate symptoms, divided into 10 nonoverlapping categories.

The psychosocial aspect has to do with the notion that hysterics often appear to be caricatures of the stereotyped male or female sex role. The Personality Research Form Androgyny Scale, now known as the Interpersonal Disposition Inventory (Berzins, Welling, & Wetter, 1978), was used to assess this facet of the construct. This is an 85-item scale containing 29 masculine items, 27 feminine items, 20 self-esteem items, 5 infrequency items, and 4 filler items.

Familial interactions, which are assumed to include a passive-aggressive style, especially with the opposite sex, were tapped by the Parent Behavior Form (Worell & Worell, 1974). This test consists of 270 items; 135 are related to the father, 135 to the mother. Scores can be obtained for 15 scales. For this study, only warmth/acceptance and strict control for the father and warmth/acceptance and hostile control for the mother were scored.

Hysterical personalities are said to be excessively field dependent. To assess this perceptual-cognitive style, the Grays Embedded Figures Test (Witkin, Oltman, Raskin, & Karp, 1971) was used. Basically the subject's task was to find simpler figures hidden in more complex forms.

Subjects for this study were 102 females enrolled in undergraduate psychology courses. Females were focused on mainly because the literature suggests that hysterical personality in its different forms is more apt to be manifested by females than by males.

TABLE 5.6
Correlations Among *Hy, Hy* Subscales and
Hysteria Criteria

Criteria	Hy	Hy-O	Hy-N	Hy-S
Symptom Checklist	.33**	.66***	.58***	-.38***
IDI (Masculine)	-.08	-.18	-.18	.13
IDI (Feminine)	.07	.09	.08	-.03
Mother (Warm)	-.08	-.10	-.04	.00
Mother (Hostile)	.11	.21*	.13	-.09
Father (Warm)	-.14	-.28*	-.21*	.14
Father (Strict)	.03	.32**	.29*	-.34**
Embedded Figures	-.06	-.05	-.18	.07

$*p < .05$
$**p < .01$
$***p < .001$

The results of this study are summarized in Table 5.6. Examination of this table shows no significant relationships between any of the scale 3*(Hy)* scores and performance on the Embedded Figures or the Masculinity–Feminity scale. Perception of the mother's warmth or hostility was, for all practical purposes, also not related to scale 3 scores, although father's warmth or strictness was. The most powerful relationships, clearly, were between scale 3 scores and the Symptom Checklist. This is not surprising because there is undoubtedly item overlap between scale 3 and the checklist. One could say that all of the other criteria were based on inferences about what the hysterical personality *ought* to be like, derived from this or that piece of evidence.

If we focus strictly on the issue of the comparative predictive power of obvious and subtle items, it appears that an edge must be given the obvious items. These results resemble those for scale 4*(Pd)*, where obvious items were superior, but subtle items had a unique contribution to make. It is also worth noting that *Hy-O* is a much better predictor than the full *Hy* scale ($t[100] = 4.56$, $p < .001$). Intercorrelations between the *Hy* subscales showed a pattern similar to that found for the *D* subscales. That is, *Hy-O* and *Hy-N* had high positive correlations ($r = .60$), *Hy-O* and *Hy-S* had significant negative correlations ($r = -.35$), and *Hy-N* and *Hy-S* were not significantly correlated ($r = -.18$).

ANOTHER VIEW OF SUBTLETY

Our definitions of subtlety and obviousness with regard to MMPI items are not shared by Jackson. To illustrate that viewpoint, Holden and Jackson (1979) ask one to consider the item: ''I would enjoy the occupation of a butcher.'' Without a context, this item's underlying construct may be obscure. In other words, it might be deemed subtle or not face valid. However, if one is given a theoretical definition of sadism, its substantive link becomes apparent. For Holden and Jackson (1979) then: "face validity involves the ability of test respondent to relate item content to a hypothesized behavior dimension, [while] item subtlety is concerned with the respondent's ability to relate an item to its actual, keyed scale [p. 461]." Their study is not directly relevant to our concerns about MMPI items because they worked with items from the Personality Research Form. However, what Jackson is saying about subtlety means that our definitions may be too general. If we were to follow his recommendations, subtle–obvious ratings would have to be derived on a scale-by-scale basis. In other words, one would not ask whether endorsement of an item implies the presence of a psychological problem, but rather whether endorsement of an *Ma* or a *Pd* item indicates the presence of behaviors associated with hypomania or psychopathy, respectively.

Studies along these lines with the MMPI should be carried out. There certainly are items defined as subtle within a general context of psychopathology but, in terms of a specific dimension, these items appear to be obvious (cf. "When I get bored I like to stir up some excitement" for scale 9). Whether such items account for the predictive power our studies attributed to subtlety in certain cases is an empirical question.

SUBTLE ITEMS RECONSIDERED

Pending future clarification of the utility of Jackson's definitions, how might one evaluate the status of subtle items within the more general framework we have used? Does the incremental validity associated with subtle items in the *Pd* study, for example, justify the inclusion of 12 such items in that scale? If one were to substitute an equivalent number of the more powerful obvious items, presumably the predictive validity of the scale would be enhanced above the current maximum value (i.e., .40 - .45). Retention of subtle items does not seem defensible on purely statistical grounds.

However, subtle items may function as "corrections" for certain kinds of response sets. We have already mentioned that subtle items are endorsed in the direction opposite to that intended when subjects are instructed to fake bad or fake good (Burkhart, Christian, & Gynther, 1978). Norman (1972) has pointed out that there are many kinds of response sets, some of which may be unique to a particular trait. If this is the case, an overall correction such as the *K* scale may not be as effective as a set of subtle items derived from the specific content domain.

Furthermore, subtle items may be useful in the assessment of certain kinds of people. Wiener (1948) demonstrated that both ability and psychological sophistication influence the pattern of obvious–subtle scores obtained. As stated earlier in this chapter, Burkhart, Gynther, and Christian (1978) obtained similar results (i.e., psychologically minded subjects endorsed more subtle and fewer obvious items than subjects not so characterized). These results suggest that an index of subtlety could be devised to evaluate and/or classify persons on that dimension in an unobtrusive way.

On a more speculative level, subtle items may be especially appropriate for assessing sensitive areas of personality functioning. On the MMPI, the three most objectionable types of questions have been those dealing with bodily elimination processes, sexual functioning, and religious values (Butcher & Tellegen, 1966). Most people find very few items—even in these categories—to be offensive, but some people object to many items. Subtle items should be less threatening and arouse fewer concerns about invasion of privacy, especially for low-trust externals who are reactive to these intrusions into their affairs (Gynther & Ullom, 1976; Hoerl, 1971).

There may also be criteria not predictable in whole or part by obvious items. For example, if people have feelings or conflicts that they have been unable to articulate to themselves or to others, it is unlikely that responding to obvious items would provide any sudden revelations. Subtle items, however, might be able to assess these areas that the subject is not fully aware of (cf. Meehl, 1945).

SUMMARY AND CONCLUSIONS

On the basis of these four studies, what answer should be given to the question: Should subtle items be retained or excluded? It depends on what criterion is employed. If depression is the criterion, subtle items clearly could be omitted with no loss of predictive power. Indeed, D-0 predicts significantly better than the full D scale. Also, in the case of hysteria, subtle items supply no information not better given by obvious items. For psychopathy, subtle items do have a small, but unique, contribution to make. And, in the case of hypomania, subtle items supply information not available from the obvious items alone.

If one's judgment on this matter is restricted to psychometric considerations, it appears that subtle items cannot compete with obvious items with regard to predictive validity. However, there are other potential uses for subtle items. Some are supported by research, but others have not yet been investigated. Future studies in this area should make more use of clinical diagnostic groups. Relationships found with normal subjects may not necessarily hold for deviant persons. Patients diagnosed as conversion reactions, for example, obtain high scores on both the admission and denial components of the Hy scale, whereas the combination is rare for normal subjects (Dahlstrom, 1969). Also, criteria need strengthening. Fishbein and Ajzen (1974) have shown that dispositional measures do poorly in predicting single acts, but they are much better in predicting multiple acts. Epstein (1979) has demonstrated that it is difficult, if not impossible, to predict single instances of behavior, but that it is possible to predict behavior averaged over a sample of situations and/or occasions. Although we are not optimistic about the worth of subtle items, a final resolution of this question should be postponed until the results of such studies have been carefully evaluated.

REFERENCES

Anthony, N. C. Comparison of clients' standard, exaggerated, and matching MMPI profiles. *Journal of Consulting and Clinical Psychology*, 1971, *36*, 100–103.

Beck, A. T. *Depression: Clinical, experimental, and theoretical aspects.* New York: Harper & Row, 1967.

Berg, I. A. Deviant responses and deviant people: The formulation of the deviation hypothesis. *Journal of Counseling Psychology*, 1957, *4*, 154–161.

Berzins, J. I., Welling, M. A., & Wetter, R. E. A new measure of psychological androgyny based on the personality research form. *Journal of Consulting and Clinical Psychology*, 1978, *46*, 126–138.

Burkhart, B. R., Christian, W. L., & Gynther, M. D. Item subtlety and faking on the MMPI: A paradoxical relationship. *Journal of Personality Assessment*, 1978, *42*, 76–80.

Burkhart, B. R., Gynther, M. D., & Christian, W. L. Psychological mindedness, intelligence, and item subtlety endorsement patterns on the MMPI. *Journal of Clinical Psychology*, 1978, *34*, 76–79.

Burkhart, B. R., Gynther, M. D., & Fromuth, M. E. The relative predictive validity of subtle versus obvious items on the MMPI depression scale. *Journal of Clinical Psychology*, 1980, *36*, 748–751.

Butcher, J. N., & Tellegen, A. Objections to MMPI items. *Journal of Consulting Psychology*, 1966, *30*, 527–534.

Cattell, R. B., Eber, H. W., & Tatsuoka, M. M. *Handbook for the sixteen personality factor questionnaire (16PF).* Champaign, Ill.: Institute for Personality and Ability Testing, 1970.

Christian, W. L., Burkhart, B. R., & Gynther, M. D. Subtle–obvious ratings of MMPI items: New interest in an old concept. *Journal of Consulting and Clinical Psychology*, 1978, *46*, 1178–1186.

Cofer, C. N., Chance, J. E., & Judson, A. J. A study of malingering on the MMPI. *Journal of Psychology*, 1949, *27*, 491–499.

Cronbach, L. J. *Essentials of psychological testing* (3rd ed.). New York: Harper & Row, 1970.

Dahlstrom, W. G. Recurrent issues in the development of the MMPI. In J. N. Butcher (Ed.), *MMPI: Research developments and clinical applications.* New York: McGraw-Hill, 1969.

Duff, F. L. Item subtlety in personality inventory scales. *Journal of Consulting Psychology*, 1965, *29*, 565–570.

Elion, V. H., & Megargee, E. I. Validity of the MMPI *Pd* scale among black males. *Journal of Consulting and Clinical Psychology*, 1975, *43*, 166–172.

Epstein, S. The stability of behavior: I. On predicting most of the people much of the time. *Journal of Personality and Social Psychology*, 1979, *37*, 1097–1126.

Fishbein, M., & Ajzen, I. Attitudes toward objects as predictors of single and multiple behavior criteria. *Psychological Review*, 1974, *81*, 59–74.

Goldberg, L. R., & Slovic, P. Importance of test item content: An analysis of a corollary of the deviation hypothesis. *Journal of Counseling Psychology*, 1967, *14*, 462–472.

Guze, S. B., Woodruff, R. A., Jr., & Clayton, P. Sex, age, and the diagnosis of hysteria. *American Journal of Psychiatry*, 1972, *129*, 121–124.

Gynther, M. D., Burkhart, B. R., & Hovanitz, C. Do face-valid items have more predictive validity than subtle items? The case of the MMPI *Pd* scale. *Journal of Consulting and Clinical Psychology*, 1979, *47*, 295–300.

Gynther, M. D., & Ullom, J. Objections to MMPI items as a function of interpersonal trust, race and sex. *Journal of Consulting and Clinical Psychology,* 1976, *44,* 1020.

Harris, R. E., & Lingoes, J. C. *Subscales for the MMPI: An aid to profile interpretation.* Mimeographed materials. Department of Psychiatry, University of California, 1955. (Corrected version, 1968.)

Hoerl, J. B. *Objections to selected MMPI items as a function of sex, internal versus external locus of control and procedures for objecting.* Unpublished doctoral dissertation, St. Louis University, 1971.

Holden, R. R., & Jackson, D. N. Item subtlety and face validity in personality assessment. *Journal of Consulting and Clinical Psychology,* 1979, *47,* 459–468.

Hovanitz, C., & Gynther, M. D. The prediction of impulsive behavior: Comparative validities of obvious versus subtle MMPI hypomania (Ma) items. *Journal of Clinical Psychology,* 1980, *36,* 422–427.

Jackson, D. N. The dynamics of structured personality tests: 1971. *Psychological Review,* 1971, *78,* 229–248.

Koss, M. P., & Butcher, J. N. A comparison of psychiatric patients' self-report with other sources of clinical information. *Journal of Research in Personality,* 1973, *7,* 225–236.

Koss, M. P., Butcher, J. N., & Hoffman, N. The MMPI critical items: How well do they work? *Journal of Consulting and Clinical Psychology,* 1976, *44,* 921–928.

Lachar, D., & Wrobel, T. A. Validation of clinicians' hunches: Construction of a new MMPI critical item set. *Journal of Consulting and Clinical Psychology,* 1979, *47,* 277–284.

MacPhillamy, D. J., & Lewinsohn, P. M. Depression as a function of levels of desired and obtained pleasure. *Journal of Abnormal Psychology,* 1974, *83,* 651–657.

McCall, R. J. Face validity in the D scale of the MMPI. *Journal of Clinical Psychology,* 1958, *14,* 77–80.

McNair, D. M., Lorr, M., & Droppleman, L. F. *Manual for the profile of mood states.* San Diego, Cal.: Educational and Industrial Testing Service, 1971.

Meehl, P. E. The dynamics of "structured" personality tests. *Journal of Clinical Psychology,* 1945, *1,* 296–303.

Meehl, P. E. Reactions, reflections, projections. In J. N. Butcher (Ed.), *Objective personality assessment: Changing perspectives.* New York: Academic Press, 1972.

Meehl, P. E., & Hathaway, S. R. The K factor as a suppressor variable in the MMPI. *Journal of Applied Psychology,* 1946, *30,* 525–564.

Messick, S., & Jackson, D. N. Desirability scale values and dispersions for MMPI items. *Psychological Reports,* 1961, *8,* 409–414.

Norman, W. T. Psychometric considerations for a revision of the MMPI. In J. N. Butcher (Ed.), *Objective personality assessment: Changing perspectives.* New York: Academic Press, 1972.

Perley, M., & Guze, S. B. Hysteria: The stability and usefulness of clinical criteria. *New England Journal of Medicine,* 1962, *266,* 421–426.

Riddle, M., & Roberts, A. H. Delinquency, delay of gratification, recidivism, and the Porteus maze test. *Psychological Bulletin,* 1977, *84,* 417–425.

Seeman, W. "Subtlety" in structured personality tests. *Journal of Consulting Psychology,* 1952, *16,* 278–283.

Seeman, W. Concept of "subtlety" in structured psychiatric and personality tests: An experimental approach. *Journal of Abnormal and Social Psychology,* 1953, *48,* 239–247.

Stone, L. A. Subtle and obvious response on the MMPI as a function of acquiescence response style. *Psychological Reports,* 1965, *16,* 803–804.

Vesprani, G. J., & Seeman, W. MMPI *X* and zero items in a psychiatric out-patient group. *Journal of Personality Assessment,* 1974, *38,* 61–64.

Wales, B., & Seeman, W. A new method for detecting the fake good response set on the MMPI. *Journal of Clinical Psychology,* 1968, *24,* 211–216.

Wales, B., & Seeman, W. What do MMPI zero items really measure? An experimental investigation. *Journal of Clinical Psychology,* 1969, *25,* 420–424.

Wiener, D. N. Subtle and obvious keys for the Minnesota multiphasic personality inventory. *Journal of Consulting Psychology,* 1948, *12,* 164–170.

Wiener, D. N., & Harmon, L. R. *Subtle and obvious keys for the MMPI: Their development* (Advisement Bulletin No. 16). Minneapolis, Minn.: Regional Veterans Administration Office, 1946.

Wilson, R. L. *A comparison of the predictive validities of subtle versus obvious MMPI items: Predicting the elusive neurosis.* Unpublished Master's thesis, Auburn University, 1980.

Witkin, H. A., Oltman, P. K., Raskin, E., & Karp, S. A. *A manual for the embedded figures tests.* Palo Alto, Cal.: Consulting Psychologists Press, 1971.

Worell, L., & Worell, J. *The parent behavior form.* Manual in preparation, University of Kentucky 1974.

Zuckerman, M. *Preliminary manual with scoring keys and norms for form V of the sensation seeking scale.* Unpublished manuscript, University of Delaware, 1977.

6

Bender-Gestalt Recall: A Review of the Normative Data and Related Issues

James C. Schraa
Medical Psychology Program
Division of Psychobiology
National Jewish Hospital/National Asthma Center
Denver, Colorado

Nelson F. Jones
School of Professional Psychology
University of Denver
Denver, Colorado

Jerald F. Dirks
Medical Psychology Program
Division of Psychobiology
National Jewish Hospital/National Asthma Center
Denver, Colorado

The normative data on the recall of Bender-Gestalt designs by adults are consolidated and organized for the first time. The relationships of intelligence, personality variables, and age to Bender recall are discussed. The relationship of Bender recall to the Wechsler Memory Scale and other measures of functioning are also described. The experimental data on the utility of Bender recall as a screening measure for brain damage are reviewed. The extensive variation in how Bender recall has been operationalized is described, and desirable characteristics for a standardized operational definition of Bender recall are outlined. The recall of Bender-Gestalt designs is analyzed in terms of a model of memory.

Recent surveys of test utilization have revealed that the Bender-Gestalt Test is among the three most frequently used psychological tests and that it is the most widely used test in institutional settings (Klopfer & Taulbee, 1976; Lubin, Wallis, & Paine, 1971). The popularity of the standard administration of the Bender appears to be due to the fact that it affords a convenient way of assessing visuoconstructional skills by having the patient directly copy the designs (Billingslea, 1963). Since 1938, psychologists have also used recall of the Bender-Gestalt designs as a way of testing immediate visual memory by having patients recall the designs as soon as they have finished copying them (Bender, 1938). The importance of assessing visual memory has recently received increasing recognition (Erickson & Scott, 1977). However, the lack of a conventionally accepted system for scoring Bender recall and the lack of readily obtainable published norms has limited the utility of the Bender recall procedure. The deficiencies in the literature on Bender recall are unfortunate since having patients recall the Bender designs immediately after they have finished copying them is an efficient way of obtaining a measure of visual memory. Adding the recall procedure to the standard copy phase of the Bender requires little additional administration time, with patients typically requiring one to five minutes to copy the designs from memory. (An examination of the recall procedure on 201 chronic respiratory patients found the mean time to be 201.78 seconds, with a standard deviation of 140.55 seconds.) Thus, Bender recall, if its validity were clearly established, could provide a cost effective way of adding a measure of visual memory to test batteries in institutional and other settings where none may currently be obtained or adding depth to assessment batteries that include only one measure of visual memory.

Bender recall and other measures of figural memory are primarily mediated by the right temporal lobe and the right hippocampus (Russell, 1975, 1980). The procedure of having patients immediately reproduce the Bender designs from memory after they have copied them may be conceptualized as a test of free recall (the designs can be recalled in any order) that reflects the processes involved in both short term and long term memory (Glanzer & Clark, 1979). Short term memory has been described as a temporary holding and organizing process that plays a crucial control function when information is registered into and retrieved from long term memory (Craik, 1977; Russell, 1980). Short-term memory has a limited capacity, a length of 20-30 seconds without rehearsal, and has been described as constituting conscious awareness (Craik, 1977; Russell, 1980). Long term memory is more permanent in character than short term memory and is involved whenever the limited span of short term memory has been exceeded. Goodstein, Spielberger, Williams and Dahlstrom (1955) demonstrated that the recall of a particular Bender design is a function of both its difficulty level and its position in the order of presentation. It has consistently been found that design 8 (the last design administered) is most frequently recalled in standard administrations of the test (Armstrong, 1963). The superior recall by patients of design 8 is consistent with the serial position effect in which the last stimulus presented is recalled from short term memory (Glanzer & Clark, 1979). Thus Bender recall may be regarded as reflecting short term memory (the recall of design 8) and long term memory (the recall of designs that are no longer in conscious awareness).

This paper has two objectives. The first, since the norms for Bender recall are presently scattered in over 26 journal articles, is to consolidate and organize the normative data on Bender recall so that researchers and clinicians can readily compare their data and local norms with related published data. The second objective is to provide a brief summary of the research on the recall of Bender-Gestalt designs in hopes of stimulating more systematic research to correct major deficiencies in the existing literature.

To compile the normative data presented in this paper, a search of Buros' *Mental Measurements Yearbooks* and *Psychological Abstracts* was undertaken. The results of the search for normative data are presented in five tables by diagnostic category: Table 6.1, "Normals;" Table 6.2, Medical Patients; Table 6.3, Psychiatric Patients; Table 6.4, "Organic" Patients; Table 6.5, Seizure Disorder Patients. For the convenience of the reader, the distinction between medical and organic patients is made on the basis of the type of setting or service in which the patients were found. Obviously, medical conditions may directly affect brain functioning. The tables should be read in conjunction with the text since diagnostic and selection factors and the operational definitions of what constituted correct recall varied from study to study. The normative data on Bender recall are presented in terms of the number of designs recalled. Since the few articles that used modifications of standardized Bender scoring systems also simply reported the number of Bender designs recalled, the normative data for Bender recall will not be presented in terms of the specialized scoring systems. Standardized scoring systems, in fact, reportedly do not increase the validity of the Bender for any purpose (Lyle & Quast, 1976).

DIAGNOSIS OF SUBJECT GROUPS

The normative data presented in Tables 6.1–6.5 are all drawn from studies in which the reliability of the diagnosis of the patient groups was not addressed. The majority of the studies did not even delineate the specific diagnostic criteria which were utilized to categorize patients. Exceptions to the paucity of explicit diagnostic criteria did occur. Schwartz and Dennerll (1969) confirmed the diagnosis of epilepsy by seizure history, EEG's, and neurological exams. However, Schwartz and Dennerll did not report etiologic data on their subjects. Lyle and Quast (1976) identified their subjects as the descendants of individuals with Huntington's disease. Hanvik and Andersen (1950) reported that the locus of brain injury in their patients was verified by x-rays or surgery. Only Holland and Wadsworth (1979) reported that their nonorganic group of schizophrenics received neurological exams. Heaton, Baade, and Johnson (1978) pointed out that failure to examine individuals with functional disorders neurologically may have a confounding effect on comparisons with groups having cerebral dysfunctions. The presence of cerebral dysfunctions among patients with functional diagnoses may reduce intergroup differences since neurological disorders can be expected to occur in psychiatric patients at rates greater than the overall incidence rate (Heaton, *et al.*, 1978).

OPERATIONAL DEFINITIONS OF RECALL

In Tables 6.1–6.5, the values for the number of Bender designs recalled are drawn from studies which defined recall in various ways. Many of the definitions of recall require a substantial amount of clinical judgment on the part of raters. However, the available reliability data suggest that psychologists can determine the number of Bender-Gestalt designs recalled with acceptable degrees of reliability.

In addition, the figures presented in Tables 6.1–6.5 are based in part upon a number of studies that described recall in relatively global terms and some in which more elaborate operational definitions of what constituted appropriate recall were given. The recall score used by Peek and Olson (1955) represented the number of designs completely recalled plus half credits where clearly recognizable design elements were produced. Tolor (1956) stated that both whole and part figures were counted in arriving at the total number of designs recalled. Lyle and Quast (1976) awarded one point for each design correctly reproduced and a half point was given when only part of a design with overlapping segments or distinct parts were drawn. Armentrout (1976) scored full credit when all major components were present with no more than minor distortions and half credit when all major components were present but moderate distortions occurred or when just one major component from a design was reproduced. Reznikoff and Olin (1957) and Schwartz and Dennerll (1969) reported three different scores. Designs which were reproduced from memory with no major distortions, omissions, or rotations constituted Good Recall. Weighted Recall was based upon Good Recall plus half credit for each design in which a distortion, omission, or rotation occurred. The Total Recall score criterion was very liberal, and any design in which any portion of the original stimulus was present was counted. In the papers presented by Olin and Reznikoff (1957, 1958), a design was scored as having been recalled if it could be scored by their modification of the Pascal and Suttell scoring system. Freed (1966) scored protocols by the Pascal and Suttell system, but did not make clear how the numerical value of the number of designs recalled was arrived at. Similarly, Armstrong (1965) developed and utilized a revision of the Pascal and Suttell system, but how this was translated into a figure for the number of designs recalled was not explicitly stated. Holland and Wadsworth (1979) reported recall as the number of designs receiving less than the maximum deviation score in Canter's scoring system. For first year university students, Weiss (1970) reported good recall as the number of figures recalled with no more than one slight distortion. Obviously, the variability in the definitions of Bender recall points up the need for specification of a simple standardized procedure for scoring Bender recall.

Several aspects of the literature are pertinent to operationalizing the scoring of Bender recall. Rogers and Swenson (1975) compared a stringent operational definition of Bender recall and a more liberal one and found that the two methods of scoring recall yielded correlations with the Wechsler Memory Scale that did not differ significantly. However, Reznikoff and Olin (1957) reported that their organic and schizophrenic groups were significantly different when their most stringent measure of recall, Good Recall, was used but not when more liberal operational definitions of Bender recall were used. Olin and Reznikoff (1957) found significant positive correlations between the overall quality of designs reproduced from memory and the quality of the design reproductions obtained in the copy phase for normal, organic, and schizophrenic groups. These studies and other aspects of the literature suggest that a useful definition of Bender recall would be stringent and require that all major components of the designs as illustrated on the original stimulus cards, or as illustrated in a patient's efforts to directly copy the design, be present with no more than minor distortions for the patient to receive credit for recalling the design. Such an operational definition has the advantage of not underestimating the visual memory of individuals with poor constructional skills and still maintaining a rigorous measure of visual memory.

THE NORMATIVE DATA ON BENDER RECALL

Tables 6.1–6.5 summarize all of the published data we could find on Bender recall. In the tables, the normative data are presented on a study-by-study basis since the literature essentially consists of a series of reports of local norms. Attempts to collapse the norms that are summarized here would obscure their meaning and eliminate their utility for clinicians working in specific settings. All of the local normative data reviewed in this paper appear to have been collected from readily available subjects rather than from well planned samplings. Readers should carefully review the tables to determine which set of norms is most appropriate for the use they have in mind. Many of the characteristics that are desirable for normative data (e.g., ethnic mix, socioeconomic level, locale) are simply not available for Bender recall, and, as has already been noted, the degree of accuracy in the criterion diagnosis of most of the parient groups is unknown. The vast majority of the studies cited in the tables used the simple procedure of asking patients to recall as many designs as possible as soon as they had finished copying them. All variations in administration procedures are noted in the tables.

TABLE 6.1

Characteristics of Normal Subjects on Bender Recall

Authors/date	Subjects	Age	Education	IQ	Bender recall
Gobetz (1953	258 white male WWII non-disability veterans in aptitude testing and vocational counseling	M = 24.22 SD = 4.70	M = 12.47 SD = 1.72	—	M = 6.28 SD = 1.15
Olin & Reznikoff (1957); Olin & Reznikoff (1958)	33 student nurses	Range 19-23	—	—	M = 6.52 SD = 1.26
Stewart & Cunningham (1958	20 student nurses	—	—	—	Values calculated from a table M = 6.95 SD = 1.05
Spielberger, Goodstein & Dahlstrom (1958)	44 undergraduates scoring high on the Taylor Manifest Anxiety Scale	—	—	—	Recall after a 6 minute delay; 40 second limit on copying time and altered order of presentation M = 5.05
	44 undergraduates scoring low on Taylor Manifest Anxiety Scale	—	—	—	M = 5.50
Weiss (1970)	65 adult nonclinical subjects	—	9-14 years of education	"Normal intelligence"	Only 5% recalled fewer than 6 whole designs, while 60% recalled at least 8
	77 first year Israeli university students	M = 22.6	—	—	"Good Recall" M = 5.85 Range 2.5-8.5 Median 6.55

Gobetz (1953) provided the one set of normative data on Bender recall in "normals" that was composed of a large enough sample to provide truly stable values. His subjects were native born, white, male, World War II veterans who were availing themselves of aptitude testing and vocational counseling under the G.I. Bill. They were not suffering from physical or psychiatric disabilities. Additional characteristics of this group are listed in Table 6.1. The mean and standard deviation provided by Gobetz permit the conceptualization of Bender recall scores in terms of a normal distribution. Using the values provided by Gobetz, a Bender recall value of 7.43 is one standard deviation above the mean, 6.28 is the mean, 5.13 is one standard deviation below the mean, and 3.98 is two standard deviations below the mean. Rounding from these units to whole numbers, it is reasonable to designate recall of 8 or more designs as superior, 6-7 designs as average, 5 designs as low average, and 4 designs or less as impaired. Utilizing the mean and standard deviation for the group of 33 student nurses provided by Olin and Reznikoff (1957) yields values for standard deviation cuts that are very similar to those generated from Gobetz' data. The data provided by Stewart and Cunningham (1958) are based on 20 student nurses in the upper half of their class. In turn, these presumably more intelligent student nurses generated a higher mean and smaller standard deviation which would yield higher cut points. Means and standard deviations are not available for any of the other "normal" groups.

An inspection of Table 6.2 reveals that all of the groups of medical patients recalled fewer Bender designs than the normal groups. The means for the medical groups range from 3.2 to 5.57. Although several of the studies reporting data on medical patients provided little or no information on the diagnostic characteristics of their subjects, when taken as a group these studies do provide some support for the inference that Bender recall is sensitive to the neuropsychological effects of medical conditions and treatments. The work of Jacobs, Winter, Alvis, and Small (1969) also provides support for the inference that Bender recall is sensitive to changes in medical status. They reported that intermittent exposures to 100 percent oxygen at 2.5 atmospheres of absolute pressure brought about large and significant increases in the number of Bender designs recalled in a group of intellectually deteriorated elderly patients. These studies suggest that Bender recall may potentially constitute one way of establishing whether particular medical conditions or medical procedures affect visual memory.

Table 6.3 summarizes the available normative data on Bender recall in psychiatric patients. An inspection of the data from all of the studies using standard administration procedures reveals that the groups with less severe diagnoses (e.g., character disorders, neuroses) generally recalled more Bender designs and had smaller standard deviations than the groups with more severe diagnoses (e.g., psychoses, schizophrenia). However, there is a substantial degree of overlap between the two groups.

TABLE 6.2
Characteristics of Medical Patients on Bender Recall

Authors/date	Subjects	Age	Education	IQ	Bender recall
Hanvik & Andersen (1950)	37 male Veterans Administration patients with verified or psychogenic low back pain	—	—	—	$M = 5.57$ $SD = 1.73$
Goldstein, Ewert, Randall, & Gross (1968)	8 Wilson's disease (hepatolenticular degeneration) prior to treatment	$M = 67$ $SD = 4.2$ Range 55-81	$M = 8$	WAIS Full Scale IQ $M = 100$ $SD = 13$ Range 76-145	$M = 3.2$ $SD = 2$ Range 0-8
Levine & Feirstein (1972)	18 medical patients with no history of substance abuse, psychiatric illness, or head injury. Length of hospitalization 26 months	$M = 44.7$	$M = 10.6$	WAIS Vocabulary $M = 10.7$	$M = 4.7$
Schraa, Dirks, Jones, & Kinsman (in press)	95 adult asthmatic inpatients	$M = 37$ Range 21-55	—	—	53% of the patients recalled 4 or fewer designs; 26% recalled 5 or 6 designs; 21% recalled 7 or more designs

TABLE 6.3
Characteristics of Psychiatric Patients on Bender Recall

Authors/date	Subjects	Age	Education	IQ	Bender recall
Gobetz (1953)	108 white male neurotic WWII veterans in VA outpatient treatment	$M = 29.76$ $SD = 5.74$	$M = 10.74$ $SD = 2.89$	–	$M = 5.93$ $SD = 1.60$
Peek & Olson (1955)	193 state hospital inpatients	$M = 34.67$ $SD = 12.85$ Range 14-72	–	Shipley Hartford conceptual quotient mean $M = 83.06$ $SD = 16.30$ Shipley Hartford raw score mean $M = 28.81$ $SD = 5.67$	$M = 5.09$ $SD = 2.08$
	Lowest third of patients on Shipley-Hartford;	–	–	–	$M = 4.53$
	Highest third of patients on Shipley-Hartford;	–	–	–	$M = 5.40$
	35 individuals with Shipley-Hartford conceptual quotents over 100	–	–	–	$M = 6.19$
Tolor (1956)	49 "psychogenic patients" 3 psychotic 46 personality disorders	$M = 35.4$ $SD = 14.2$ Range 12-64	–	Wechsler-Bellevue Form 1 $M = 110.8$ $SD = 13.1$ Range 79-136	$M = 5.98$ corrected by covariance for intelligence $M = 5.53$

(Continued)

141

TABLE 6.3 (Continued)

Authors/date	Subjects	Age	Education	IQ	Bender recall
Reznikoff & Olin (1957); Olin & Reznikoff (1957); Olin & Reznikoff (1958)	50 hospitalized schizophrenics	M = 30.9 Range 18-49	—	"Wechsler IQ" M = 107.5 Range 80-128	"Good Recall" M = 4.16: "Weighted Recall" M = 5.09: "Total Recall" M = 5.30 SD = 1.48
Stewart (1957)	21 newly admitted female psychotic patients	For all 39 patients M = 33 Range 16-52	—	—	Standard recall was preceded by a 5 second recall M = 5.57 Range 2-8
	18 newly admitted female nonpsychotics	—	—	—	M = 7.73 Range 4-9
Tolor (1958)	18 male patients with character and behavior disorders	M = 25.4 Range 19-40	—	WAIS Full Scale IQ M = 99.5 Range 77-124	M = 6.3 SD = 1.28
	18 schizophrenics who were difficult diagnostic cases	M = 25.8 Range 19-41	—	WAIS Full Scale M = 99.4 Range 78-123	M = 5.8 SD = 1.53
Stewart & Cunningham (1958)	16 female personality disorders and neurotics	—	—	—	Values calculated from a table M = 5.62 SD = .96
	18 female psychotics	—	—	—	M = 4.56 SD = 1.58

Study	Sample description				
Armstrong (1963)	Consecutively referred patients in a private psychiatric hospital diagnosed functionally psychotic 15 - sample 1 9 - sample 2 16 - sample 3 40 - total	—	—	—	Sample 1 M = 5.80; Sample 2 M = 5.61; Sample 3 - order of presentation was changed M = 6.25; Total M = 5.94
	Consecutively referred patients in a private psychiatric hospital diagnosed nonpsychotic i.e. neurotic and character disorders 5 - sample 1 7 - sample 2 7 - sample 3 19 - total	—	—	—	Sample 1 - M = 6.60; Sample 2 - M = 5.57; Sample 3 - order of presentation was changed M = 7.14; Total M = 6.42
Armstrong (1965); Armstrong (1969) reports that these findings were replicated	Hospitalized patients who were consecutively referred for psychological testing. 32 - schizophrenic	M = 25.72	M = 13.31	WAIS Full Scale IQ M = 112.66; WAIS Verbal IQ M = 117.53; WAIS Performance IQ M = 104.66	M = 6.00

(Continued)

TABLE 6.3 (Continued)

Authors/date	Subjects	Age	Education	IQ	Bender recall
	7 - depressive	M = 53.57	M = 11.14	WAIS Full Scale IQ M = 113.83; WAIS Verbal IQ M = 117.17; WAIS Performance IQ M = 106.00	M = 5.57
	11 - Neurotic	M = 35.00	M = 13.36	WAIS Full Scale IQ M = 120.18; WAIS Verbal IQ M = 120.45; WAIS Performance IQ M = 117.18	M = 6.09
	17 - Character Disorder	M = 29.41	M = 13.94	WAIS Full Scale IQ M = 118.94; WAIS Verbal IQ M = 122.65; WAIS Performance IQ M = 111.42	M = 6.06
Freed (1966)	33 newly admitted male psychiatric patients; 67% schizophrenic;	M = 40.00 SD = 8.64	M = 11.03 SD = 2.42	Shipley Hartford	M = 3.79 SD = 2.00

	Median of 8 days of hospitalization				Vocabulary IQ $M = 112.09$ $SD = 13.16$
	30 male psychiatric patients who had been hospitalized for a mean of 3.30 years and were about to be discharged; 83% schizophrenic	$M = 38.57$ $SD = 8.40$	$M = 10.03$ $SD = 2.30$	Shipley Hartford vocabulary IQ $M = 106.23$ $SD = 20.28$	$M = 3.80$ $SD = 2.07$
Gilbertstadt (1970)	116 psychiatric cases	$M = 34.00$	—	$M = 105$ (type unknown)	Only 6% of the sample had a recall score of 3 or less
Levine & Feirstein (1972)	18 schizophrenics who were selected because of unequivocal diagnosis and ability to cooperate; length of hospitalization 27 months	$M = 43.2$	$M = 11.1$	WAIS Vocabulary $M = 11.1$	WAIS $M = 4.6$
Armentrout (1976)	111 vocational rehabilitation clients that had either physical, mental, or emotional disabilities that hampered employment	$M = 22.6$ $SD = 8.1$ Range 17-54	—	WAIS Full Scale IQ $M = 92.7$ $SD = 13.8$; Verbal IQ $M = 92.4$ $SD = 14.9$; Performance IQ $M = 93.9$ $SD = 12.9$	$M = 5.7$ $SD = 1.5$ Range 2.5-9
Holland & Wadsworth (1979)	20 male veteran schizophrenic inpatients	$M = 46.0$ $SD = 9.64$	$M = 11.15$ $SD = 2.98$	WAIS Full scale IQ $M = 101.25$ $SD = 12.29$	$M = 5.05$ $SD = 1.23$ Recall after the Background Interference procedure $M = 5.55$ $SD = 1.61$

TABLE 6.4
Characteristics of Organic Patients on Bender Recall

Authors/date	Subjects	Age	Education	IQ	Bender Recall
Hanvik & Anderson (1950)	Male Veterans Administration in-patients; 20 dominant hemisphere lesions; 20 nondominant hemisphere lesions	— — —	— — —	— — —	$M = 3.90$, $SD = 1.97$ $M = 4.67$, $SD = 1.58$
Tolor (1956)	91 patients having varied types of intercranial pathology	$M = 44.1$ $SD = 15.1$ Range 12-72	—	Wechsler-Bellevue Form 1 $M = 90.8$ $SD = 16.7$ Range 54-129	$M = 3.48$ corrected by covariance for intelligence $M = 3.69$
Tolor (1958)	18 male organic patients with physical etiology, structural changes in the brain or encephalopathy	$M = 28.0$ Range 18-40	—	WAIS Full Scale IQ $M = 98.8$ Range 77-125	$M = 4.9$ $SD = 2.01$
Armstrong (1963)	Consecutively referred patients in a private psychiatric hospital diagnosed organic. 5 - sample 1 4 - sample 2 2 - sample 3 11 - Total	— — — —	— — — —	— — — —	Sample 1 $M = 3.80$ Sample 2 $M = 3.50$ For Sample 3 the order of presentation was changed. $M = 3.00$ Total $M = 3.55$
Armstrong (1965);	13 hospitalized patients who had	$M = 48$	$M = 13.85$	WAIS Full	$M = 3.85$

Study	Description				
Armstrong (1969)	reports that these findings were replicated.	been consecutively referred for psychological testing			Scale IQ M = 101.31; WAIS Verbal IQ M = 106.92; WAIS Performance IQ M = 93.69	
Levine & Feirstein (1962)	18 unequivocal diagnoses of diffuse brain disease by a staff neurologist in white male hospitalized patients; Length of hospitalization 22 months	M = 43.9	M = 10.7	WAIS Vocabulary IQ M = 10.0	M = 2.5
Lyle & Quast (1976)	All subjects were offspring of Huntington's disease victims.				
	23 normals who remained free of Huntington's disease	M = 31	—	—	M = 5.89 SD = 1.46 Range 4-9
	23 normals who remained free of Huntington's disease	M = 31	—	—	M = 5.44 SD = 1.07 Range 3-8
	22 premorbids who developed Huntington's disease after testing	M = 31	—	—	M = 4.34 SD = 2.35 Range 0-9
	21 patients who manifested signs of Huntington's disease at the time of testing	M = 38	—	—	M = 4.60 SD = 1.93 Range 0-7.5
Holland & Wadsworth (1979)	20 male brain damaged veterans.	M = 46.0 SD = 9.64	M = 11.15 SD = 2.98	WAIS Full Scale IQ M = 88.60 SD = 16.51	M = 3.15 SD = 1.50 Recall after the Background Interference Procedure M = 2.70 SD = 1.87

TABLE 6.5
Characteristics of Seizure Disorder Patients on Bender Recall

Authors/date	Subjects	Age	Education	IQ	Bender recall
Tolor (1956)	35 patients with varied seizure disorders	$M = 27.6$ $SD = 11.9$ Range 12-56	—	Wechsler-Bellevue Form 1 $M = 94.2$ $SD = 15.4$ Range 61-121	$M = 5.06$ Correct by covariance for intelligence $M = 5.15$
Aaronson (1957)	N - 104. An epileptic state hospital population with a high incidence of feeble mindedness	$M = 31.5$ $SD = 14.0$ Range 12-72	—	Porteus Maze $M = 72.9$ $SD = 23.0$ Range 20-123	$M = 3.1$ $SD = 3.6$ Range 0-9
Schwartz & Denneryll (1969)	129 patients with grand mal seizures	$M = 26.61$ $SD = 9.18$	$M = 11.39$ $SD = 2.15$	Full Scale IQ $M = 96.37$ $SD = 14.75$	"Good Recall" $M = 4.13$ $SD = 1.84$; "Weighted recall" $M = 4.73$ $SD = 1.70$; "Total Recall" $M = 5.56$ $SD = 1.56$
	6 patients with petit mal seizures	$M = 25.32$ $SD = 8.82$	$M = 12.33$ $SD = 1.70$	Full Scale IQ $M = 100.83$ $SD = 16.63$	"Good Recall" $M = 3.83$ $SD = .90$; "Weighted Recall" $M = 4.67$ $SD = 1.07$; "Total Recall" $M = 5.50$ $SD = 1.26$
	22 patients with psychomotor seizures	$M = 27.17$ $SD = 8.13$	$M = 10.59$ $SD = 1.61$	Full Scale IQ $M = 96.86$ $SD = 12.65$	"Good Recall" $M = 3.86$ $SD = 1.78$; "Weighted Recall" $M = 4.45$ $SD = 1.80$;

Group			Full Scale IQ	Recall measures
36 patients with grand mal and psychomotor seizures	$M = 26.03$ $SD = 8.17$	$M = 11.33$ $SD = 1.75$	$M = 96.86$ $SD = 10.43$	"Total Recall" $M = 5.32$ $SD = 1.69$ "Good Recall" $M = 3.64$ $SD = 1.34$; "Weighted Recall" $M = 4.11$ $SD = 1.35$; "Total Recall" $M = 4.89$ $SD = 1.20$
9 patients with grand mal and petit mal seizures	$M = 26.89$ $SD = 11.23$	$M = 12.67$ $SD = 1.89$	$M = 102.44$ $SD = 11.93$	"Good Recall" $M = 4.75$ $SD = 1.20$; "Weighted Recall" $M = 4.83$ $SD = 1.86$; "Total Recall" $M = 5.56$ $SD = 1.64$
31 patients with grand mal plus akinetic, myoclonic, sensory, or unclassifiable seizures	$M = 25.64$ $SD = 8.86$	$M = 12.03$ $SD = 1.49$	$M = 100.29$ $SD = 12.81$	"Good Recall" $M = 4.81$ $SD = 2.16$; "Weighted Recall" $M = 5.53$ $SD = 1.34$; "Total Recall" $M = 6.26$ $SD = 1.66$
6 patients with akinetic, myoclonic, sensory, or unclassifiable seizures	$M = 24.02$ $SD = 10.04$	$M = 11.33$ $SD = 2.13$	$M = 106.33$ $SD = 15.90$	"Good Recall" $M = 4.33$ $SD = 1.25$; "Weighted Recall" $M = 4.92$ $SD = 1.37$; "Total Recall" $M = 5.50$ $SD = 1.61$

149

In Table 6.4, all of the available normative data on Bender recall in patients who have been diagnosed as having some form of cerebral dysfunction or "organicity" are presented. A review of these "organic" groups reveals that their means are generally lower than those reported for other diagnostic categories. The means range from 4.9 to 2.5. Research on the recall of Bender-Gestalt designs could readily be improved by discarding the unitary construct of "organicity" which has generally been used to date and by relating Bender recall to more specific types of cerebral dysfunctions. Table 6.4 provides as much diagnostic information as is available about the composition of the organic groups. Variables which need to be studied in relationship to Bender recall are the localization of lesions, the static vs. progressive nature of lesions, the rate at which various lesions progress, the etiology of lesions, and age of onset (Heaton et al., 1978).

Useful normative data on the Bender recall of patients with seizure disorders are presented in Table 6.5. Schwartz and Dennerll (1969) reported their normative data by seizure type. Their epileptic subjects were all outpatients who volunteered for participation in the study. The subjects were obtained from general practitioners, neurologists, schools, self-referrals, hospitals, the Department of Vocational Rehabilitation, and the Michigan Epilepsy Center. Schwartz and Denerll found that the poorest recall occurred in the group with grand mal and psychomotor seizures. They concluded that the psychomotor component was the critical factor in reducing the short term visual memory of this group relative to the other groups of epileptics.

BENDER RECALL AS A SCREENING MEASURE FOR ORGANICITY

Reporting the normative data in tables grouped by diagnostic category rather than on a study-by-study basis does neglect the relatively consistent patterns in the intergroup comparisons both within studies and across studies. In the seven independent sets of data reporting Bender recall which included organics, the groups of organic patients always ranked last in the number of designs recalled in comparison with groups of patients with functional disorders. In terms of a "box score," all seven sets of data showed that the organic groups recalled significantly fewer designs than the functional groups. Six of the seven studies included schizophrenic or functionally psychotic groups. The seventh study had a mixed group of psychogenic patients. When Reznikoff and Olin (1957) and Olin and Reznikoff (1958) used more liberal operational definitions of recall, their schizophrenic group no longer differed signifcantly from their organic group. One other study also provided support for the inference that individuals with cerebral dysfunctions tend to have impaired performances on Bender recall. Neibuhr and Cohen (1956) presented each Bender design for 10 seconds and then asked each subject to recall it. Their group of 10 hospitalized, neurologically impaired veterans received significantly lower ratings of their recall performance than chronic shcizophrenics, acute schizophrenics, and student nurses. Taken as a group, this series of studies would appear to indicate that the reduction in the capacity of individuals with cerebral disorders to recall Bender designs from memory is a relatively dependable and powerful phenomenon. Tversky and Kahneman (1971) suggest that a series of such near replications is relatively rare.

Earlier researchers and reviewers have generally concluded that the significant differences between functional and organic groups on Bender recall were not large enough to permit judgments concerning the presence of brain damage in individual cases (Reznikoff & Olin, 1957; Tolor & Schulberg, 1963). However, an analysis of the effect of sizes of three Bender recall studies supports the conclusion that further research on Bender recall is in order to clearly establish its effectiveness as a screening measure for brain damage. Effect size is a measure of the degree of departure from the null hypothesis or the extent to which the null hypothesis is false (Cohen, 1977). The effect size is the difference between two means divided by the standard deviation of the control group (Smith & Glass, 1977). In this case, the standard deviations that are utilized are those of the functional groups since the area of interest is how far the organic groups deviate from them (Kulik, Kulik & Cohen, 1979). For example, an effect size of $-.68$ would represent a .68 standard deviation inferiority of an organic group relative to a functional group. Cohen (1977) classifies a small effect size as .2, a medium effect size as .5, and a large effect size as .8. An analysis of effect sizes provides a worthwhile way to analyze the utility of Bender recall as a screening measure since the studies on Bender recall have not generally reported hit rates.

Means and standard deviations could be located for three studies on Bender recall which included organic groups. In all of the following comparisons, the organic groups are inferior to the functional groups in terms of Bender recall. Tolor's (1958) study yields an effect size of $-.59$ for the organic vs. schizophrenic comparison and -1.09 for the organic vs. character-behavior disorder comparison. The organic vs. functional differences and the effect sizes for Tolor's study were no doubt reduced because he matched his subjects on WAIS IQ which would result in a spuriously low estimate of Bender recall effectiveness as a screening measure (Heaton et al., 1978). Holland and Wadsworth's (1979) paper produces a -1.54 effect size for the organic versus schizophrenic comparison on recall and an effect size of -1.77 based upon recall from the Background Interference Procedure. Even Olin and Reznikoff's (1958) means and standard deviations for Total Recall result in effect sizes of $-.32$ for the organic versus schizophrenic comparison and -1.36 when the organic group was compared with a group of nurses. A reading of Cohen (1977) permits the conclusion that the effect sizes of Bender recall studies are quite promising in view of the primitive controls that many of these studies had. Cohen (1977) indicated that when better experimental designs are developed, random variation is reduced and effect size increases. The effect sizes reported here suggest that further research on Bender recall as a screening measure for organicity is in order.

Holland and Wadsworth (1979) recently reported that Bender recall, as well as Bender recall obtained after the administration of Canter's Background Interference Procedure, discriminated significantly between schizophrenic and brain damaged groups. They also found that the recall procedures discriminated between the two groups independently of IQ whereas the Background Interference Procedure did not. Thus, Holland and Wadsworth provide another type of evidence indicating that additional research on Bender recall as a screening measure for brain damage is in order because Bender recall appears to be superior to the copy performance as a screening measure for organicity. Similarly, Lyle and Quast (1976) found that Bender recall discriminated significantly between the disease free, impaired, and premorbid status of descendants of Huntington's disease victims, while global evaluations of Bender protocols by experienced clinicians did not.

Relationships Between Bender Recall and Personality Variables

Little additional research has been reported on the relationship between Bender recall and personality variables since Billingslea's (1963) review of the area. A number of early studies attempted to determine if there were differences in the number of Bender designs recalled by groups of "normals," and groups of patients carrying functional diagnoses. One of the best of these early research efforts was conducted by Gobetz (1953) who compared the recall performance of a group of 108 neurotic, white, male, World War II veterans who were in treatment at a Veterans Administration mental hygiene clinic and 285 control subjects who were white, male, World War II veterans with no known psychiatric problems availing themselves of aptitude testing under the GI Bill. The diagnoses of the neurotic subjects were based upon the judgments of one or more staff psychiatrists who utilized case histories, clinical interviews, and an extensive battery of psychological tests to arrive at a dignosis. The Bender Gestalt was not utilized in establishing a patient's diagnosis, although it was administered with the other tests. Gobetz failed to report whether the differences between the two groups on age, education, and marital status were statistically significant, although relevant descriptive statistics were provided. The difference in the number of Bender designs recalled by the two groups was not statistically significant. Further, Gobetz found only six qualitative signs that were capable of discriminating between the neurotic and control groups, and these failed to hold up under cross validation.

Levine and Feirstein (1972) reported that there was not a significant difference between a group of medical patients and a group of schizophrenic patients on Bender recall. The schizophrenic patients were selected on the basis of "unequivocal diagnosis" and the medical patients all had "uncomplicated medical problems'' and no history of psychopathology. There were no significant differences between the groups on age, education, IQ, and length of hospitalization. In a brief communication, Hanvik (1951) reported that Bender recall did not differentiate patients with funcational complaints of backache from patients with backache from surgically verified herniated disks. Hanvik did not report whether age, education, and IQ were controlled for in this study. Niebuhr and Cohen (1956) evaluated the Bender recall performance of groups of student nurses, acute schizophrenics, and chronic schizophrenics. The diagnostic procedures used to categorize the patients were not described. The authors attempted to control for intelligence but did not relate the method that they used to do so. No effort was made to control for age. In this study, each of the Bender designs was exposed for ten seconds, and the subject was then asked to draw the designs from memory. Bender recall was scored on the basis of ratings of the quality of reproductions. The group of student nurses had significantly better Bender recall than the group of chronic schizophrenics but not the group of acute schizophrenics. Stewart and Cunningham (1958) found that a group of academically superior student nurses had significantly better Bender recall than groups of female state hospital patients classified as Psychotic and nonpsychotic by criteria that were not reported. However, there were no controls for age, education, IQ, or socioeconomic status. Olin and Reznikoff(1957) compared the Bender recall performance of a group of student nurses and a group of hospitalized schizophrenics. The diagnostic criteria used to identify the schizophrenics were not reported, and the groups were not equated on age and IQ. Not surprisingly, the student nurses had significantly better recall than the schizophrenics.

Overall, there is no convincing evidence that Bender recall varies significantly between ''normal'' and functional groups. Those studies that report such differences tend to be poorly controlled and the differences that are found tend to disappear when minimal (Gobetz, 1953) or appropriate controls are imposed (Levine & Feirstein, 1972).

Several studies have explored whether Bander recall would differentiate between groups of patients with different functional disorders. Tolor (1958) found that Bender recall did not vary sinificantly between a group of schizophrenics and a group composed of parients diagnosed as having character and behavior disorders. Tolor's groups were matched on age and intelligence. Bernstein (1963) compared the Bender recall of a schizophrenic group and a nonschizophrenic group that was composed mainly of personality and character disorders. All of the subjects were drawn from the acute wards of public psychiatric hospitals and the groups were matched on age, schooling, sex, and intelligence. In this study, each Bender design was presented for five seconds, and then the subject was asked to draw the design from memory. There was a significant difference between the groups, with the nonschizophrenic group having better recall than the schizophrenic group. Armstrong (1963, 1965) reported two studies which lacked appropriate controls for age, intelligence, and chronicity. Armstrong (1965) failed to find any significant differences in the number of Bender designs recalled by schizophrenic, depressive, neurotic, and character disorder groups. Armstrong (1963) reported that a small group of "functionally psychotic" patients did not differ from a small group of nonpsychotic patients in the number of Bender designs recalled. In neither of her studies did Armstrong specify the diagnostic criteria that were utilized. The literature that has explored whether Bender recall varies as a function of diagnosis for functional groups is flawed by a number of inadequacies. Two of the more salient deficiencies are the lack of operationalized criteria for making the diagnoses on which group assignments are based and a total failure to consider the influence of psychotropic medications on Bender recall performance.

Surprisingly, the more fruitful question of how personality characteristics (e.g., depression and anxiety) as measured by standard methods of assessment (e.g., the MMPI) influence Benter recall has received little attention. Spielberger, Goodstein, and Dahlstrom (1958) contributed the only meaningful study in this area. They compared the recall performance of undergraduate volunteers who scored low and high on the Taylor Manifest Anxiety Scale (TMAS). They presented the Bender designs in an order that had been empirically determined to maximize the range of task difficulty. The recall of specific designs was also empirically categorized as being hard, medium, or easy. Presentation of the designs was followed by a six-minute exposure to an unrelated task. There was a significant interaction between design difficulty and level of anxiety as measured by the TMAS. Subjects who scored low on the TMAS recalled more hard Bender designs than the high scorers on the TMAS, while the high scorers on the TMAS recalled more easy designs. However, only performance on recall of the hard designs was actually significantly different. Recall of the designs of medium difficulty did not vary significantly between the two groups. There was no significant difference between the two groups in the total number of designs recalled. The results were interpreted as being consistent with Hullian learning theory. The hard designs were conceptualized as producing more competing responses which was regarded as being detrimental to the group scoring high on TMAS (high drive) and as beneficial to the group scoring low on the TMAS (low drive). The experiment by Spielberger, Goodstein, and Dahlstrom (1958) demonstrates that personality variables may influence Bender recall and suggests that studies of how such personality variables (e.g., Depression, Psychasthenia, Welsh's Anxiety Scale on the MMPI) influence Bender recall are appropriate and indicated in those settings where Bender recall is used clinically.

THE RELATIONSHIP OF BENDER RECALL TO OTHER VARIABLES

Several studies have reported moderate correlations between Bender recall and the Wechsler Scales. Tolor (1956) found an overall significant correlation of .50 between the Wechsler-Bellevue Form I and Bender recall for his organic, convulsive, and psychogenic patients as a group. This combined group of patients had IQs ranging from 54–136. Inglis, Shapiro, and Post (1956) reported a significant correlation of .69 between Bender recall and a prorated Wechsler-Bellevue Form I. IQ for a group of elderly functional patients, and a significant correlation of .87 for a group of elderly organic patients. The prorated Wechsler IQ was calculated from the Vocabulary, Picture Completion, and Block Design subtests. The recall scores were derived from a "slightly modified" form of the Bender-Gestalt Test. The functional group had an average age of 66.9 (SD = 5.6), and the average age of the organic group was 69.7 (SD = 8.65). Armstrong (1965) reported a correlation for all of her psychiatric and organic subjects of −.48 between WAIS Full Scale IQ and her revised scoring system which yields an error score (i.e., high IQs were associated with low error scores and low IQs with high error scores). For 65 patients referred for the evaluation of possible intellectual deficits, Rogers and Swenson (1975) reported a correlation of .63 for Bender recall and the WAIS Verbal Scale Score totals and .63 with WAIS Performance Scale Score totals. Armentrout (1976) studied the relationship between Bender recall and WAIS scores for 111 vocational rehabilitation clients. He found a correlation of .34 with Verbal IQ, .52 with Performance IQ, and .44 with Full Scale IQ. The correlations between Bender recall and Performance IQ and between Bender recall and Verbal IQ did not differ significantly.

Aaronson, Nelson, and Holt (1953) failed to find significant relationships between Bender recall and either Shipley-Hartford Mental Age or the Shipley-Hartford Conceptual Quotient. However, Peek and Olson (1955) found a significant correlation between Bender recall and the Conceptual Quotient (.34) in a group of state hospital inpatients. They also reported a correlation of .19 between Shipley-Hartford raw scores and Bender recall. Aaronson (1957) reported a correlation of .46 between Bender recall and Porteus Maze Test Quotient. His subjects were spileptics with Porteus Maze Test Quotients ranging from 20 to 123 with a mean of 72.9.

A review of all of these correlations leads to the general impression that Bender recall is moderately related to intelligence. More systematic research needs to be conducted to clearly establish the number of Bender designs that may reasonably be expected to be recalled at different levels of intelligence.

Rogers and Swenson (1975) investigated the relationship between Bender recall and the Wechsler Memory Scale. Bender recall correlated .73 with Wechsler Memory Scale Visual Reproduction scores. They reported that Bender recall correlated signficantly higher with a factor of the Wechsler Memory Scale considered to reflect memory (.76) than a factor reflecting freedom from distractability (.40). The overall correlation on Bender recall with the Wechsler Memory Scale total was .74. The final conclusion of Rogers and Swenson was the Bender recall is a valid measure of memory. The high correlation of Bender recall with the visual memory portion of the Wechsler Memory Scale supports the inference that Bender recall provides a valid measure of immediate visual memory.

Age-related norms are not available for Bender recall (Rogers & Swenson, 1975). However, several studies have reported correlations between age and Bender recall. Aaronson (1957) reported a nonsignificant correlation of −.13 between Bender recall and age in a sample of epileptic subjects ranging in age from 12–72. Reznikoff and Olin (1957) also failed to find significant relationships between Bender recall and age for a group of organics (−.07) and a group of schizophrenics (−.04). Both groups had an age range of 18–49. Armstrong (1963) reported significant negative correlations of −.34 and −.48 between age and the number of Bender designs recalled for two mixed groups of psychiatric and organic patients. The first group had a mean age of 37.6 and a standard deviation of 14.67, and the second group had a mean age of 39 and a standard deviation of 16.87. For another mixed group of psychiatric and organic patients, Armstrong (1965) reported a correlation of .49 between age and a recall error score. The positive direction of the correlation indicates that older subjects had poorer recall. The contradictions in these correlations and the lack of clear information about the samples from which they were drawn made it apparent that the effects of aging on Bender recall have yet to be clearly established. Similarly, there is no worthwhile information on the effects of education and sex on Bender recall.

The available data on the relationship of Bender recall scores to daily behaviors are quite limited. However, correlational data have been published on the relationship of Bender recall to several dimensions reflecting the daily behaviors of elderly, hospitalized psychiatric patients. Inglis *et al* (1956) reported data for a sample of 61 functional and 17 organic patients. For the functionals, Bender recall correlated .38 with memory for remote personal events, .35 with memory for recent general events, .57 with memory for time and routine, and .52 with orientation on the ward. All of these correlations are significant. For the organics, the correlations were respectively .80, .73, .67, and .73. All of these correlations are significant.

Further research on how Bender recall relates to human functioning and significant behaviors is needed. Promising examples exist. Gilberstadt (1968) found that Bender recall was significantly related to social functioning at two-year follow-up in a sample of 101 elderly veterans. Gilberstadt also reported that recall scores of 1 or 0 were obtained from 67% of the subjects who died within two years of testing.

The literature on Bender recall reflects the era in which the majority of studies were conducted. Since most of the studies were completed in the early 1950s and 1960s, they often lack the methodological sophistication that would be expected today. The literature to date has failed to establish how age, education, and sex affect Bender recall. The number of Bender designs that should be recalled at different levels of intelligence remains to be empirically established. A review of the literature reveals that surprisingly little is known about the relationship of Bender recall to personality variables. The impact of personality variables on the number of Bender designs recalled would appear to be a fruitful area for further research. The inconsistent and frequently negative findings reported to date suggest that further research on whether Bender recall varies significantly by functional diagnosis holds little promise of producing significant or particularly meaningful results. In spite of the many weaknesses in the literature on Bender recall, the procedure does have promise as a screening measure for brain damage and for identifying deficits in immediate visual memory. The general consistency and convergent validation inherent in the comparisons of "organic groups" with other groups of subjects is impressive. This conclusion is bolstered by the more recent findings of Holland and Wadsworth (1979) and Lyle and Quast (1976). Clearly the studies reported to date suggest that further research on how specific forms of cerebral dysfunction affect Bender recall would be worthwhile.

In the majority of studies on Bender recall there are methodological problems which cast doubt on the conclusions drawn from the group comparisons in any single study. Nevertheless, many of the early studies provide worthwhile normative data on particular groups of subjects.

The normative data which have been summarized here should be of considerable assistance to researchers and clinicians seeking appropriate norms against which to compare the performance of individual clients and groups. The popularity of the Bender-Gestalt Test, the relative ease with which Bender recall scores can be obtained, and the overwhelming consistency of normative data which different investigators have obtained for particular diagnostic groups all suggest that further research on Bender recall is in order, and that it might have a particularly strong impact since many clinicians apparently use the procedure for assessing visual memory (Schulberg & Tolor, 1961; Lezak, 1976.) It is also important to note that the effectiveness of Bender recall as either a measure of visual memory or as a screening measure for organicity has not been experimentally evaluated in comparison with other measures of immediate visual memory.

ACKNOWLEDGMENTS

Supported in part by Grants AI-15392 and HL-22065 from the National Institutes of Health.

REFERENCES

Aaronson, B. S. The Porteus Mazes and Bender Gestalt recall. *Journal of Clinical Psychology,* 1957, *13,* 186–187.

Aaronson, B. S., Nelson, S. E., & Holt, S. On the relation between Bender Gestalt recall and Shipley-Hartford scores. *Journal of Clinical Psychology,* 1953, *9,* 88.

Armstrong, R. G. Recall patterns on the Bender-Gestalt: A re-evaluation. *Journal of Projective Techniques and Personality Assessment,* 1963, *27,* 418–422.

Armentrout, J. A. Bender-Gestalt recall: Memory measure or intelligence estimate? *Journal of Clinical Psychology*, 1976, *32*, 832–834.

Armstrong, R. G. A re-evaluation of copies and recalled Bender-Gestalt reproductions. *Journal of Projective Techniques and Personality Assessment*, 1965, *29*, 134–139.

Armstrong, R. G. The Bender-Gestalt: A replication of comparisons of recalled reproductions and an investigation of effects of varying instructions. *Newsletter for Research in Psychology*, 1969, *11*, 39.

Bender, L. A visual motor gestalt test and its clinical use. *American Orthopsychiatric Association Research Monographs*, 1938, No. 3.

Bernstein, I. H. A comparison of schizophrenics and nonschizophrenics on two methods of administration of the Bender-Gestalt Test. *Perceptual and Motor Skills*, 1963, *16*, 757–763.

Billingslea, F. Y. The Bender Gestalt: A review and perspective. *Psychological Bulletin*, 1963, *60*, 233–251.

Cohen, J. *Statistical power analysis for the behavioral sciences* (Rev. ed.). New York: Academic Press, 1977.

Craik, F. I. Age differences in human memory. In J. Birren & K. Schaie (eds.), *Handbook of the psychology of aging*. New York: Van Nostrand Reinhold, 1977.

Erickson, R. C., & Scott, M. L. Clinical memory testing: A review. *Psychological Bulletin*, 1977, *84*, 1130–1149.

Freed, E. X. Comparison on admission and discharge of Bender-Gestalt performance by hospitalized psychiatric patients. *Perceptual and Motor Skills*, 1966, *23*, 919–922.

Gilberstadt, H. Relationships among scores of tests suitable for the assessment of adjustment and intellectual functioning. *Journal of Gerontology*, 1968, *23*, 483–487.

Gilberstadt, H. Detection of organicity with a Bender recall sign. *Newsletter for Research in Psychology*, 1970, *12*, 58–61.

Glanzer, M., & Clark, E. O. Cerebral mechanisms of information storage: The problem of memory. In M. S. Gazzaniga (Ed.), *Handbook of behavioral neurobiology* (Vol. 2: *Neuropsychology*). New York: Plenum Press, 1979.

Gobetz, W. A quantification, standardization, and validation of the Bender-Gestalt test on normal and neurotic adults. *Psychological Monographs*, 1953, *67* (6, Whole No. 356).

Goldstein, N. P., Ewert, J. C., Randall, R. V., & Gross, J. B. Psychiatric aspects of Wilson's Disease (Hepatolenticular Degeneration): Results of psychometric tests during long-term therapy. *American Journal of Psychiatry*, 1968, *124*, 1555–1561.

Goodstein, L. D., Spielberger, C. D., Williams, J. E., & Dahlstrom, W. G. The effect of serial position and design difficulty on recall of the Bender-Gestalt test designs. *Journal of Consulting Psychology*, 1955, *19*, 230–234.

Hanvik, L. J. A note on the limitations of the use of the Bender-Gestalt test as a diagnostic aid in patients with a functional complaint. *Journal of Clinical Psychology*, 7, 1951, 194.

Hanvik, L. J., & Andersen, A. L. The effects of focal brain lesions on recall and on the production of rotations in the Bender Gestalt test. *Journal of Consulting Psychology*, 1950, *14*, 197–198.

Heaton, R. K., Baade, L. E., & Johnson, K. L. Neuropsychological test results associated with psychiatric disorders in adults. *Psychological Bulletin*, 1978, *85*, 141–162.

Holland, T. R., & Wadsworth, H. M. Comparison and combination of recall and Background Interference Procedures for the Bender Gestalt Test with brain-damaged and schizophrenic patients. *Journal of Personality Assessment*, 1979, *43*, 123–127.

Inglis, J., Shapiro, M. B., & Post, F. "Memory function" in psychiatric patients over sixty, the role of memory in tests discriminating between "functional" and "organic" groups. *Journal of Mental Science*, 1956, *102*, 589–598.

Jacobs, E. A., Winter, P. M. Alvis, H. J., & Small, S. M. Hyperoxygenation effect on cognitive functioning in the aged, *New England Journal of Medicine*, 1969, *281*, 753–757.

Klopfer, W. G., & Taulbee, E. S. Projective tests. *Annual Review of Psychology*, 1976, *27*, 543–567.

Kulik, J. A., Kulik, C.-L. C., & Cohen, P. A. A meta-analysis of outcome studies of Keller's personalized system of instruction. *American Psychologist,* 1979, *34,* 307–318.

Levine, J., & Feirstein, A. Differences in test performance between brain damaged, schizophrenic, and medical patients. *Journal of Consulting and Clinical Psychology,* 1972, *39,* 508–511.

Lezak, M. D. *Neuropsychological assessment.* New York: Oxford University Press, 1976.

Lubin, B., Walls, R., & Paine, C. Patterns of psychological test usage in the United States: 1935–1969. *Professional Psychology* 1971, *2,* 70–74.

Lyle, O., & Quast, W. The Bender Gestalt: Use of clinical judgment versus recall scores in prediction of Huntington's disease. *Journal of Consulting and Clinical Psychology,* 1976, *44,* 229–232.

Niebuhr, H., & Cohen, D. The effect of psychopathology on visual discrimination. *Journal of Abnormal and Social Psychology,* 1956, *53,* 173–177.

Olin, T. D., & Reznikoff, M. Quantification of the Bender-Gestalt recall: A pilot study. *Journal of Projective Techniques,* 1957, *21,* 265–277.

Olin, R. D., & Reznikoff, M. A comparison of copies and recalled reproductions of the Bender-Gestalt designs. *Journal of Projective Techniques,* 1958, *22,* 320–327.

Peek, R. M., & Olson, G. W. The Bender Gestalt recall as an index of intellectual functioning. *Journal of Clinical Psychology,* 1955, *11,* 185–188.

Reznikoff, M., & Olin, T. D. Recall of the Bender-Gestalt designs by organic and schizophrenic patients: A comparative study. *Journal of Clinical Psychology,* 1957, *13,* 183–186.

Rogers, D. L., & Swenson, W. M. Bender-Gestalt recall as a measure of memory versus distractability. *Perceptual and Motor Skills,* 1975, *40,* 919–922.

Russell, E. W. A multiple scoring method for the assessment of complex memory functions. *Journal of Consulting and Clinical Psychology,* 1975, *43,* 800–809.

Russell, E. W. The pathology and clinical examination of memory. In S. Filskov & T. Boll (Eds.), *Handbook of clinical neuropsychology.* New York: Wiley, 1980.

Schraa, J. C., Dirks, J. F., Jones, N. F., & Kinsman, R. A. Bender-Gestalt performance and recall in an asthmatic sample. *Journal Asthma,* 1981, *18,* 7–9.

Schulberg, H. C., & Tolor, A. The use of the Bender-Gestalt in clinical practice. *Journal of Projective Techniques,* 1961, *25,* 345–351.

Schwartz, M. L., & Dennerll, R. D. Immediate visual memory as a function of epileptic seizure type. *Cortex,* 1969, *5,* 69–74.

Smith, M. L., & Glass, G. V. Meta-analysis of psychotherapy outcome studies. *American Psychologist,* 1977, *32,* 752–760.

Spielberger, C. D., Goodstein, L. D., & Dahlstrom, W. G. Complex incidental learning as a function of anxiety and task difficulty. *Journal of Experimental Psychology,* 1958, *56,* 58–61.

Stewart, H. F. A note on recall patterns using the Bender Gestalt with psychotic and non-psychotic patients. *Journal of Clinical Psychology,* 1957, *13,* 95–97.

Stewart, H., & Cunningham, S. A note on scoring recalled figures of the Bender Gestalt test using psychotics, non-psychotics and controls. *Journal of Clinical Psychology,* 1958, *14,* 207–208.

Tolor, A. A comparison of the Bender-Gestalt test and the Digit Span test as measures of recall. *Journal of Consulting Psychology,* 1956, *20,* 305–309.

Tolor, A. Further studies on the Bender-Gestalt test and the Digit Span test as measures of recall. *Journal of Clinical Psychology,* 1958, *14,* 14–18.

Tolor, A., & Schulberg, H. C. *An evaluation of the Bender-Gestalt test.* Springfield, Illinois: Charles C. Thomas, 1963.

Tversky, A., & Kahneman, D. Belief in the law of small numbers. *Psychological Bulletin,* 1971, *76,* 105–110.

Weiss, A. A. Reproduction from memory and frequency of recall of Bender-Gestalt figures in non-clinical subjects of different ages. *The Israel Annals of Psychiatry and Related Disciplines,* 1970, *8,* 143–145.

7 Assessment of Anger: The State-Trait Anger Scale

C. D. Spielberger, G. Jacobs, S. Russell, and R. S. Crane
University of South Florida, Tampa

INTRODUCTION

Anger, hostility and aggression are central concepts of many theories of personality. In psychopathology, the maladaptive effects of anger are traditionally emphasized as important in the etiology of psychoneurosis, depression, and schizophrenia. Recent research findings also suggest that anger and hostility contribute to the pathogenesis of hypertension (e.g., Crane, 1981; Harburg, Erfurt, Hauenstein, Chape, Schull, & Schork, 1973), coronary heart disease (Friedman & Rosenman, 1974; Matthews, Glass, Rosenman, & Bortner, 1977; Spielberger & London, 1982), and cancer (Greer & Morris, 1975).

Although much has been written about the negative impact of anger and hostility on physical and psychological well-being, definitions of these constructs are ambiguous and sometimes contradictory. Moreover, anger, hostility and aggression are often used interchangeably in the research literature, and this conceptual confusion is reflected in a diversity of measurement operations of questionable validity (Biaggio, Supplee, & Curtis, 1981).

The major goal of this chapter is to describe the development and validation of a new psychometric instrument for the assessment of anger, the *State-Trait*

[1]The research reported in this chapter was supported, in part, by grants from the Advanced Research Projects Agency, United States Department of Defense (MDA903-77-0190) and R. J. Reynolds, Inc. We would like to express our appreciation to Dr. Harold F. O'Neil, Jr., of ARPA, and to H. C. Roemer, Esquire, Senior Vice President and General Counsel of R. J. Reynolds, Inc., for their encouragement and support of this work.

Anger Scale. The chapter is organized into four sections. Definitions and concepts of anger, hostility and aggression are examined in the first section. In Section II, a number of psychological measures of hostility and anger are briefly reviewed and evaluated. The construction and the psychometric properties of the *State-Trait Anger Scale (STAS)* are described in Section III. Research findings based on efforts to validate the *STAS* are reported in the final section.

I. ANGER, HOSTILITY AND AGGRESSION: CONCEPTS AND DEFINITIONS

Anger is generally considered to be a simpler concept than hostility or aggression. The concept of anger usually refers to an emotional state that consists of feelings that vary in intensity, from mild irritation or annoyance to fury and rage. Although hostility usually involves angry feelings, this concept has the connotation of a complex set of attitudes that motivate aggressive behaviors directed toward destroying objects or injuring other people.

While anger and hostility refer to feelings and attitudes, the concept of aggression generally implies destructive or punitive behavior directed towards other persons or objects. It should be noted, however, that aggression and hostility are often used interchangeably. A useful convention for distinguishing between these concepts is the distinction between hostile and instrumental aggression. Whereas hostile aggression refers to behavior motivated by anger, instrumental aggression refers to aggressive behavior directed toward removing or circumventing an obstacle that stands between an aggressor and a goal, when such behavior is not motivated by angry feelings.

The physiological correlates of anger and hostility, and the behavioral manifestations of aggression have been investigated in numerous studies. In contrast, anger, that is, the phenomenological experience of angry feelings, has been largely neglected in psychological research. Moreover, most psychometric measures of hostility confound angry feelings with the mode and direction of the expression of anger.

An important limitation in research on the measurement of anger and hostility is that the state-trait distinction has typically not been taken into account. First introduced by Cattell and Scheier (1961), this distinction has proved especially useful in anxiety research (Spielberger, 1966, 1972). Applying the state-trait distinction to research on anger and hostility requires clarification of whether these constructs refer to transitory emotional states and/or relatively stable individual differences in personality traits. The utility of the state-trait distinction for research on anger and hostility is further considered after briefly reviewing and evaluating a number of psychometric measures that have been developed to assess these concepts.

II. ASSESSMENT OF ANGER AND HOSTILITY

The earliest attempts to assess anger and hostility were based on clinical interviews, behavioral observations and projective techniques. Although interviews and behavioral rating scales can be flexibly structured to facilitate gathering relevant information, the interview method is highly dependent on the skills and training of the interviewer and the responsiveness of the subject. Research findings based on interviews are also highly vulnerable to subjective interpretation (Morris, 1976; Wiggins, 1973). Behavioral rating scales provide a potentially more objective systematic means for encoding and quantifying information, but distortions due to halo effects, and leniency and proximity errors, are difficult to control in such ratings (Wiggins, 1973).

During the 1950's and 1960's, projective techniques were widely employed in the assessment of hostility and aggression. The *Rorschach Inkblot Tests* (Rorschach, 1921) and the *Thematic Apperception Test (TAT)* (Murray, 1943) are the projective measures most widely used for this purpose. Formal scoring of the Rorschach has not yielded measures that are consistently related to aggression, but scores of hostility content (e.g., De Vos, 1952) have been shown to be related to aggressive behavior in both assaultive and psychiatric populations (Buss, 1961). Although the *Rorschach* and *TAT* have shown some promise in distinguishing between extremely violent and nonaggressive groups, there are several major problems associated with their use in measuring anger, hostility and aggression. Administration is time consuming, scoring systems are often complex and influenced by subjectivity, reliability is low, and there is only limited evidence of the validity of these projective tests (Anastasi, 1982; Buss, 1961).

The Rosenzweig (1945) *Picture-Frustration Study (P-F Study)* is a semiprojective technique developed specifically for the measurement of hostility and aggression. Conceptually derived from frustration-aggression theory, the *P-F Study* was designed to assess characteristic reactions to frustrating everyday interpersonal situations. Responses to 24 cartoon-like pictures that represent a variety of frustrating interpersonal situations are scored for direction and type of aggression. While some evidence of the validity of the *P-F Study* has been reported in studies with delinquent populations (Kaswan, Wasman, & Freedman, 1960; Rosenzweig, 1963) and psychosomatic patients (Guyotat & Guillaumin, 1960), this instrument is difficult to score and has been used only sparingly in research over the past two decades.

MMPI Measures of Hostility

Several self-report scales for measuring hostility have been derived from the *Minnesota Multiphasic Personality Inventory (MMPI)*. The *Iowa Hostility In-*

ventory (IHI) (Moldawsky, 1953) was constructed on the basis of psychologists' intuitive judgments about the content reflected in *MMPI* items. A similar rational strategy was employed by Cook and Medley (1954) in developing the Hostility *(Ho)* scale. A third rationally-derived *MMPI* hostility measure, the *Manifest Hostility Scale (MHS)* (Siegel, 1956) consists of items judged by clinicians to reflect manifest hostility, as defined in a 1947 Veterans Administration technical bulletin on psychiatric nomenclature.

All three scales were developed in the early 1950's, but have been used only rarely over the past 20 years. Buss, Durkee and Baer (1956) investigated the psychometric properties of the *IHI* and concluded that clinical evaluations were more useful in the assessment of hostility. The *Ho* scale has adequate stability as reflected in a test-retest correlation of .86 (Cook & Medley, 1954), but relatively little information is available on the psychometric properties and validity of this measure (Youseff, 1968). While Hokanson and Gordon (1958) and Berkowitz (1960) found some evidence of the validity of the *MHS,* other investigators have reported contradictory findings (e.g., Johnson, 1973; Shipman & Marquette, 1963).

Schultz (1954) used an empirical strategy to derive separate measures of overt hostility and hostility control. Ratings of Veterans Administration patients and University Counseling Center clients were obtained in order to identify individuals at the extremes of a dimension of overt hostility. Through item analyses of the patients' *MMPI* records, 14 items were selected for the *Overt Hostility (Hv)* scale. Schultz found a correlation of .38 between scores on the *Hv* scale and therapist ratings on the frequency of expression of overt hostility for a sample of University Counseling Center clients, but little additional research has been reported for this scale.

The *Hostility and Direction of Hostility Questionnaire (HDHQ)* is perhaps the best known MMPI-derived hostility measure (Foulds, Caine, & Creasy, 1960). Based on Foulds' conception of hostility as a unitary entity that can be directed inward toward the self (intropunitiveness) or outward against other people or objects (extrapunitiveness), the *HDHQ* is scored for total hostility and direction of hostility. In addition, Acting-out Hostility (AH), Criticism of Others (CO), and Projected and Delusional Hostility (PH) subscales measure extrapunitiveness, and Self-criticism (SC) and Guilt (G) scales measure intropunitiveness. Test-retest reliability coefficients of .73 for the total hostility score and .51 for the direction of hostility score have been reported for normals (Caine, Foulds, & Hope, 1967).

The *HDHQ* has been used with neurotics (Caine, 1965) and depressives (Foulds, 1965; Mayo, 1967), who showed a decrease in *HDHQ* general hostility and intropunitiveness scores with therapy. Psychiatric patients, medical and surgical patients, and suicidal patients were found to differ in terms of their *HDHQ* scores (Vinoda, 1966). Cockett (1970) and Crawford (1977) found no association between *HDHQ* hostility scores and total criminality or institutional misbehavior for a sample of criminals, which led them to question the validity of the instrument. Since the *HDHQ* was validated with psychiatric patients as criterion groups, its validity may be restricted to this type of population. On the basis of a comprehensive review of research with the *HDHQ*, Philip (1969) concluded that the research findings were inconsistent, and that the scale required revision and the collection of more normative data.

The Buss-Durkee Hostility Inventory (BDHI)

A combined rational-empirical strategy was employed in developing the *BDHI* (Buss & Durkee, 1957), which is generally regarded as the most carefully constructed psychometric measure of hostility. Buss (1961) conceptualized hostility as a multidimensional concept and developed the *BDHI* to assess the following seven subclasses:

1. Assault—physical violence against others;
2. Indirect—roundabout and undirected aggression;
3. Irritability—readiness to explode with negative affect at the slightest provocation;
4. Negativism—oppositional behavior, usually directed against authority;
5. Resentment—jealousy and hatred of others;
6. Suspicion—projection of hostility onto others;
7. Verbal—negative affect expressed in both the style and content of speech.

In addition, the *BDHI* includes a Guilt subscale to assess feelings of having done wrong and suffering pangs of conscience.

Using the above definitions of guilt and the seven subclasses of hostility, a preliminary set of 105 items was rationally selected for the first version of the *BDHI*. The items were administered to samples of college students; those items were retained that met specified frequency criteria and correlated .40 or higher with the subscale for which the items were rationally selected. After eliminating 45 items that failed to meet these criteria and writing a number of new items, a revised 94-item *BDHI* was administered to another sample of college students. Further item analyses were employed to select the final set of 75 items, which included 66 hostility and 9 guilt items.

Test-retest stability was relatively high ($r = .82$) for the Total Hostility score which is obtained by summing the scores for the seven hostility subscales, and moderate for the *BDHI* subscales ($r = .46$ to .78). Intercorrelations among the *BDHI* subscales range from $-.07$ to .58. Evidence of the validity of the *BDHI* has been reported in studies of the perception of violence (Petzel & Michaels, 1973), the effects of smoking deprivation on hostility and aggression (Schechter & Rand, 1974), and aggressive behavior as reflected in the administration of shock (Knott, 1970). The *BDHI* has also proved useful in the assessment of hostility in male psychiatric patients (Young, 1976), and in violent and non-violent chronic alcohol abusers (Renson, Adams, & Tinklenberg, 1978). Extensive normative data are available for the *BDHI* for college students and psychiatric populations.

The factorial validity of the *BDHI* subscales was investigated in two studies in which the responses of college students to individual *BDHI* items were factored. In contrast to the seven clearly defined subcategories of hostility on the basis of which Buss and Durkee rationally selected their items, Bendig (1962) identified only two major factors, which he labeled overt and covert hostility. Russell (1981) also factor-analyzed responses to individual *BDHI* items, identifying three meaningful factors which were invariant for both sexes on the basis of the factor loadings of marker variables that were included to provide independent measures of anger, hostility, anxiety and psychopathology. These factors were labeled: (1) Neuroticism; (2) General Hostility; and (3) Expression of Anger. Thus, although the *BDHI* items were carefully selected and retained only if each item correlated with its subscale score, factor analyses do not provide empirical support for the validity of the *BDHI* subscales as measures of the seven types of hostility originally postulated by Buss and Durkee (1957).

Psychometric Measures of Anger

The assessment of anger has received much less attention than the measurement of hostility, as was previously noted. Moreover, those measures that have been developed tend to confound anger and hostility as these constructs were defined in the preceeding section of this paper. Three instruments that purport to assess anger have been reported in the literature over the past decade. Each of these measures are briefly described; the three measures are then compared and evaluated.

Reaction Inventory (RI): The *RI* was developed by Evans and Stangeland (1971) to assess the extent to which specific stimulus situations evoke anger reactions. This inventory consists of 76 items that were selected by the authors on an intuitive basis. In responding to each item, subjects are instructed to report the amount of anger provoked by each situation by rating themselves on a five-point scale, from "not at all" to "very much." Item-total score correlations for four independent samples indicated reasonably good internal consistency.

Since the *RI* was developed primarily for use in clinical assessment (Biaggio, Supplee, & Curtis, 1981), its potential as a research instrument has not been extensively explored. In two samples, moderate positive correlations ($r = .52, .57$) were obtained between the *RI* "Degree of Anger" score and the Total score of the *BDHI*, providing evidence of the concurrent validity of the *RI*. On the basis of a factor analysis of the responses to individual *RI* items, the following ten factors were identified: (1) minor chance annoyances; (2) destructive people; (3) unnecessary delays; (4) inconsiderate people; (5) self-opinionated people; (6) frustration in business; (7) criticism; (8) major chance annoyances; (9) people being personal; and (10) authority. Evans and Stangeland (1971) concluded that the large number of factors identified in the *RI* demonstrated ". . . that there are numerous specific stimulus situations which produce anger and thus aggressive behavior.'' (p. 414)

Anger Self-Report (ASR): This 64-item questionnaire was developed by Zelin, Adler, and Myerson (1972) to assess angry feelings and the expression of anger. The *ASR* is comprised of the following seven subscales: "Awareness of Anger;'' three subscales for measuring the "Expression of Anger'' (General, Physical and Verbal); "Guilt;'' "Condemnation of Anger;'' and "Mistrust.''

Zelin et al. (1972) reported split-half reliabilities for psychiatric patients and college students that ranged from .64 to .82. They also found that the *ASR* scores of psychiatric patients correlated significantly with psychiatrists' ratings and that the "Awareness of Anger'' scores of college students correlated significantly with peer ratings of the extent that acquaintances "feel anger.'' Zelin et al. (1972) concluded that "the validities found herein support the value of utilizing the *ASR* in future studies of aggression, (p. 340) but this conclusion seems premature because the predictive and construct validity of the *ASR* has not been firmly established by the authors and the scale has been infrequently used by other investigators.

Anger Inventory (AI): The *AI* was developed by Novaco (1974) to assess the extent to which a broad range of situations provoke anger reactions. In its original form, the scale consisted of 90 statements, each describing potentially anger-provoking incidents. These incidents were derived in interviews with university students which focused on identifying specific events that made them angry. In responding to the *AI,* subjects are instructed to respond to each statement by indicating, on a five-point scale, from "not at all'' to "very much,'' the amount of anger the individual would have experienced if a particular incident actually occurred.

Novaco (1975) has reported high internal consistency for the original 90-item *AI* (Cronbach's alpha = .96), but the test-retest reliability for the 80-item revised form (Novaco, 1977) reported by Biaggio et al. (1981) was only .17. Furthermore, no significant correlations were found between *AI* scores and self-report ratings of anger in provocative imaginal and roleplay laboratory situations, nor with the number of anger-provoking incidents experienced during a two-week period.

In a series of recent studies, Biaggio (1980) and her colleagues (Biaggio et al., 1981) examined and compared the reliability, concurrent and predictive validity, and correlates of the *BDHI* and the three anger scales described above. Biaggio (1980) also reported the results of a factor analysis based on the total scores for the four measures and the 15 subscales of the *BDHI* and *ASR*. Although there were only 19 measures in the factor matrix, five factors were identified. The names given to these factors were: Willingness to experience and express anger; Overt anger expression; Resentment, mistrust and guilt; Anger-provoking incidents; and Negativism.

The *BDHI* and the *ASR* were factorially complex, with subscale loadings on four of the five factors. The fourth factor was defined entirely by the loadings of the total scores on the *RI* and *AI* scales; factor 5 was defined entirely by the *BDHI* Total and Negativism scores. Moreover, the eigenvalues for the fourth and fifth factors were less than 1.00, which raises questions about the legitimacy of the five-factor solution.

The measures of anger and hostility described above tend to confound the experience of anger with situational determinants of angry reactions. Furthermore, none of these scales explicitly takes the state-trait distinction into account. The *ASR* Awareness subscale comes closest to examining the extent to which subjects experience angry feelings, but does not assess the intensity of these feelings at a particular time. While a number of *BDHI* items implicitly assess individual differences in anger as a personality trait by inquiring about the *frequency* that anger is experienced (e.g., "I *sometimes* show my anger; "*Almost every week,* I see someone I dislike;" "I *never* get mad enough to throw things"), most *BDHI* items assess hostile attitudes, such as resentment, negativism and suspicion rather than feelings of anger.

On the basis of her review of the *RI, ASR, AI,* and *BDHI,* Biaggio (1980) concluded that evidence of the validity of these measures was both fragmentary and limited. It is also apparent that the phenomena assessed by the existing scales are heterogeneous and complex. A coherent theoretical framework that distinguishes between anger, hostility and aggression as psychological concepts and that takes the state-trait distinction into account is required in order to validate psychometric measures of these constructs.

III. CONSTRUCTION OF THE STATE-TRAIT ANGER SCALE

In examining the conceptual ambiguity with regard to anger, hostility and aggression as psychological constructs, we concluded that anger refers to phenomena that are both more fundamental and less complex than hostility and aggression. Anger can be readily conceptualized as an emotional state that varies in intensity and as a relatively stable personality trait. However, most of the available measures of anger tend to confound the experience of anger with aggressive behavior and anger-provoking situations: None of these measures takes the state-trait distinction into account. Therefore, we decided to construct a state-trait anger measure that was analogous in conception and similar in format to the *State-Trait Anxiety Inventory* (Spielberger, Gorsuch, & Lushene, 1970).

The first step in constructing a scale to measure state and trait anger was to formulate working definitions of these constructs. State anger (S-Anger) was defined as an emotional state or condition that consists of subjective feelings of tension, annoyance, irritation, fury and rage, with concomitant activation or arousal of the autonomic nervous system. We further assumed that S-Anger can vary in *intensity* and fluctuate over time as a function of perceived affronts or injustice, or frustration resulting from the blocking of goal-directed behavior.

Trait anger (T-Anger) was defined in terms of individual differences in the *frequency* that S-Anger was experienced over time. It was assumed that persons high in T-Anger were more likely to perceive a wide range of situations as anger-provoking (e.g., annoying, irritating, frustrating), and to respond to such situations with elevations in state anger. In addition to experiencing the arousal of S-Anger more often, persons high in T-Anger were expected to experience more intense elevations in S-Anger whenever annoying or frustrating conditions were encountered.

In order to relate our test construction efforts to previous research, we attempted to identify an underlying anger factor in the *BDHI,* which is widely regarded as the most carefully constructed and best validated instrument for measuring anger and hostility. The *BDHI* has also been used more often in research than any other psychometric measure of anger or hostility. If an anger factor could be identified in the *BDHI,* items with the strongest loadings on this factor could be revised in the state-trait format to provide a nucleus for developing a new psychometric measure of state and trait anger. A similar rational-empirical approach proved successful in extracting a general test anxiety factor from Sarason's (1972) *Test Anxiety Scale* (Spielberger, Gonzalez, Taylor, Algaze, & Anton, 1978); items with high loadings on this factor were rewritten to provide the nucleus for constructing the *Test Anxiety Inventory* (Spielberger, 1980), a situation-specific measure of test anxiety as a personality trait.

The *BDHI* was administered to 347 students enrolled in undergraduate psychology courses in the Spring of 1978 and the responses of these students were factored in separate analyses for males and females (Russell, 1981). The scree-breaks criterion suggested that six factors could be extracted. However, inspection of the six-, five- and four-factor solutions revealed that the resulting factors were either lacking in simple structure or psychological meaning, and/or were *not* invariant for males and females. Although three meaningful *BDHI* factors that were invariant for both sexes were identified, there was no underlying anger factor. Therefore, it was not possible to identify specific *BDHI* items that could be adapted for use in new scales for measuring state and trait anger.

Given the disappointing results in the factor analyses of the *BDHI* items, we proceeded to write new items that were consistent with our working definitions of anger as an emotional state and a personality trait. For the preliminary T-Anger scale, a pool of 22 items was assembled. Some of these items were adapted from the *BDHI* and other measures of anger and hostility, and a number of entirely new items were formulated.

The next step in scale construction was to administer the T-Anger items (e.g., "I am a hotheaded person;" "It makes me furious when I am criticized in front of others'') to a sample of 146 college students who were instructed to rate themselves according to "how you generally feel" on the following four-point scale: (1) Almost never; (2) Sometimes; (3) Often; (4) Almost always. The rating scale format and procedures were the same as those used with the *STAI* Trait Anxiety scale (Spielberger et al., 1970).

Alpha coefficients and Item-remainder correlations for the T-Anger items were computed separately for men and women, and correlations of each T-Anger item with measures of trait anxiety (Spielberger et al., 1970) and trait curiosity (Spielberger, Peters, & Frain, 1981) were determined for both sexes. The 15 items with the highest item-remainder correlations and with relatively low correlations with measures of anxiety and curiosity were selected for the T-Anger scale. The alpha coefficients for the 15 item T-Anger scale were .87 for both males and females, indicating an acceptable level of internal consistency.

In developing the State Anger (S-Anger) scale, *Roget's International Thesaurus* (1977) and several standard dictionaries were consulted to identify synonyms and idioms for describing anger. A pool of 20 items consistent with our working definition of anger as an emotional state was then generated. In responding to the S-Anger items (e.g., "I am furious;" "I feel angry"), the subjects were asked to report the *intensity* of their feelings "right now" by rating themselves on the following four-point scale: (1) Not at all; (2) Somewhat; (3) Moderately so; (4) Very much so. The instructions and the format for responding to the S-Anger items were the same as those employed by Spielberger et al. (1970) in the *STAI* State Anxiety scale.

The 20 preliminary S-Anger items were administered to 270 Navy recruits along with the 15 T-Anger items. Item-remainder correlations and alpha coefficients were computed separately for men and women for both scales. Correlations were also determined for each S-Anger item with measures of state anxiety and state curiosity, and for each T-Anger item with measures of trait anxiety and trait curiosity. The 15 S-Anger items with the highest item-remainder correlations and lowest correlations with anxiety and curiosity are reported in Table 7.1. The item-remainder correlations for the S-Anger scale were uniformly high for both sexes, except for one item ("I am resentful") for which the correlation was only .29 for females.

Item-remainder correlations and correlations of each T-Anger item with measures of trait anxiety and trait curiosity are reported in Table 7.2. Although these correlations were somewhat lower than for the S-Anger items, all of the item-remainder correlations were .35 or greater for both sexes. Moreover, it is interesting to note that the item-remainder correlations for the state and trait anger subscales were substantially higher than those obtained for the STAI S-Anxiety and T-Anxiety scales, even though much more extensive test-development work was carried out in selecting the anxiety items (Spielberger et al., 1970).

The correlations of individual S-Anger and T-Anger items with state and trait anxiety scores were substantially higher than anticipated, especially for the S-

TABLE 7.1
Item-Remainder Correlations for the 15-Item State Anger Scale and
Correlations of the S-Anger Items with the State Anxiety and
State Curiosity Scales

	Item-Remainder S-Anger		Item-Scale Correlation			
			S-Anxiety		S-Curiosity	
S-Anger Scale	M	F	M	F	M	F
1. I am mad	.79	.62	.51	.57	-.52	-.36
2. I feel angry	.76	.77	.55	.55	-.55	-.12
3. I am burned up	.71	.63	.45	.52	-.50	-.14
4. I feel irritated	.67	.71	.60	.57	-.54	-.05
5. I feel frustrated	.69	.71	.71	.64	-.53	-.19
6. I feel aggravated	.67	.66	.52	.65	-.40	-.16
7. I feel like I'm about to explode	.68	.67	.49	.62	-.44	-.09
8. I feel like banging on the table	.64	.76	.49	.50	-.38	-.26
9. I feel like yelling at somebody	.64	.80	.40	.54	-.33	-.27
10. I feel like swearing	.68	.51	.50	.40	-.42	.11
11. I am furious	.59	.65	.40	.45	-.33	-.23
12. I feel like hitting someone	.63	.54	.30	.27	-.33	-.11
13. I feel like breaking things	.56	.73	.30	.45	-.41	-.04
14. I am annoyed	.49	.70	.34	.47	-.35	-.28
15. I am resentful	.57	.29	.41	.29	-.47	-.26
Median Item-Correlation	.64	.67	.49	.52	-.42	-.16

Anger items. Moreover, the correlations of several S-Anger items (e.g., "I feel irritated;" "I feel frustrated") with S-Anxiety were approximately the same as the item-remainder correlations for these items. Similarly, a number of T-Anger items were moderately correlated with T-Anxiety. Given the content validity of the T-Anger items (e.g., "I feel irritated;" "I feel angry"), these findings suggested an intrinsic relationship between anger and anxiety that cannot readily be eliminated from psychometric measures of these constructs.

The means, standard deviations and alpha coefficients for the T-Anger scale for the original sample of college students is reported in Table 7.3. Similar data for the T-Anger and S-Anger scales of the Navy recruits are also reported in this table. In both groups, males scored slightly higher in T-Anger than the females. The male recruits also scored higher in S-Anger than the females. The alpha coefficients for the T-Anger scale were relatively high for both groups. For the recruits, the alpha coefficients for the S-Anger scale were even higher than for the T-Anger scale.

The internal consistency of the S-Anger scale is especially impressive when it is recalled that the items for this scale were generated entirely on the basis of their content validity. In addition to providing evidence of the utility of the

TABLE 7.2
Item-Remainder Correlations for the 15-Item Trait Anger Scale and
Correlations of the T-Anger Items with the Trait Anxiety and
Trait Curiosity Scales

| | | Item-Remainder T-Anger | | Item-Scale Correlation | | | |
| | | | | T-Anxiety | | T-Curiosity | |
T-Anger Scale		M	F	M	F	M	F
1.	I have a fiery temper	.62	.62	.38	.12	-.27	-.10
2.	I am quick-tempered	.65	.62	.37	.09	-.22	-.04
3.	I am a hotheaded person	.49	.62	.32	.24	-.34	-.25
4.	I get annoyed when I am singled out for correction	.64	.55	.30	.28	-.31	-.28
5.	It makes me furious when I am criticized in front of others	.36	.66	.15	.28	-.10	-.35
6.	I get angry when I'm slowed down by others mistakes	.56	.53	.15	.16	-.10	-.06
7.	I feel infuriated when I do a good job & get poor evaluation	.52	.54	-.07	.32	.12	-.03
8.	I fly off the handle	.42	.59	.22	.19	-.33	-.21
9.	I feel annoyed when I am not given recognition for doing good work	.54	.50	.14	.15	.04	-.10
10.	People who think they are always right irritate me	.53	.46	.15	.05	-.18	-.12
11.	When I get mad, I say nasty things	.45	.47	.22	.15	-.27	-.14
12.	I feel irritated	.40	.47	.38	.36	-.36	-.37
13.	I feel angry	.43	.44	.44	.33	-.28	-.41
14.	When I get frustrated, I feel like hitting someone	.58	.35	.30	.19	-.23	-.18
15.	It makes my blood boil when I am pressured	.48	.41	.16	.20	-.10	-.24
	Median Item-Correlation	.52	.50	.30	.19	-.23	-.21

working definition of S-Anger which guided the item-selection process, the high degree of internal consistency of the S-Anger scale also suggested that people are quite sensitive to experiences of anger as an emotional state, and are highly consistent in reporting the level of intensity of state anger at a particular time.

The high degree of internal consistency reflected in the item-remainder correlations and the alpha coefficients for both the S-Anger and T-Anger scales suggested that these constructs could be measured with fewer items. It was also considered highly desirable to construct measures of anger that were relatively independent of anxiety. Therefore, the psychometric characteristics of each S-Anger and T-Anger item were examined in order to identify those items with the highest item-remainder correlations and the lowest correlations with anxiety.

TABLE 7.3
Means, Standard Deviations and Alpha Coefficients for the
15-Item State-Trait Anger Scale

	Trait Anger		State Anger	
	Male	Female	Male	Female
College Students				
Mean	31.04	30.96		
SD	7.30	7.46		
Alpha	.87	.87		
N	48	98		
Navy Recruits				
Mean	31.66	30.10	27.14	23.56
SD	7.63	6.92	9.39	10.52
Alpha	.87	.84	.93	.93
N	192	71	192	71

Except for items 14 and 15, the item-remainder correlations for the S-Anger items were .50 or higher for both sexes, and items 4, 5 and 6 had the highest correlations with the S-Anxiety scale (.60 or higher for one or both sexes), as can be seen in Table 7.1. The two items with the lowest item-remainder coefficients and the three items with the highest correlations with S-Anxiety were eliminated in reducing the number of S-Anger items from 15 to 10.

In order to reduce the number of T-Anger items from 15 to 10, the item-remainder coefficients and the correlations of each T-Anger item with measures of anxiety and curiosity were examined for both the original college student sample and the Navy recruits. The T-Anger item-remainder correlations were .35 or higher for both sexes in the Navy sample, but were less than .35 for two items (4,10) in the original sample. The correlations of items 12 and 13 with T-Anxiety were relatively high in both samples and for item 15 in the original sample. Therefore, these five items were eliminated in forming the 10-item T-Anger scale.

It is interesting to note that two of the T-Anger items that were eliminated (e.g., # 12, "I feel irritated;" #13, "I feel angry") have excellent content validity as measures of anger. Since the correlations of these items with T-Anxiety were almost as high as their item-remainder coefficients (see Table 7.2), these findings suggested that feelings of anger and irritation are frequently associated with symptoms of anxiety.

Correlations between the 10-item and 15-item State and Trait Anger scales for the Navy recruits and a new sample of college students are reported in Table 7.4. These correlations were uniformly high, ranging from .95 to .99. Even though there was complete item overlap between the 10- and 15-item forms, the exceedingly high correlations further suggested that the scores on the 10-item forms provide essentially the same information as do scores for the longer forms. An

TABLE 7.4
Correlations of the 15-Item and 10-Item State and Trait
Anger Scales

| | Navy[1] | | College[2] | |
	Male	Female	Male	Female
State Anger	.98	.99	.98	.97
Trait Anger	.97	.95	.96	.97

[1] Based on 198 males and 72 females for all measures.
[2] Based on 95 males and 185 females for the trait measures, and 66 males and 133 females for the state measures.

added advantage of the 10-item form is that the items with the highest correlations with anxiety have been eliminated, resulting in lower correlations with measures of state and trait anxiety.

Factor Structure of the Trait Anger Scale

The factor structure of the 10-item S-Anger and T-Anger scales were investigated for 280 undergraduate college students (95 males; 185 females) enrolled in introductory psychology courses and 270 Navy recruits (198 males; 72 females) who were tested on their fifth day of basic training as part of another study (Spielberger & Barker, 1979). These scales were administered as part of the *State-Trait Personality Inventory (STPI)* (Spielberger, Jacobs, Crane, Russell, Westberry, Barker, Johnson, Knight, & Marks, 1979), which consists of six 10-item subscales for measuring state and trait anger, anxiety, and curiosity. The items for the *STPI* anxiety and curiosity subscales were selected, respectively, from the *State-Trait Anxiety Inventory* and the *State-Trait Curiosity Inventory* on the basis of large item-remainder correlations and relatively small correlations with the S-Anger and the T-Anger scales.

In order to investigate whether the S-Anger and T-Anger scales measured unitary psychological constructs, the items for each scale were factored in separate analyses for the males and females in the college and Navy samples. Initial extraction was by the principal factor method, utilizing iterations to squared multiple correlations as estimates of the commonalities (Nie, Hull, Jenkins, Steinbrenner, & Bent, 1975). The following criteria were utilized for determining the number of factors to be extracted: (a) Guttman's (1954) latent roots greater than 1.00; and (b) Cliff and Hamburger's (1967) 'breaks' criterion. Kaiser's (1958) varimax procedure was used to facilitate orthogonal rotation to simple structure of factors to be extracted. A factor solution was considered to have good simple structure when each item loaded unambiguously on one and only one factor (Kaiser, 1958; Thurstone, 1947). Salient items were identified as possessing factor loadings equal to or greater than .30.

TABLE 7.5
Item-Remainder Correlations, Alpha Coefficients and Factor Loadings for the Trait Anger Scale

	Item-Remainder Correlations				Factor Loadings			
	Males		Females		Factor I		Factor II	
					Angry Temperament		Angry Reaction	
	College (N=95)	Navy (N=198)	College (N=185)	Navy (N=72)	Males	Females	Males	Females
Angry Temperament								
I have a fiery temper	.78	.72	.77	.75	.81	.80	.21	.23
I am quick-tempered	.69	.76	.77	.63	.79	.75	.18	.21
I am a hotheaded person	.64	.74	.79	.75	.74	.87	.24	.05
I fly off the handle	.58	.63	.68	.59	.64	.70	.28	.10
Alpha Coefficient	.84	.86	.89	.84				
Angry Reaction								
Infuriated when get poor evaluation	.48	.56	.55	.61	.14	.10	.67	.71
Furious when criticized	.55	.50	.47	.54	.34	.07	.57	.63
Annoyed when not given recognition	.42	.49	.48	.60	.21	.09	.54	.58
Angry when slowed down by others	.53	.44	.43	.44	.19	.34	.56	.47
Alpha Coefficient	.70	.71	.70	.75				
Other Trait Anger Items								
When I get mad, I say nasty things					.45	.45	.27	.29
When frustrated, feel like hitting					.41	.28	.30	.34

In the factor analysis of the S-Anger items, both the latent roots and the "breaks" criteria were in agreement in suggesting only a single factor for both males and females. These results were consistent with the very high item-remainder correlations found for the S-Anger scale (median r=.64 and .67, respectively, for males and females, See Table 7.1), and with the alpha coefficients of .93 obtained for both sexes (See Table 7.3), providing further evidence of a high degree of internal consistency. Thus, the S-Anger scale appears to measure anger as a unitary emotional state that varies in intensity.

The latent roots and breaks criteria were also in agreement in suggesting a two-factor solution for the T-Anger scale, for both males and females. The T-Anger items that defined the underlying factors are grouped in Table 7.5, in which the factor loadings for each item are reported. Four items had high loadings on each of these factors, with low loadings on the other. The loadings of the two remaining items were spread across both factors. On the basis of the content of the four items loading each factor, the factors were labeled Angry Temperament (T-Anger/T) and Angry Reaction (T-Anger/R).

The T-Anger/T items describe individual differences in the disposition to express anger, without specifying any provoking circumstances. In contrast, the T-Anger/R items describe anger responses in situations that involve frustration and/or negative evaluations. The T-Anger items for which the variance was spread across both factors appear to describe reactions when someone feels angry or frustrated, but do not specify the anger-provoking circumstances.

On the basis of the factor analyses of the T-Anger items, item-analyses were carried out to evaluate the internal consistency of the 4-item T-Anger/T and T-Anger/R subscales. The item-remainder correlations and alpha coefficients obtained in these analyses are reported in Table 7.5. The median item-remainder coefficients for the T-Anger/T subscale was .73; the alpha coefficients for this scale ranged from .84 to .89. The median item-remainder correlation for the T-Anger/R subscale was .50; the alphas ranged from .70 to .75. Considering the fact that the T-Anger subscales were comprised of only four items, the internal consistency for both males and females was surprisingly good. The psychometric properties of the T-Anger scale and its subscales are further examined in the following section.

Psychometric Characteristics of the State-Trait Anger Scale

In developing norms for the *State-Trait Anger Scale (STAS)*, the *STAS* was administered to large samples of junior and senior high school students, military recruits, college students, and working adults. The school sample consisted of more than 3000 students enrolled in junior and senior high schools in nine counties in Central and South Florida. The students were tested in regular classroom settings; approximately one-third were in the eighth grade and the remaining students were in the tenth grade at the time they were tested.

Approximately 2500 military recruits were tested at the Navy Recruit Training Command, Orlando, Florida and the Air Force Basic Military Training School, Lackland Air Force Base, Texas. The *STAS* was administered to entire companies of recruits within five days of their reporting for the training programs. Approximately 85 percent of the sample was comprised of Air Force recruits; most of the military recruits were high school graduates.

The college sample consisted of more than 1600 students enrolled in psychology courses at the University of South Florida and the Hillsborough Community College. Both institutions serve the same large urban metropolitan area; the University also attracts students from the entire state of Florida and a small proportion of out-of-state students. The college student sample was relatively heterogeneous in terms of the socio-economic background of the students, with most students coming from upper-lower and middle-class backgrounds.

The means, standard deviations and alpha coefficients for the *STAS* S-Anger and T-Anger scales, and for the T-Anger/T and T-Anger/R subscales, are reported in Table 7.6 for junior and senior high school students, military recruits, and college students. The high school students scored slightly higher in S-Anger than the other two samples. The male recruits had slightly higher S-Anger scores

TABLE 7.6
Means, Standard Deviations and Alpha Coefficients for the
State-Trait Anger Scale for High School and College Students
and Military Recruits

	High School Students		Military Recruits		College Students	
	Females (N=1424)	Males (N=1592)	Females (N=700)	Males (N=1660)	Females (N=995)	Males (N=622)
State Anger						
Mean	14.52	14.64	13.12	14.15	13.62	13.08
SD	6.10	6.08	4.78	5.86	5.58	4.83
Alpha	0.89	0.88	0.88	0.91	0.95	0.95
Trait Anger						
Mean	23.35	23.65	18.61	19.91	19.56	19.28
SD	6.22	5.93	5.11	5.46	5.05	4.98
Alpha	0.82	0.81	0.82	0.84	0.91	0.89
Angry Temperament						
Mean	8.20	8.07	6.12	6.40	6.33	6.15
SD	3.22	3.11	2.56	2.62	2.57	2.35
Alpha	0.83	0.81	0.88	0.87	0.92	0.88
Angry Reaction						
Mean	10.47	10.64	9.39	9.82	9.86	9.58
SD	2.90	2.77	2.72	2.73	2.63	2.55
Alpha	0.66	0.64	0.71	0.71	0.87	0.81

than the females, whereas the female college students had slightly higher scores than the males.

The alpha coefficients for the S-Anger scale were uniformly high, ranging from .88 to .95, indicating a surprisingly high degree of internal consistency for a 10-item scale. The alphas for the college students were substantially higher than for the other groups, suggesting that persons with a higher level of education respond in a more consistent manner to the S-Anger scale than persons with less education.

The high school students scored substantially higher on T-Anger and its subscales than the other two samples, for which the psychometric properties were quite similar. As was the case for the S-Anger scale, the male military recruits scored somewhat higher than the females, whereas the female college students scored slightly higher than the males. The alpha coefficients for the T-Anger scale and its 4-item T-Anger/T scale were quite high, varying from .81 to .92. The alpha coefficients for the T-Anger/R subscale were also relatively high for the college students, but substantially lower for high school students and military recruits. The finding that the latter groups were less consistent in responding to this subscale suggested that the language or concepts conveyed by the items are influenced to some extent by educational level.

TABLE 7.7

Means, Standard Deviations and Alpha Coefficients for the
State-Trait Anger Scale for Working Adults

	18-22 Years Old		23-32 Years Old		33 or Older	
	Females (N=180)	*Males (N=112)*	*Females (N=189)*	*Males (N=138)*	*Females (N=129)*	*Males (N=128)*
State Anger						
Mean	13.41	14.79	13.71	14.28	13.67	13.29
SD	5.25	5.91	5.72	6.03	5.24	4.93
Alpha	0.94	0.94	0.93	0.94	0.93	0.93
Trait Anger						
Mean	20.19	20.33	18.45	18.49	18.13	17.41
SD	5.21	5.09	4.51	4.98	4.82	5.19
Alpha	0.91	0.92	0.89	0.91	0.90	0.88
Angry Temperament						
Mean	6.62	6.80	5.99	5.90	5.95	5.80
SD	2.57	2.73	2.25	2.55	2.58	2.38
Alpha	0.91	0.90	0.90	0.92	0.91	0.91
Angry Reaction						
Mean	10.03	9.86	9.48	9.50	9.26	8.86
SD	2.72	2.53	2.58	2.55	2.70	2.87
Alpha	0.84	0.87	0.82	0.83	0.82	0.78

TABLE 7.8
Item-Remainder Correlations and Alpha Coefficients for the
State Anger Scale

Items	High School Students		Military Recruits		College Students		Working Adults	
	Females (N=1424)	Males (N=1592)	Females (N=700)	Males (N=1660)	Females (N=999)	Males (N=622)	Females (N=839)	Males (N=413)
I am furious	53	50	57	62	69	68	87	71
Feel like banging table	58	59	58	66	81	74	85	72
Worrying over misfortunes	70	65	73	76	80	80	87	74
Feel like yelling	73	72	69	68	81	79	87	72
Feel like breaking things	66	69	62	67	81	81	86	76
I am mad	68	67	70	76	85	84	89	85
I feel irritated	56	49	62	65	81	85	85	81
Feel like hitting someone	70	69	59	66	80	76	83	75
I am burned up	67	61	62	67	81	81	86	79
I feel like swearing	60	59	54	60	79	78	86	79
Alpha Coefficients	89	88	89	91	95	95	97	93

TABLE 7.9
Item-Remainder Correlations and Alpha Coefficients for the Trait Anger Scale and the Angry Temperament and Angry Reaction Subscales

	High School Students		Military Recruits		College Students		Working Adults	
	Females (N=1424)	Males (N=1592)	Females (N=700)	Males (N=1660)	Females (N=999)	Males (N=627)	Females (N=839)	Males (N=413)
Angry Temperament								
I have a fiery temperament	59	58	61	64	72	70	86	72
I am quick-tempered	55	58	60	63	73	71	86	69
I am a hot-headed person	54	54	60	62	72	67	85	76
I fly off the handle	61	55	59	59	74	67	86	72
Subscale Alpha Coefficients	83	81	88	87	92	89	95	91
Angry Reaction								
Infuriated when get poor evaluation	44	41	49	49	70	59	84	60
Furious when criticized	40	40	46	51	65	63	82	58
Annoyed when not given recognition	40	41	44	42	68	60	85	64
Angry when slowed down by others	44	45	40	44	70	65	85	68
Subscale Alpha Coefficients	66	64	71	71	87	81	93	83
Other Trait Anger Items								
When I get mad, I say nasty things	52	47	49	50	68	62	84	69
When frustrated, feel like hitting	54	49	51	54	59	62	80	66
Full Scale Alpha Coefficients	82	81	82	84	91	89	96	90

The means, standard deviations, and alpha coefficients for the *State-Trait Anger Scale* are reported in Table 7.7 for a sample of 1252 working adults, ranging in age from 18 to 63. Most of the subjects in this sample were employed in various governmental agencies in Hillsborough County, Florida and were tested on the job as part of another study. Approximately 30 percent of the sample consisted of persons employed full-time in the Tampa Bay area, who were tested in night school classes. In order to examine the relationship between anger scores and age, the subjects were divided into three age groups, approximately equal in size.

The S-Anger scores for the three age groups were similar, and the alpha coefficients for this scale were uniformly high for all three groups. The T-Anger scores for the younger group were somewhat higher than for the other two groups, and slightly lower for the older males. The alpha coefficients for the T-Anger scale and T-Anger/T subscale were uniformly high, ranging from .88 to .92. Although the alpha coefficients for the T-Anger/R subscale were somewhat lower, they were quite satisfactory and comparable to those of the college students.

The item-remainder correlations and alpha coefficients for the individual items in the S-Anger scale are reported in Table 7.8 for the four normative groups. The item-remainders for the S-Anger items were very high for both females and males in all four groups. Most of the coefficients for individual S-Anger items were larger in those samples in which the subjects were older and had more education, as can be noted in Table 7.8. The influence of age and educational level were also reflected in the alpha coefficients, which were higher for the college students and working adults than for the high school students and military recruits.

Item-remainder correlations and alpha coefficients for the T-Anger scale and its subscales are reported in Table 7.9. The item-remainders and alpha coefficients for the 4-item T-Anger/T scale were uniformly high for all four normative groups. The two items that failed to have clear-cut loadings on the T-Anger subscales were nevertheless relatively high, especially for the working adults. The T-Anger/R coefficients were also high for the college students and working adults, but somewhat lower for high school students and military recruits. The same pattern of increasing internal consistency for older, better-educated subjects that was previously noted for the S-Anger scale (See Table 7.8) can also be seen in Table 7.9 for the T-Anger scale.

IV. RESEARCH FINDINGS WITH THE STATE-TRAIT ANGER SCALE

Since the *STAS* was recently constructed, only limited data are available on the validity of the scale. In order to obtain information about the concurrent, convergent, and discriminant validity, the *State-Trait Personality Inventory*, which included the 10-item S-Anger and T-Anger scales, was administered to the samples of 280 undergraduate college students and 270 Navy recruits that were previously described. Data were also available for these same subjects on T-Anxiety and T-Curiosity, and the *Eysenck Personality Questionnaire* (Eysenck & Eysenck, 1975), which includes Extraversion, Neuroticism, Psychoticism and Lie subscales, and three hostility measures: the *Buss-Durkee Hostility Inventory* and two *MMPI* hostility scales, the *Hostility (Ho) Scale* developed by Cook and Medley (1954) and the *Overt Hostility (Hv) Scale* constructed by Schultz (1954). Since most of these measures seem to assess personality traits, our main interest was in the correlations between the T-Anger scale and the other measures.

The correlations of the T-Anger scale with S-Anger and the three hostility measures are reported in Table 7.10 for males and females in the college and Navy samples. The highest correlations were with the *BDHI* Total score and the *Ho* scale. Although the correlations of the T-Anger scale with the *Hv* scale were statistically significant, they were substantially lower than with the other hostility measures. Since the scales were administered under relatively nonthreatening, neutral conditions, only small-to-moderate correlations were expected between the T-Anger and S-Anger scales.

These findings provide evidence that the *BDHI*, and *Ho* and the T-Anger scale measure a hostility trait. Since the correlations of the *Hv* scale with the other hostility measures were also quite low, and comparable to the correlations found for this scale with the T-Anger scale, it is apparent that the *Hv* scale shares relatively little common variance with the other measures.

Correlations of the Trait and State Anger scales with the *STPI* Trait and State Anxiety and Curiosity scales, and with the *EPQ* and its subscales, are reported in Table 7.11 for large samples of college students (545 females; 334 males). The moderate correlations between the T-Anger scale and the *STPI* T-Anxiety and the

TABLE 7.10
Correlations of the Trait Anger Scale With Measures of
Hostility and Other Personality Measures

	College		Navy	
	Males *(N=95)*	*Females* *(N=185)*	*Males* *(N=198)*	*Females* *(N=72)*
Hostility Measures				
Buss-Durkee Hostility Invent. Total	.71***	.66***	.66***	.73***
Hostility Scale (Ho)	.59***	.43***	.49***	.48***
Overt Hostility Scale (Hv)	.32***	.27***	.31***	.30**
S-Anger Scale	.38***	.22**	.34***	.41***

*p < .05
**p < .01
***p < .001

EPQ Neuroticism scales are consistent with clinical observations and theory that persons high in neuroticism and trait anxiety frequently experience angry feelings that they cannot readily express.

The low positive correlations reported in Table 7.11 between the T-Anger scale and the *EPQ* Psychoticism scale indicate that persons with high scores on the latter experience anger somewhat more frequently than persons with low Psychoticism scores. The small negative correlations of T-Anger with the *EPQ* Lie scale suggest that anger scores may be slightly reduced by test-taking attitudes that lead some people to inhibit reports of negative characteristics such as anger. The correlations of the T-Anger scale with Extraversion and State and Trait Curiosity were essentially zero.

Low-to-moderate correlations were found between the S-Anger scale and the *STPI* T-Anxiety and the *EPQ* Neuroticism and Psychoticism scales. These findings would seem to indicate that individuals with psychopathological personality traits experienced more intense angry feelings than emotionally stable people at the time they were tested. The moderately high correlations between S-Anger and S-Anxiety that were found for both sexes may reflect an important aspect of the socialization process in American society. If aggressive behaviors in young children are motivated by angry feelings, and such behaviors are consistently punished, through learning, an association will develop between feelings of anger and anxiety so that feeling angry will elicit elevations in S-Anxiety in anticipation of punishment.

Evidence of the concurrent validity of the T-Anger scale as a measure of hostility was reported in Table 7.10. Since the research literature suggested important differences between anger and hostility as personality constructs, the relationship between the T-Anger scale and the hostility measures was further evaluated in a factor analysis of the individual items of the *STPI* T-Anger scale. For this analysis, the 30 items of the *STPI* Trait Personality scale (10 T-Anger items; 10 T-Anxiety items; 10 T-Curiosity items) were factored with the following marker variables: T-Anger Total score, the *BDHI* Total and subscale scores, and scores for the *Ho* and *Hv* scales and the *STPI* T-Anxiety and T-Curiosity scales.

The factor analysis procedures were essentially the same as those used in factoring the individual items on the S-Anger and T-Anger scales, that were previously described. The latent roots criteria indicated that as many as 10 factors could be extracted for both sexes. However, the "breaks" criteria suggested that no more than three or four factors should be extracted. Therefore, three-, four- and five-factor solutions were considered. Since the five-factor solution did not have good simple structure and was lacking in psychological meaningfulness, it will not be further considered.

The three- and four-factor solutions are reported in Table 7.12; these solutions were quite similar for both males and females. In the three-factor solution, the first factor was clearly an anger-hostility factor; the T-Anger and Buss-Durkee

TABLE 7.11
Correlations Between the State-Trait Anger Scale, the STPI State and Trait Anxiety and Curiosity Scales, and the Eysenck Personality Questionnaire for College Students

	Trait Anger		Angry Temperament		Angry Reaction		State Anger	
	Males	Females	Males	Females	Males	Females	Males	Females
State-Trait Personality Inventory								
Trait Anxiety	.37***	.38***	.26***	.26***	.37***	.33***	.35**	.30***
State Anxiety	.19***	.25***	.17**	.15***	.17**	.00	.63***	.63***
Trait Curiosity	-.08	-.07	-.10	-.06	-.04	.21***	-.20***	-.12**
State Curiosity	-.15**	-.08	-.11*	-.04	-.12*	-.05	-.07	-.18***
Eysenck Personality Questionnaire								
Extraversion	.06	-.07	.09	-.05	-.02	-.05	-.03	-.08
Neuroticism	.50***	.49***	.40***	.34***	.47***	.42***	.43***	.27***
Psychoticism	.21***	.20***	.15**	.13**	.14**	.15***	.26***	.27***
Lie	-.20***	-.25***	-.15**	-.16***	-.13*	-.22***	-.11	-.04

*p < .05
**p < .01
***p < .001

TABLE 7.12
Factor Analyses of the Items of the Trait Anger Scale with Marker Variables

	Three Factor Solution						Four Factor Solution							
	Factor I		Factor II		Factor III		Factor I		Factor II		Factor III		Factor IV	
Items and Scales	M	F	M	F	M	F	M	F	M	F	M	F	M	F
Trait Anger Total	92	92	19	19	-16	-01	84	81	23	18	-09	00	41	50
I have a fiery temper	67	67	16	13	-24	02	69	75	19	16	-19	02	25	22
I am a hotheaded person	66	63	06	-03	-19	-05	70	75	10	00	-14	-05	22	16
I am quick-tempered	67	63	10	12	-19	05	72	74	14	15	-13	06	23	17
When mad, I say nasty things	58	60	09	09	-06	-08	41	43	05	06	-06	-07	44	42
I fly off the handle	63	57	06	08	-21	-04	67	65	10	11	-16	-04	22	17
Angry when slowed down	47	54	06	-04	00	00	46	45	07	-04	04	01	22	30
Frustrated feel like hitting	54	48	10	08	-14	-20	41	29	07	04	-14	-20	38	39
Infuriated when poor evaluation	49	44	19	23	10	07	41	23	19	19	14	08	29	41
Annoyed when not given recognition	44	38	25	19	03	12	45	21	30	16	09	12	18	34
Furious when criticized	50	33	27	28	-18	-01	50	20	31	26	-14	00	22	29
Median Item Factor Loading	58	57	10	12	16	05	50	45	14	15	13	05	22	30
Buss-Durkee Total	81	85	36	33	-04	-04	33	34	23	22	-10	-03	87	89
Assault	52	64	11	07	-05	03	24	28	02	-02	09	04	56	64
Verbal	58	60	00	-09	01	05	31	33	-09	-15	-02	05	57	51
Indirect	50	58	12	20	03	06	26	42	05	18	02	07	50	41
Negativism	39	36	14	07	-07	-14	17	08	08	01	-10	-14	44	43
Irritability	62	62	36	47	-07	00	31	35	29	42	-09	00	62	56
Suspicion	45	42	42	35	-05	-16	10	03	34	27	-09	-16	60	60
Resentment	49	47	51	50	-09	-09	15	09	43	42	-12	-08	61	61
Guilt	13	20	55	41	-04	-02	-03	-02	52	36	-06	-01	26	34
Hostility (Ho) Scale	59	56	51	43	-07	-12	22	11	42	33	-11	-11	68	72
Overt Hostility (Hv) Scale	34	37	29	15	-10	-05	15	14	25	10	-11	-05	37	40
Trait Anxiety	25	25	85	90	-38	-29	23	17	82	89	-35	-28	18	24
Trait Curiosity	-20	-09	-31	-25	91	95	-18	-01	-32	-23	85	95	-14	-14

Total scores had the highest loadings for this factor. Moreover, the *Ho* and *Hv* scales, all 10 T-Anger items, and all but the Guilt subscale of the BDHI had salient loadings on this factor. The highest loadings on Factor II, labeled "Trait Anxiety," were the *STPI* T-Anxiety scale, the *Ho* scale, and the *BDHI* Guilt, Irritability, Suspicion and Resentment scales. The third factor, defined primarily by the *STPI* T-Curiosity scale, with a secondary negative loading on T-Anxiety, was labeled "Trait Curiosity."

In the four-factor solution, Factors II and III were quite similar to the second and third factors in the three-factor solution, and the "Anger-Hostility" factor in the three-factor solution divided into separate "Anger" (Factor I) and "Hostility" (Factor IV) factors. The T-Anger Total score and most of the individual T-Anger items had the highest loadings on the new "Anger" factor, and the new "Hostility" factor was defined by high loadings on the Buss-Durkee and *Ho* Total scores, and by salient loadings for all of the Buss-Durkee subscales except Guilt. Moreover, most of the T-Anger items had secondary loadings on the "Hostility" factor and several of the Buss-Durkee subscales had secondary loadings on the "Anger" factor. It is interesting to note, however, that the *Ho* scale and the *BDHI* Irritability, Suspicion and Resentment subscales had higher secondary loadings in the four-factor solution on the T-Anxiety (Factor II) than on anger, suggesting that some hostile persons use neurotic defense mechanisms for projecting or indirectly expressing anger.

Additional information about the psychometric properties and the factor structure of the anger scales were reported by Westberry (1980). Crane (1981) found that hypertensive patients had higher T-Anger and T-Anger/R scores than a control group of medical and surgical patients. She also found that hypertensives reported higher scores on the *STPI* T-Anxiety scale, and also had higher scores on the S-Anger and S-Anxiety scales after performing on a mildly frustrating task.

SUMMARY

The concepts of anger, hostility and aggression were examined in this chapter. The psychometric properties and the validity of a number of psychological scales for measuring hostility and anger were also reviewed and evaluated. The construction and development of a new inventory, the *State-Trait Anger Scale*, were described in detail, and the psychometric properties and factor structure of this instrument were examined. Research findings from recent studies that have evaluated the validity of the *State-Trait Anger Scale* were also reported.

REFERENCES

Anastasi, A. *Psychological testing* (5th ed.). New York: MacMillan, 1982.

Bendig, A. W. Factor analytic scales of covert and overt hostility. *Journal of Consulting Psychology*, 1962, *26*, 200.

Berkowitz, L. Manifest hostility level and hostile behavior. *Journal of Social Psychology*, 1960, *52*, 165–171.

Biaggio, M. K. Assessment of anger arousal. *Journal of Personality Assessment*, 1980, *44*, 289–298.

Biaggio, M. K., Supplee, K., & Curtis, N. Reliability and validity of four anger scales. *Journal of Personality Assessment*, 1981, *45*, 639–648.

Buss, A. H. *The psychology of aggression*. New York: Wiley, 1961.

Buss, A. H., & Durkee, A. An inventory for assessing different kinds of hostility. *Journal of Consulting Psychology*, 1957, *21*, 343–349.

Buss, A. H., Durkee, A., & Baer, M. The measurement of hostility in clinical situations. *Journal of Abnormal Social Psychology*, 1956, *52*, 84–86.

Caine, T. M. Changes in symptom, attitudes, and trait measures among chronic neurotics in a therapeutic community. In G. A. Foulds, (Ed.), *Personality and personal illness*. London: Tavistock Press, 1965.

Caine, T. M., Foulds, G. A., & Hope, K. *Manual of the hostility and direction of hostility questionnaire (HDHQ)*. London: University of London Press, 1967.

Cattell, R. B., & Scheier, I. H. *The meaning and measurement of neuroticism and anxiety*. New York: Ronald Press, 1961.

Cliff, N., & Hamburger, C. D. The study of sampling errors in factor analysis by means of artificial experiments. *Psychological Bulletin*, 1967, *68*, 430–455.

Cockett, R. *Hostility in young offenders*. C. P. Report, No. 35, Prison Department, Home Office, 1970.

Cook, W. W., & Medley, D. M. Proposed hostility and pharisaic-virtue scales for the MMPI. *The Journal of Applied Psychology*, 1954, *38*, 414–418.

Crane, R. *The role of anger, hostility and aggression in essential hypertension*. Unpublished doctoral dissertation, University of South Florida, 1981.

Crawford, D. A. The HDHQ results of long-term prisoners: Relationships with criminal and institutional behavior. *British Journal of Social Clinical Psychology*, 1977, *16*, 391–394.

De Vos, G. A. A quantitative approach to affective symbolism in Rorschach responses. *Journal of Projective Techniques*, 1952, *16*, 133–150.

Endicott, J., & Spitzer, R. L. What! Another rating scale? The psychiatric evaluation form. *Journal of Nervous and Mental Disorders*, 1972, *154*, 88–104.

Evans, D. R., & Stangeland, M. Development of the reaction inventory to measure anger. *Psychological Reports*, 1971, *29*, 412–414.

Eysenck, H. J., & Eysenck, S. B. G. *Manual of the Eysenck Personality Questionnaire*. London: Hodder and Stoughton, 1975.

Foulds, G. A. *Personality and Personal Illness*. London: Tavistock, 1965.

Foulds, G. A., Caine, T. M., & Creasy, M. A. Aspects of extra and intro-punitive expression in mental illness. *Journal of Mental Sciences*, 1960, *106*, 599–609.

Friedman, M., & Rosenman, R. H. *Type A behavior and your heart*. Greenwich, Conn.: Fawcett Publications, Inc., 1974.

Greer, S., & Morris, T. Psychological attributes of women who develop breast cancer: A controlled study. *Journal of Psychosomatic Research*. 1975, *2*, 147–153.

Guttman, L. Some necessary conditions for common-factor analyses. *Psychometrika*, 1954, *19*, 149–161.

Guyotat, J., & Guillaumin, J. Un aspect de l'adaptation du malade a la situation morbide: L'etude des reactions d'un groupe de chirurgicaux au test de frustration de Rosenzweig. *Revue de Psychologie Appliquee*, 1960, *10*, 39–58.

Harburg, E., Erfurt, J. C., Hauenstein, L. S., Chape, C., Schull, W. J., & Schork, M. A. Socio-ecological stress, suppressed hostility, skin color, and black–white male blood pressure: Detroit. *Psychosomatic Medicine*, 1973, *35*, 276–296.

Hokanson, J. E., & Gordon, J. E. The expression and inhibition of hostility in imaginative and overt behavior. *Journal of Abnormal and Social Psychology*, 1958, *57*, 327–333.

Johnson, J. H. A cross-validation of seventeen experimental MMPI scales related to anti-social behavior. *Journal of Clinical Psychology*, 1973, *30*, 564–565.

Kaiser, H. F. The varimax criterion for analytic rotation in factor analysis. *Psychometrika*, 1958, *23*, 187–200.

Kaswan, J., Wasman, M., & Freedman, L. Z. Aggression and the picture frustration study. *Journal of Consulting Psychology*, 1960, *24*, 446–452.

Knott, P. D. A further methodological study of the measurement of interpersonal aggression. *Psychological Reports*, 1970, *26*, 807–809.

Matthews, K. A., Glass, D. C., Rosenman, R. H., & Bortner, R. W. Competitive drive, pattern A, and coronary heart disease: A further analysis of some data from the Western Collaborative Group Study. *Journal of Chronic Diseases*, 1977, *30*, 489–498.

Mayo, P. R. Some psychological changes associated with improvement in depression. *British Journal of Social and Clinical Psychology*, 1967, *6*, 63.

Moldawsky, P. A. *Study of personality variables in parients with skin disorders.* Unpublished doctoral dissertation, State University of Iowa, 1953.

Morris, C. J. *Psychology: An introduction* (2nd, ed.). Englewood Cliffs, N.J.: Prentice Hall, 1976.

Murray, H. A. *Thematic Apperception Test.* Cambridge: Harvard University Press, 1943.

Nie, N. H., Hull, C. H., Jenkins, J. G., Steinbrenner, K., & Bent, D. H. *Statistical package for the social sciences.* New York: McGraw-Hill Co., 1975.

Novaco, R. W. *The effect of disposition for anger and degree of provocation on self-report and physiological measures of anger in various modes of provocation.* Unpublished Manuscript, Indiana University, Bloomington, 1974.

Novaco, R. W. *Anger control: The development and evaluation of an experimental treatment.* Lexington, Mass.: Lexington Books/D. C. Heath, 1975.

Novaco, R. W. Stress innoculation: A cognitive therapy for anger and its application to a case of depression. *Journal of Consulting and Clinical Psychology*, 1977, *45*(4), 600–608.

Petzel, T. P., & Michaels, E. J. Perception of violence as a function of levels of hostility. *Journal of Consulting and Clinical Psychology*, 1973, *41*, 35–36.

Philip, A. E. The development and use of the Hostility and Direction of Hostility Questionnaire. *Journal of Psychosomatic Research*, 1969, *13*, 283–287.

Renson, G. L., Adams, J. E., & Tinklenberg, J. R. Buss-Durkee assessment and validation with violent versus nonviolent chronic alcohol abusers. *Journal of Consulting and Clinical Psychology*, 1978, *46*(2), 360–361.

Roget's International Thesaurus. New York: Thomas Y. Crowell, 1977.

Rorschach, H. *Psychodiagnostik.* Bern, Switzerland: Bircher, 1921.

Rosenzweig, S. The picture association test and its application in a study of reactions to frustration. *Journal of Personality*, 1945, *14*, 3–23.

Rosenzweig, S. Validity of the Rosenzweig picture-frustration study with felons and delinquents. *Journal of Consulting Psychology*, 1963, *27*, 535–536.

Russell, S. F. *The factor structure of the Buss-Durkee hostility inventory.* Unpublished master's thesis, University of South Florida, 1981.

Sarason, I. G. Experimental approaches to test anxiety: Attention and the uses of information. In C. D. Spielberger (Ed.), *Anxiety: current trends in theory and research* (Vol. 2). New York: Academic Press, 1972.

Schechter, M. D., & Rand, M. J. Effects of acute deprivation of smoking on aggression and hostility. *Psychopharmacologia*, 1974, *35*, 19–28.

Schultz, S. D. A differentiation of several forms of hostility by scales empirically constructed from significant items on the MMPI. *Dissertation Abstracts*, 1954, *17*, 717–720.

Shipman, W. G., & Marquette, C. H. The Manifest Hostility Scale: A validation study. *Journal of Clinical Psychology*, 1963, *19*, 104–106.

Siegel, S. The relationship of hostility to authoritarianism. *Journal of Abnormal and Social Psychology*, 1956, *52*, 368–373.

Spielberger, C. D. Theory and research on anxiety. In C. D. Spielberger (Ed.), *Anxiety and Behavior*. New York: Academic Press, 1966.

Spielberger, C. D. Anxiety as an emotional state. In C. D. Spielberger (Ed.), *Anxiety: Current Trends in Theory and Research* (Vol. 1), New York: Academic Press, 1972.

Spielberger, C. D. *Test anxiety inventory: Preliminary professional manual*. Palo Alto, California: Consulting Psychologists Press, 1980.

Spielberger, C. D., & Barker, L. R. *The relationship of personality characteristics to attrition and performance problems of navy and air force recruits*. (TAEG Report No. 75). Naval Training Center, Orlando, Florida: Training Analysis and Evaluation Group, 1979.

Spielberger, C. D., Jacobs, G., Crane, R., Russell, S., Westberry, L., Barker, L., Johnson, E., Knight, J., & Marks, E. *Preliminary Manual for the State-Trait Personality Inventory (STPI)*. Tampa: University of South Florida Human Resources Institute, 1979.

Spielberger, C. D., & London, P. Rage boomerangs: Lethal Type-A anger. *American Health*, 1982, *1*, 52–56.

Spielberger, C. D., Gonzalez, H. P., Taylor, C. D., Algaze, B., & Anton, W. D. Examination stress and test anxiety. In C. D. Spielberger and I. G. Sarason (Eds.), *Stress and anxiety* (Vol. 5). Washington, D.C.: Hemisphere/Wiley, 1978.

Spielberger, C. D., Gorsuch, R. L., & Lushene, R. E. *Manual for the State-Trait Anxiety Inventory (Self-Evaluation Questionnaire)*. Palo Alto, California: Consulting Psychologists Press, 1970.

Spielberger, C. D., Peters, R. A., & Frain, F. Curiosity and anxiety. In H. G. Voss and H. Keller (Eds.), *Curiosity research: Basic concepts and results*. Weinheim, Federal Republic of Germany: Beltz, 1981.

Thurstone, L. L. *Multiple factor analysis*. Chicago: University of Chicago Press, 1947.

Vinoda, K. S. Personality characteristics of attempted suicides. *British Journal of Psychiatry*, 1966, *112*, 1143.

Westberry, L. G., *Concurrent validation of the trait-anger scale and its correlation with other personality measures*. Unpublished master's thesis, University of South Florida, 1980.

Young, L. Personality characteristics of high and low aggressive adolescents in residential treatment. *Journal of Clinical Psychology*, 1976, *32*, 814–817.

Youseff, Z. I. The role of race, sex, hostility, and verbal stimulus in inflicting punishment. *Psychonomic Science*, 1968, *12*, 285–286.

Wiggins, J. S. *Personality and prediction: Principles of personality assessment*. Reading, Mass.: Addison-Wesley, 1973.

Zelin, M. L., Adler, G., & Myerson, P. G. Anger self-report: An objective questionnaire for the measurement of aggression. *Journal of Consulting and Clinical Psychology*, 1972, *39*, 340.

Author Index

Biele, A. M., 2, *12*
Billingslea, F. Y., 134, 152, *158*
Birchall, P. M. A., 85, 87, 89, 90, 92, 93, 96, *111, 112*
Bishop, D. V. M., 75, *111*
Bleuler, E., 72, *111*
Block, J., 75, *111*
Borkenau, P., 44, *65*
Bortner, R. W., 161, *188*
Březinová, V., 84, *111*
Brislin, R., 42, *66*
Browne, J., 44, *67*
Bryant, E., 25, *39*
Buchsbaum, M. S., 91, 95, *111, 113*
Burkhart, B. R., 118, 119, 120, 122, 128, *130*
Buss, A. H., 163, 164, 165, 166, *187*
Butcher, J. N., 42, *66*, 118, 129, *130, 131*

C

Caine, T. M., 164, *187*
Caird, W. K., 50, *67*
Callaway, E., 91, *111*
Carlier, M., 44, *66*
Carpenter, W., 91, *113*
Cattell, R. B., 44, 51, *66*, 123, *130*, 162, *187*
Chan, J., 47, 48, *67*
Chance, J. E., 116, 118, *130*
Chape, C., 161, *187*
Chapman, J. P., 107, *111*
Chapman, L. J., 107, *111*
Chappa, H. J., 80, 85, 86, *112*
Choungourian, A., 50, *66*
Choynowski, M., 50, *66*
Christian, W. L., 118, 119, 120, 128, *130*
Ciborowski, R., 42, *68*
Claridge, G. S., 72, 74, 76, 80, 81, 84, 85, 86, 87, 89, 90, 92, 93, 96, 100, 101, *111, 112, 114*
Clark, E. O., 134, *158*
Clark, K., 85, *112*
Clayton, P., 126, *130*
Cliff, N., 174, *187*
Cockett, R., 164, *187*
Cofer, C. N., 116, 118, *130*
Cohen, D., 150, 153, *159*
Cohen, J., 151, *158*
Cohen, P. A., 151, *159*
Comrey, A., 44, *66*
Cook, W. W., 164, 182, *187*

Coursey, R. D., 95, *113*
Court, J., 50, *69*
Craik, F. I., 134, *158*
Crane, R., 161, 174, 186, *187, 189*
Crawford, D. A., 164, *187*
Creasy, M. A., 164, *187*
Cronbach, L. J., 118, *130*
Cunningham, S., 138, 139, 142, 151, *159*
Curtis, N., 161, 166, 167, *187*
Curtis, R. H., 76, 78, 80, *113*

D

Dahlstrom, W. G., 129, *130*, 134, 138, 154, *158, 159*
Dasen, R., 42, *66*
Dawson, J., 42, *66*
Demaree, R., 44, *69*
Dennerll, R. D., 135, 136, 148, 150, *159*
DeVos, G. A., 163, *187*
Diaz-Guerrero, R., 42, *69*
Dimitriou, E. C., 47, 49, *66*
Dirks, J. F., 140, *159*
Donald, J. R., 96, *112*
Droppleman, L. F., 122, *131*
Duff, F. L., 117, 118, *130*
Duffy, A., 44, *66*
Durkee, A., 164, 165, 166, *187*
Dyk, R. B., 98, *114*
Dykes, M., 104, *112*

E

Eaves, L., 64, *66*
Eber, H. W., 123, *130*
Edell, W. S., 107, *111*
Edwards, D., 50, *66*
Elion, V. H., 120, *130*
Endicott, J., 33, 34, *40*, 102, *114*
Epstein, S., 129, *130*
Erfurt, J. C., 161, *187*
Erickson, R. C., 134, *158*
Escolar, V., 47, *67*
Evans, D. R., 166, 167, *187*
Ewert, J. C., 140, *158*
Exner, J. E., 13, 14, 15, 16, 17, 18, 19, 20, 21, 23, 24, 25, 26, 27, 28, 29, 32, 34, 35, 37, *39, 40*
Eysenck, H. J., 44, 45, 46, 47, 48, 49, 58, 64, *66, 67, 68, 69*, 73, 74, 75, 76, 78, 79, 80, 82, 83, 84, 99, 101, 110, *112, 114*, 182, *187*

Subject Index